The Reader's Digest Good Health Cookbooks

Fish, Poultry and Game

The Reader's Digest Good Health Cookbooks

FISH, POULTRY AND GAME

PUBLISHED BY THE READER'S DIGEST ASSOCIATION LIMITED LONDON SYDNEY CAPE TOWN

FISH, POULTRY AND GAME
was edited and designed by
The Reader's Digest Association,
and is based on The Cookery Year,

First Edition

Printed in Great Britain

Contents

How to use

The Good Health Cookbooks

Dieting need not be dreary. Whatever diet you may follow, you can still enjoy the classic dishes. Often, all you need are alternative ingredients that suit the recipe and suit the requirements of your diet. This book gives you the recipes for those classic dishes from *The Cookery Year*. It also gives you those vital alternatives. It has, in fact, several features unique in cookery books. In the special "Alternatives" column on each page, we identify how high each recipe is in salt, sugar, fat, cholesterol and fibre. We also give the calorie count. We check if it is gluten-free and wholefood. Then we suggest how you could adapt the recipe to any diet you, your family, or your guests might want to follow.

We do not lay down what diet you should follow. That is your decision. The book assumes that you yourself know what you want to do and tries to help you to do it by making suggestions (not commands), some or all of which you may want to follow. Perhaps you have been told to cut down drastically on salt; perhaps you have been thinking for some time that you should eat a little less sugar; perhaps you have a friend coming to a meal who cannot eat gluten or who is avoiding food high in cholesterol. You do not have to buy a new cookbook for each diet. You do not have to produce alternative meals for every guest. With these books, you can simply adapt the existing recipes to suit your needs.

You will find that we make use of a few conventions. This is mainly in order to avoid constant repetition. **The asterisk** (*) is used as follows:

1) Salt* indicates that this item may be omitted for those on a low-salt diet; the salt level of the recipe as given in the "Alternatives" column is calculated on the assumption that this salt has been omitted and that any ingredients that sometimes contain salt and sometimes don't (e.g. tinned tomatoes) have been bought in their salt-free version.

2) Gluten-free* indicates that the recipe is free of gluten so long as gluten-free flour (or bread or breadcrumbs) is used where appropriate.

3) Wholefood* indicates that the recipe is wholefood if wholemeal flour (or bread or breadcrumbs), brown rice and unrefined sugar are used where appropriate.

The levels of salt, **sugar**, **fat**, **cholesterol** and **fibre** for each recipe are denoted by symbols in the "Alternatives" column:

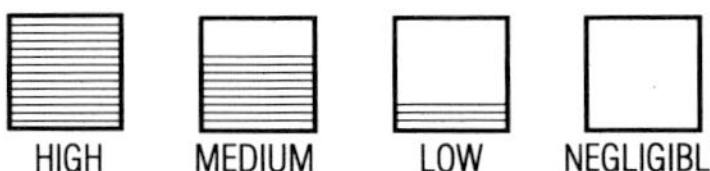

For definitions of what constitutes a high threshold level of any one of these, see under the appropriate diet on the following pages. Less than half this threshold level is considered low.

Calorie counts are given, firstly for the recipe as a whole and secondly as an indication of how many calories may be avoided as a result of following particular alternative suggestions.
Calories are automatically lost when either sugar or fat is significantly reduced. The calculations for calorie-

loss can be no more than approximate, and occasionally are omitted, as so many factors can vary: the fat level of fish and meat at different times of the year, the exact amount of fat trimmed off a cut of meat, or the amount of sugar that will make a dish acceptably sweet to a particular palate.
To convert calories to kilojoules, multiply the figure for calories by 4·18.

Cooking hints on when it is appropriate or helpful to use a pressure cooker, slow cooker, food processor, freezer or microwave are indicated by a tick, together with any further information required. With a microwave it is always essential that you also consult the manufacturer's instructions, as cooking times vary from cooker to cooker.

Measurements are expressed in both imperial and metric units. The figures are rounded up or down as necessary. As this is an international publication, we have borne in mind that teaspoons and tablespoons vary in capacity from country to country, but in any recipe where we have used these measurements, the dish should not be affected by such variations. For a check on the comparative values of these measures, consult the tables on the inside of the book's covers.

With practice you should find that the technique and alternatives recommended in this book will work with recipes from other books. In this way it becomes simple to adapt recipes so that they are both healthy and delicious. That is how it ought to be.

The Diets

Low-salt diet

Sodium is acknowledged to be a contributory factor in hypertension (high blood pressure) and thus in coronary heart disease and strokes; it can also be involved in some kidney disorders.

By far the most concentrated source of sodium is common salt (sodium chloride), and many processed foods contain a lot of added salt.

Diets which are very severely restricted in sodium are on occasion prescribed, but we are not concerned with them here. A certain minimum of both sodium and chloride is essential to good health, and the majority of salt-conscious people will simply want to cut out excessive consumption.

While setting an exact figure is very difficult, as the total level of salt in a meal depends on the combination of foods eaten, a target of 5 grams a day (generally considered to be not excessive) can usually be reached by cutting down on cooking or table salt as well as on monosodium glutamate. Foods such as salted or cured pork products and most cheeses should be eaten only in small quantities. Then the sodium occurring naturally in meat and fish, even in sodium-rich shellfish, need not be avoided.

It is important to check the labels on tins. Some tomatoes, for instance, are canned with added salt, others not. Egg whites and dried fruit are also relatively high in sodium and should not be overindulged in.

Salt substitutes are available but we do not specify them: they do not taste like salt and anyone suffering from heart or kidney disease should not take them without medical approval.

Many of those wishing to cut down on salt will also want to combine this with cutting down on fat. Therefore, for example, although double cream contains much less sodium than single cream or milk does, we do not advocate replacing milk with double cream.

Salt is used to to mean both common salt (sodium chloride) and sodium in general. Where the level of salt in the recipe is given, this takes into account sodium occurring naturally in the ingredients; in the list of ingredients, salt refers, as usual, to the sodium chloride commonly used for seasoning.

The salt content of a recipe is taken to be high if it contains the equivalent of more than 2 egg whites or $\frac{1}{2}$ pint (300 ml) of milk per person.

Low-sugar diet

Sugar is "empty calories": it provides no nutrients, but concentrated calories for a very little weight of food.

Sugar is the first thing to go if you are on a calorie-controlled diet. It is also known to encourage tooth decay; and high consumption, especially of refined sugar, has been correlated with certain diseases.

Refined sugar is pure sucrose, the form of sugar which is the least desirable. Sugar occurs naturally in other forms – for example, fructose in fruit, lactose in milk, dextrose (glucose) and maltose. These do not always have the same harmful effect on the body as sucrose, and are not eaten in anything like the same sort of quantity.

A low-sugar diet, therefore, usually aims at cutting out as much refined sugar as possible. This can be done simply by using less of it and deliberately cultivating a less sweet tooth, or by replacing it to some extent with other forms of sugar. Honey, for instance (which is mainly fructose and glucose, with little sucrose) is sweeter than sugar so less of it is needed. In this way you can cut down on both sucrose and the total quantity of sugar. Molasses, although a form of sucrose, has a very strong taste and again a teaspoon of it can sometimes be used instead of a tablespoon or more of sugar.

In this book, when the level of sugar in a recipe is indicated, it takes into account both the general level of sugar, including all its various forms – sucrose, fructose, glucose etc. – as well as any added sugar specified in the recipe. In the list of ingredients, sugar refers to the added sugar which is virtually pure sucrose. The suggestions for decreasing the sugar content of a recipe almost always refer to sucrose.

We are not concerned here with sugar substitutes nor with special diabetic sweeteners and jams. We do not aim to preserve an ultra-sweet taste. What we aim to do is to cut down the amount of refined sugar and to make more use of fruit and of small quantities of honey and molasses. The results will be definitely less sweet but still delicious.

The sugar content of a recipe is taken to be high if it contains the equivalent of more than 1 tablespoon of sugar per person.

Low-fat and low-cholesterol diets

One of the most common reasons for eating less fat and cholesterol is that there appears to be an undisputed link between the presence of cholesterol in the blood and liability to heart attacks.

Populations who eat less fat have lower levels of heart disease, although their consumption of oil may be high, as in many Mediterranean countries. The exact link has not yet been established, and it appears that other foods, for example garlic, onions and polyunsaturated fat, as well as fibre, have the ability to lower blood cholesterol. However, more and more people are coming to the conclusion that cutting down on fats, especially saturated fats, cannot do them any harm. Certainly it will help calorie control: fat contains twice as many calories per ounce as protein or carbohydrate.

Whether you want to lose weight or reduce the risk of a heart attack, low-fat and low-cholesterol diets are similar in many ways. Both encourage cutting down on the saturated fats which contain cholesterol.

Saturated fats are usually of animal origin but not always: coconuts, for example, have a saturated fat content of 83%. Unsaturated fats are mainly of vegetable origin and are further divided into monounsaturated and polyunsaturated fats. (These terms refer to the way in which their molecules are chemically bonded.) They are generally liquid at room temperature.

Monounsaturated fats (the most usual example is olive oil, which is 73% monounsaturated fat) have no effect on the level of cholesterol in the blood. Polyunsaturated fats can in fact, as stated above, actually lower the blood cholesterol level. There are a few foods which are very high in cholesterol relative to their fat content, notably shellfish, fish roes, and organ meats such as liver, kidney, brains and sweetbreads.

Those on a low-fat diet will want to cut down on all fats and oils. Those aiming at a low-cholesterol intake will want to eliminate as far as possible all saturated fats and will be cautious about eating shellfish and offal. This book shows you how to do either or both of these.

However the book does not purport to give a diet which actually lowers blood cholesterol. For instance, in the recipes olive oil is often specified. Those on such a diet will replace olive oil with safflower, soya or sunflower oils. Nor does this book attempt to give a fat-free diet. Such a diet should only be attempted under medical supervision, and even then it is bound to have a minimal fat content. Some fat is necessary in our diet, particularly linoleic acid, an essential fatty acid, which cannot be manufactured by the body: it is found in vegetable oils, particularly safflower oil.

Some particular foods that will be found useful in both low-fat and low-cholesterol diets are:

- skimmed milk, both liquid and dried
- low-fat cheese, particularly cottage cheese and low-fat curd cheese, such as quark or fromage blanc
- smetana (5–10% fat as opposed to 18% in sour cream)

For low-cholesterol diets:

- safflower, soya, sunflower and walnut oils
- (for frying over high heat): corn or peanut oils. It is, however, better to avoid frying over high heat as far as possible, since this changes the composition of the oils into something resembling saturated fat
- soft margarines with a high percentage of polyunsaturated oils (all margarines labelled "all vegetable" are virtually cholesterol-free)

The fat and cholesterol content of eggs is found only in the yolks, but in many cases yolks can be decreased or omitted, sometimes with a proportionate increase in the number of whites used.

The fat content of a recipe is taken to be high if it contains the equivalent of more than any 2 of the following per person:

$\frac{1}{2}$oz (1 tablespoon) double cream or oil
$\frac{1}{4}$oz (7 grams) butter, lard, suet or margarine
1 egg yolk
$\frac{1}{2}$oz (10–15 grams) ham, bacon, pork or cheese

The above applies also to the cholesterol content of a recipe, except that unsaturated oils are freely allowed, and over $\frac{1}{2}$ an egg yolk is considered to be high.

Fibre

The importance of fibre in the diet is now widely recognised, and many people pursue a high-fibre diet.

Since one of the best and easiest ways of increasing fibre intake is to eat a slice or two of wholemeal bread with your meal, the recipes themselves have not (except in one or two cases) been modified to include more fibre. The original versions of the recipes are always based on fresh ingredients, including vegetables, fruit and nuts (most of which are high in fibre), and wholefood adaptations are available for almost all the recipes, thus helping to increase the fibre level.

Gluten-free diet

As coeliac sufferers are being identified more and more frequently, so the need for a gluten-free diet for them and for other gluten-sensitive patients is becoming widely recognised.

A gluten-free diet involves complete exclusion of gluten (a protein, found mainly in wheat but also, in a different form and to a lesser extent, in rye, barley and oats). Commercial gluten-free flour is available and can be used successfully for bread, and some pastry and cakes; if it is difficult to find or expensive to buy just for one recipe, there are other flours, many of which are familiar to those on wholefood diets, which are gluten-free. Chick pea flour, brown rice flour, cornflour, potato flour and soya flour are perhaps the best known.

All labels on tins and jars must be carefully read, as wheat flour is a common ingredient not just in the obvious breads, biscuits, cakes, pastries and many cereals, but in packet soups, baking powder, sausages, stock cubes, bottled sauces and baked beans as well as in some brands of mustard, ground white pepper, curry powder and cheap chocolate.

Gluten-free grains include rice, maize, millet and buckwheat. Cornflour, chick pea flour and split pea flour are all suitable for making white sauces. For soufflés, cornflour and potato flour (the latter is denser than wheat flour and half the amount given in the recipe is usually enough) can be used. Any of these will do for coating food which is to be fried. Millet flakes make a good gluten-free alternative to a breadcrumb coating.

As a gluten-free diet is often low in fibre, it is advisable to eat plenty of brown rice, other whole grains and potatoes. Pectin (available dried from specialist suppliers) can be used as a binding agent in doughs and batters; grated fresh apple can also sometimes be used.

Intolerance of gluten is often associated with an inability to digest fats, so that a low-fat diet may also need to be followed.

Wholefood diet

Since the recipes in this book are based firmly on fresh seasonal produce, they need little alteration to be acceptable to lovers of wholefood.

The main items to avoid are refined flour and sugar. Wholemeal flour and bread, and brown rice or sugar, can be used instead as desired. When buying brown sugar, look for the name of the country of origin on the packet. If this is not given, the sugar may be white sugar that has been coloured brown with caramel.

In the case of sugar, it may also be necessary to follow any suggestion given for reducing the total amount. A high level of even the comparatively unrefined brown sugar is not usually considered wholefood. Anything other than this will be covered in the Alternatives column. Where quantities or proportions are affected, as for instance in baking, this will also be covered.

NEW ENGLAND FISH CHOWDER

The traditional chowder or fish soup cum stew is a perfect cold-weather dish which takes less than an hour to prepare and cook. Any type of white fish fillet may be used, and prawns can be substituted for the crabmeat.

PREPARATION TIME: *20 min*
COOKING TIME: *20–25 min*
INGREDIENTS *(for 4–6):*
1 lb (450 g) cod fillet
1 large onion
½ lb (225 g) potatoes
2 oz (50 g) mushrooms
3 oz (75 g) pickled belly pork
1 oz (25 g) butter
4 level teaspoons flour
½ pint (300 ml) milk
2 oz (50 g) chopped white crabmeat
Salt and black pepper*
Lemon juice
2 level tablespoons chopped parsley
GARNISH:
Bread croûtons (page 96)

Wash the fish and cut it into three or four pieces. Peel and roughly chop the onion. Peel the potatoes and cut them into ½in (1 cm) cubes; trim the mushrooms and slice them. Bring 1 pint (570 ml) of water to the boil, add 1 level teaspoon salt and the fish and simmer over low heat for 10 minutes. Drain the fish and set the liquid aside. Remove the rind and gristle and dice the pork. Fry the pork in a sauté pan over low heat until the fat runs. Add the butter and continue frying until the pork crisps.

Add the potatoes, onions and mushrooms to the pork and fry for a further 5 minutes.

Remove the pan from the heat and stir in the flour, then gradually add the milk. Bring the mixture to simmering point, then stir in ¾ pint (425 ml) of the reserved fish stock. Add the fish, which will break up naturally, and the crabmeat. Simmer for 10 minutes, season to taste with salt, freshly ground pepper and lemon juice; stir in the parsley.

Serve the chowder with a bowl of crisp bread croûtons.

PESCADO A LA MARINA

The South Americans, even more than the French, are great believers in marinating meat and fish before cooking them. The marinade, which imparts an unusual flavour to any fish fillets, is used for the sauce.

PREPARATION TIME: *1 hour 20 min*
COOKING TIME: *15 min*
INGREDIENTS *(for 4–6):*
1½ lb (700 g) haddock or cod fillet
1 egg
3–4 oz (75–100 g) fresh breadcrumbs
Oil for frying
MARINADE:
4 tablespoons olive oil
2 tablespoons lemon juice
1 small onion
1 clove garlic
1–2 bay leaves
*1 level teaspoon salt**
Black pepper and ground nutmeg
MARINA SAUCE:
4 fluid oz (100 ml) dry white wine
2 egg yolks
GARNISH:
1 heaped tablespoon finely chopped parsley

Make the marinade first, by blending together the olive oil and lemon juice; peel and finely chop the onion and garlic. Add to the oil, together with the bay leaves, salt, freshly ground pepper and a pinch of nutmeg.

Wash the fish fillets and divide into four or six portions. Place them in a shallow dish and pour over the prepared marinade. Leave for about 1 hour, turning the fish from time to time.

Lift out the fish, setting the marinade aside. Dry the fillets thoroughly on absorbent kitchen paper. Lightly beat the egg and brush it over the fish before coating with breadcrumbs. Press the crumbs well in, and shake off any surplus. Leave the coating to harden while making the sauce.

Bring the marinade to the boil, then strain it through a fine sieve into a bowl. Add the wine. Beat the egg yolks together in a separate bowl and gradually stir in the wine and marinade. Place the bowl over a saucepan of gently simmering water and stir continuously with a wooden spoon until the sauce thickens sufficiently to coat the back of the spoon. If the sauce shows signs of curdling, add a tablespoon of cold water and remove the bowl from the heat.

Heat the oil in a heavy-based pan and fry the fish until golden brown on both sides, turning once. Drain on absorbent paper.

Serve the fish hot, sprinkled with parsley. Serve the Marina sauce separately and offer creamed potatoes and buttered beans. The fillets may also be served cold with a sauce tartare (page 22) and a crisp green salad.

NEW ENGLAND FISH CHOWDER

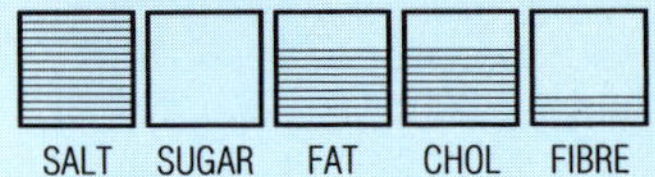

GLUTEN-FREE* WHOLEFOOD*
TOTAL CALORIES: ABOUT 1660

The **salt** can be reduced to low if the pork is reduced or omitted and unsalted butter is used. Although crabmeat is high in sodium, the amount used is very small so that omitting it would make hardly any difference. Compensate for the lack of salt by adding extra lemon juice, parsley and pepper.
To reduce the **fat** content to low, halve or omit the pork; use half the amount of butter and use skim milk (or you could substitute fish stock). Toast the croûtons instead of frying them. (Calories lost: up to 600.)
For low **cholesterol**, adapt as for low fat, and replace the butter with vegetable margarine or sunflower oil.
You can increase the **fibre** content by using a higher proportion of potatoes to fish.
As well as commercial **gluten-free** flour, cornflour, potato flour or brown rice flour could all be used similarly for thickening the soup.

Freezing: ☑ up to 1 month.

PESCADO A LA MARINA

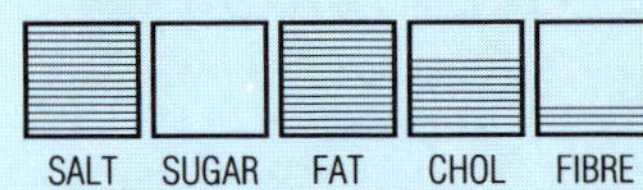

GLUTEN-FREE* WHOLEFOOD*
TOTAL CALORIES: ABOUT 1800

To reduce the **salt** content to very low, replace the added salt with more lemon juice and chopped garlic.

You can reduce the **fat** level to moderate by poaching the fish, rather than frying it in the traditional way. Poach it in the marinade and the wine for about 7 minutes, then lift it out gently and use the strained liquid to make the sauce. Use a whole egg rather than two yolks for thickening the sauce. This will give medium **cholesterol**. (Calories lost: up to 500.) If you are serving cold, the fat can be reduced still further by replacing the sauce tartare with a yogurt sauce made by stirring the chopped capers and parsley into thick low-fat plain yogurt with a little lemon juice and pepper. (Further calories lost: 400.)
Instead of **gluten-free** breadcrumbs, you can use millet flakes for coating the fish. **Wholefood:** instead of wholemeal breadcrumbs, oatmeal or millet flakes can be used for coating the fish.

FISH PIE WITH CHEESE CUSTARD

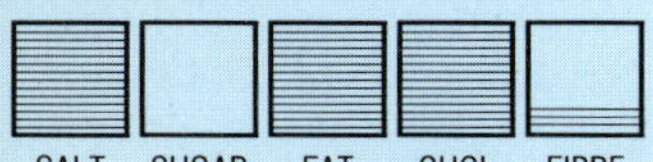

GLUTEN-FREE* WHOLEFOOD*
TOTAL CALORIES: ABOUT 2050

Minimise the **salt** by halving the amount of smoked fish and increasing the fresh fish to balance; use unsalted stock and unsalted fat in the white sauce. Reduce the **fat** to low and the **cholesterol** to medium by using only ¾ oz (20 g) butter (or soft margarine) in the sauce; use skim milk for the custard and omit the knobs of butter on the surface. (Calories lost: up to 390.) Serve with baked or boiled potatoes.

Freezing: ☑ up to 1 month.

FISH PIE WITH CHEESE CUSTARD

Smoked cod enhances the flavour of this fish pie, topped with a cheese and tomato custard.

PREPARATION TIME: *35 min*
COOKING TIME: *45 min*
INGREDIENTS *(for 6):*
1¼ lb (550 g) cod fillet
6 oz (175 g) smoked cod fillet
1½ pints (900 ml) chicken or fish stock (page 81)
1 onion
3 cloves
1 clove garlic
Salt and black pepper*
½ pint (300 ml) white sauce (page 82)
1 lb (450 g) tomatoes
2 eggs
½ pint (300 ml) milk
2 oz (50 g) Parmesan cheese
1 oz (25 g) unsalted butter

Wash and skin the fresh cod, wipe the smoked cod with a cloth and cut both into 1 in (2½ cm) wide slices. Put the fish slices in a deep sauté pan and cover with the chicken stock. Peel and finely slice the onion and add to the fish, together with the cloves and the crushed garlic. Bring slowly to the boil, and season with salt and freshly ground pepper. Simmer for 10 minutes, then remove the cod from the liquid.

Increase the heat and boil the fish liquid rapidly until it has reduced to ½ pint (300 ml); strain and use for the white sauce.

Flake the fish into a deep 8 in (20 cm) wide pie dish, pour over the hot white sauce and coat the fish thoroughly. Skin and slice the tomatoes (page 97) in a layer over the fish, and pepper well. Beat the eggs with salt and pepper; beat in the grated cheese and milk. Pour this mixture over the tomatoes and float small knobs of butter on the surface. Bake for 45 minutes or until golden brown, on the centre shelf of an oven heated to 325°F (170°C, mark 3).

Sauté potatoes and Brussels sprouts or cauliflower could be served with the pie.

FISHERMAN'S PIE

Left-over cooked fish forms the basis for this savoury dish, which is covered with a mustard-flavoured cheese scone dough.

PREPARATION TIME: *25 min*
COOKING TIME: *25–30 min*
INGREDIENTS *(for 4–6)*:
½ lb (225 g) cooked white fish
½ lb (225 g) cooked smoked haddock
Half a small green pepper
2 hardboiled eggs
Juice of a lemon
2 tablespoons chopped parsley
¾ pint (425 ml) white sauce (page 82)
Salt and black pepper*
6 oz (175 g) self-raising flour
1½ oz (40 g) butter
2 level teaspoons dry mustard
2–3 oz (50–75 g) grated Cheddar cheese
¼ pint (150 ml) milk

Skin and flake the fish; finely chop the green pepper and the hard-boiled eggs. Mix the fish, green pepper, eggs, lemon juice and parsley into the white sauce. Season with salt and pepper. Spoon the mixture into a 2 pint (1·2 litre) fireproof dish.

Sift the flour into a bowl and rub in the butter. Add the mustard and cheese and sufficient milk to make a soft pliable pastry dough. Knead this lightly on a floured surface, and roll out a circle, ¾ in (2 cm) thick, large enough to cover the dish. Cut the pastry into eight triangles and place over the fish so that the points meet in the centre. Brush with milk and bake the dish for 25 minutes, at 425°F (220°C, mark 7), or until the top of the pastry is golden.

MATELOTE OF EELS

A *matelote* – not to be confused with *matelot* (a sailor) – is the French culinary term for a fish stew. In this recipe, eels are used for a wholesome main course for lunch or supper.

PREPARATION TIME: *20 min*
COOKING TIME: *45 min*
INGREDIENTS *(for 4–6)*:
1½ lb (700 g) eels
2 small onions
3 oz (75 g) unsalted butter
½ bottle dry white wine
1 carrot
1 clove garlic
Bouquet garni (page 99)
½ level teaspoon ground mace
Salt and black pepper*
1 egg yolk
¼ pint (150 ml) double cream
GARNISH:
12 button mushrooms
12 button onions
Fried bread triangles

Have the eels skinned and cleaned. Peel and thinly slice the onions and sauté half in 2 oz (50 g) butter for 5 minutes until golden. Wash and dry the eels and cut into 2 in (5 cm) pieces, add to the onion and continue frying gently, for about 10 minutes, turning the eels until lightly browned. Pour in the wine and bring to a simmer. Peel, slice and chop the carrot, peel and crush the garlic and add these to the pan, together with the remaining onion, bouquet garni, mace and seasoning. Cover with a lid and simmer for 25 minutes.

Meanwhile, wipe and trim the mushrooms, peel the button onions and sauté both in the remaining butter; fry the bread triangles. Remove the fish and keep warm on a serving dish.

FISHERMAN'S PIE

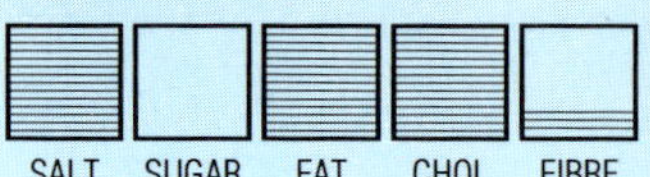

GLUTEN-FREE* WHOLEFOOD*
TOTAL CALORIES: ABOUT 2695

Minimise the **salt** by halving or omitting the smoked fish, replacing it with extra fresh fish. Compensate by adding more green pepper and seasoning with cayenne.
To reduce both **fat** and **cholesterol** to low, omit one of the eggs and use skim milk. Use half the amount of Cheddar, or replace it with a reduced-fat variety. (Calories lost: up to 465.)
Instead of using commercial **gluten-free** flour, you could make the white sauce with cornflour and cover the pie with mashed potatoes.

Microwave: ☑

MATELOTE OF EELS

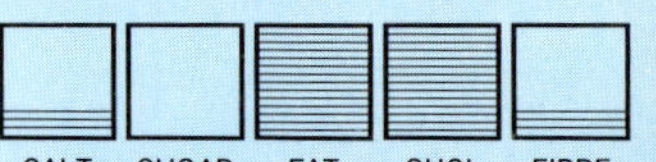

GLUTEN-FREE* WHOLEFOOD*
TOTAL CALORIES: ABOUT 3660

To reduce **salt** to almost none, substitute unsalted fish stock for the wine.
For low **fat** and **cholesterol,** sauté the eels in only 1 oz (25 g) butter, toast the bread triangles used to serve, and poach the vegetables in a little stock. Use very small eels. The fat content of eels is much less when they are tiny elvers. Substitute low-fat yogurt for the cream and thicken with cornflour instead of egg yolk. (Calories lost: up to 1205.)

Freezing: ☑ up to 1 month.

SMELTS WITH ALMONDS

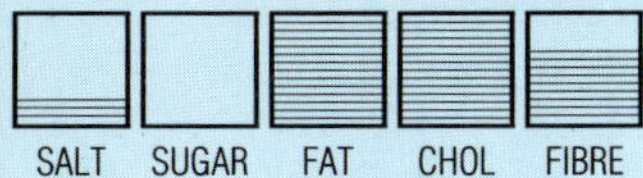

GLUTEN-FREE* WHOLEFOOD*
TOTAL CALORIES: ABOUT 2600

For medium **fat** and low **cholesterol** grill the smelts on a shallow baking tray containing one tablespoon each of oil and butter. Use smetana, low-fat yogurt or beaten egg white in place of the cream; and only 1 oz (25 g) of almonds. Toast or grill the almonds instead of frying them. (Calories lost: up to 1490.)

WHITING WITH ORANGE SAUCE

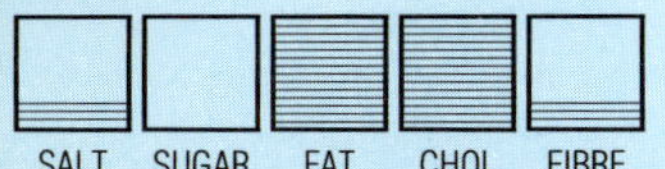

GLUTEN-FREE* WHOLEFOOD*
TOTAL CALORIES: ABOUT 2835

To reduce **fat** to low, the sauce method needs to be completely changed. Use smetana instead of cream and thicken with a tablespoon of arrowroot or cornflour mixed to a smooth paste with a little of the liquid. Heat gently and let it just simmer (on no account boil) for a few minutes with the orange and lemon juice and seasoning. Do not add any butter.
The fish could also be grilled after coating on a shallow baking tin containing 1 oz (25 g) hot oil or vegetable margarine. These measures reduce both fat and **cholesterol** level to low. (Calories lost: up to 950.)
Gluten-free: cornflour can be used for coating the fish. Serve with potatoes or rice.

Microwave: ✓ for the fish.

Beat the egg yolk and cream together and add a little of the fish liquid. Blend this into the mixture in the pan and continue gently stirring until the sauce thickens. Pour the sauce over the eels and serve garnished with the mushrooms, onions and bread triangles.

SMELTS WITH ALMONDS

These small salt-water fish are at their best when caught at spawning time in late winter. Their delicate flavour is most apparent when baked or fried. If smelts are not available, young trout or sardines can be substituted.

PREPARATION TIME: *10 min*
COOKING TIME: *10 min*
INGREDIENTS *(for 6):*
18 smelts
3 fluid oz (75 ml) single cream
Seasoned flour (page 100)
3 oz (75 g) unsalted butter
1 tablespoon olive oil
4 oz (100 g) flaked almonds

Lightly wash the smelts in cold water; cut off the heads and squeeze out the entrails. Dry the cleaned smelts on a cloth; dip the fish in the cream and roll in seasoned flour. Melt the butter in a heavy-based frying pan, add the olive oil and gently fry the smelts for 4 minutes on each side.

Remove the smelts from the pan and keep them warm. Increase the heat slightly and fry the flaked almonds in the fat in which the fish has been cooked until they turn light brown. Sprinkle the smelts with the almonds and then pour over the butter.

Serve the smelts with thin slices of wholemeal bread.

WHITING WITH ORANGE SAUCE

Fish with orange was as popular in the 18th century as fish with lemon is today. Originally, sharp Seville oranges were used, but the mixture of orange and lemon in this recipe is equally good.

PREPARATION TIME: *10 min*
COOKING TIME: *40 min*
INGREDIENTS *(for 6):*
6 whiting
Salt and black pepper*
1 lemon
1 orange
4 tablespoons double cream
¼ pint (150 ml) dry white wine
3 large egg yolks
Cayenne pepper
4 oz (100 g) unsalted butter
Seasoned flour (page 100)
GARNISH:
1 orange
Chopped parsley

Clean and wash the whiting, and fillet each into two. Dry the fillets thoroughly on absorbent kitchen paper and season with salt and pepper; sprinkle over the juice of half a lemon. Set aside. Grate the rind from the orange and set aside; squeeze the juice of the orange and remaining half lemon into a bowl.

For the sauce, stir the cream, wine and egg yolks into the fruit juices and set the bowl over a pan of simmering water. Whisk the sauce mixture continuously until it has the consistency of thin cream. Season to taste with salt, pepper and cayenne, and blend in the orange rind. Cut half the butter into knobs and beat them one by one into the sauce. Keep the sauce hot, but do not allow it to boil.

Coat the whiting fillets with seasoned flour. Melt the remaining butter in a large, heavy-based pan and fry the fillets until golden brown on both sides.

Garnish the fillets with orange wedges and chopped parsley. The sauce can be served separately or poured over the fish. Offer crusty French bread with which to mop up the sauce.

SMOKED HADDOCK MOUSSE

A mousse, whether savoury or sweet, should be chilled for several hours before serving. This recipe, suitable for a dinner party or a buffet, can also be made with smoked cod.

PREPARATION TIME: *45 min*
CHILLING TIME: *2–3 hours*
INGREDIENTS *(for 6–8):*

2 lb (900 g) smoked haddock fillet
1 small onion
¾ pint (425 ml) milk
1 bay leaf
1½ oz (40 g) unsalted butter
1½ oz (40 g) plain flour
Salt and black pepper*
Cayenne pepper
½ oz (10 g) powdered gelatine
Juice and rind of a lemon
½ pint (300 ml) double cream

ASPIC:
½ level teaspoon powdered gelatine
1 tablespoon lemon juice or vinegar

GARNISH:
½ cucumber

Cut the haddock fillet into 8–10 pieces and put them in a saucepan; peel and slice the onion and add, with the milk and bay leaf, to the fish. Cover the pan with a lid and simmer the fish over low heat for about 10 minutes. Strain the fish through a colander and set the milk aside. Remove all skin and bones, and flake the haddock flesh finely.

Melt the butter in a saucepan over low heat; stir in the flour and cook for a few minutes until this roux is light brown. Gradually stir in the milk, beating continuously to get a smooth sauce. Bring this to the boil and cook gently for 2–3 minutes. Season to taste with salt, freshly ground pepper and cayenne, then draw the pan off the heat. Pour the sauce into a large bowl, cover with buttered greaseproof paper and leave to cool. Measure 4 tablespoons of water into a saucepan and sprinkle in the gelatine. Allow to soak for 5 minutes, then stir the mixture over low heat, until the gelatine has dissolved.

Remove the buttered paper and stir the sauce; blend in the fish, melted gelatine and finely grated rind and juice from the lemon. Correct seasoning if necessary. Whip the cream lightly and fold it into the fish mixture; pour this into a 2½–3 pint (1½–1¾ litre) soufflé dish and leave until set.

For the aspic, measure 2 tablespoons of water into a saucepan and sprinkle over the gelatine. Soak for 5 minutes, then stir over low heat until the gelatine has dissolved. Draw the pan from the heat, add 2 tablespoons of water and the lemon juice. Pour a little aspic on top of the mousse. While this is setting slightly, wash and thinly slice the cucumber. Arrange the slices in a circular pattern on the aspic and leave to set. Spoon over the remaining aspic, and chill the mousse in the refrigerator until ready to serve.

Serve with a green salad tossed in French dressing (page 83).

COD GOURMET

This recipe for poaching cod in white wine, mushrooms and shallots is equally good with other firm-fleshed white fish.

PREPARATION TIME: *15 min*
COOKING TIME: *25 min*
INGREDIENTS *(for 4):*

4 cod fillets, about 5 oz (150 g) each
1–2 tablespoons plain flour
3 oz (75 g) unsalted butter
3 shallots
¼ lb (100 g) mushrooms
Salt and black pepper*
2 tablespoons dry white wine
2 teaspoons lemon juice

GARNISH:
1 tablespoon chopped parsley

Wash and skin the cod fillets. Pat them dry on absorbent paper and coat with a little flour. Grease a large, shallow, ovenproof dish with 1 oz (25 g) of the butter and arrange the fillets in this. Peel and finely chop the shallots. Melt the remaining butter in a pan and fry the shallots over low heat for 2–3 minutes, until transparent. Wipe and trim the mushrooms, slice them thinly and add to the shallots. Cook for a further 2 minutes, then season to taste with salt and freshly ground pepper.

Spoon the shallot and mushroom mixture over the cod fillets and pour over the wine. Cover the dish with a lid or foil and bake for 25 minutes in the centre of an oven pre-heated to 400°F (200°C, mark 6).

Serve the fish straight from the dish. Sprinkle with lemon juice and garnish with parsley. New potatoes and young peas go well with this dish.

SMOKED HADDOCK MOUSSE

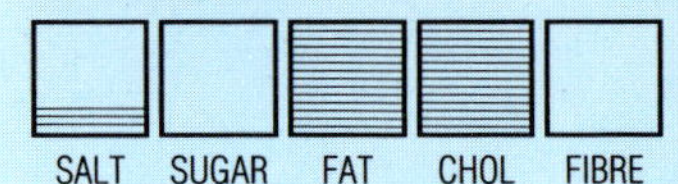

GLUTEN-FREE* WHOLEFOOD*
TOTAL CALORIES: ABOUT 2810

For low **salt**, use fresh trout or salmon, not smoked fish.
The **fat** and **cholesterol** levels of this recipe can be reduced but this involves changing the texture. For this low-fat version, use skim milk and only ¾ oz (20 g) butter for the sauce, and substitute smetana for the double cream, adding 3 stiffly beaten egg whites to make up the bulk as smetana will not whip.
(Calories lost: up to 985.)
Cornflour and potato flour are **gluten-free** flours that could be used for making the sauce.

Microwave: ✓ for cooking the haddock.

COD GOURMET

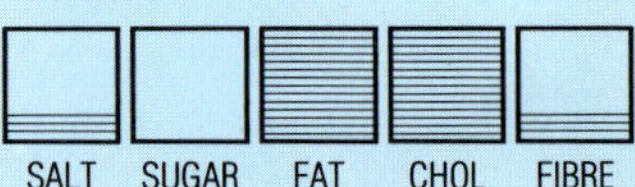

GLUTEN-FREE* WHOLEFOOD*
TOTAL CALORIES: ABOUT 1285

To reduce both **fat** and **cholesterol** to low, use only 1 teaspoon oil to grease the ovenproof dish and a further 2 teaspoons to brush the pan for sautéing the shallots and mushrooms. Serve with unbuttered vegetables.
(Calories lost: up to 500.)
Gluten-free flours: cornflour or rice flour are both suitable for coating the fish.

Freezing: ✓ up to 1 month.
Microwave: ✓

STUFFED RED SNAPPER

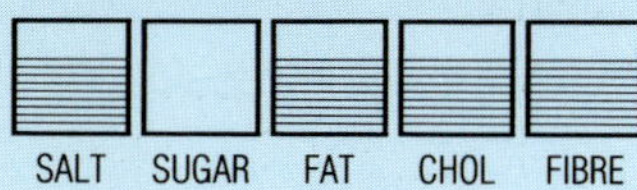

GLUTEN-FREE* WHOLEFOOD*
TOTAL CALORIES: ABOUT 5200

The **salt** can be reduced to very low by using unsalted fat and unsalted bread for the crumbs. For low **fat** and **cholesterol**, cook the onions and garlic in a pan lightly brushed with oil and halve the amount of almonds used. (Calories lost: up to 350.)

Microwave: √

FINNAN FILLED PANCAKES

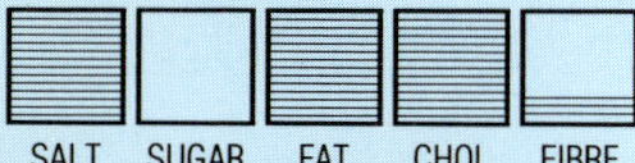

GLUTEN-FREE* WHOLEFOOD*
TOTAL CALORIES: ABOUT 2010

Reduce **salt** to low by using fresh trout or white fish in place of smoked haddock.
To reduce the **fat** and **cholesterol** to low, use skim milk in the pancake batter and replace the butter with 2 teaspoons of oil for softening the vegetables. For cooking the crêpes, brush the pan sparingly with oil. The pancake batter can be made using only white of egg. Omit the butter poured over the pancakes and use a reduced-fat Cheddar, or Edam or thinly-sliced Mozzarella. (Calories lost: up to 870.)
Gluten-free pancakes can be made using 2 eggs beaten with 4 tablespoons gluten-free flour and 6 tablespoons skim milk.

Microwave: √ to finish cooking the stuffed pancakes.

STUFFED RED SNAPPER

This superb fish adapts well to baking. The stuffing is a novel combination of cucumbers, onions, and almonds. Bream, bass and grey mullet are other suitable fish.

PREPARATION TIME: *20 min*
COOKING TIME: *40–45 min*
INGREDIENTS *(for 4–5):*
1 red snapper, 4–5lb (about 2 kg)
Salt and pepper*
1–2 oz (25–50 g) butter
2 oz (50 g) chopped almonds
1 large onion
1 clove garlic, minced
12 oz (350 g) dry breadcrumbs
½ large cucumber
1 teaspoon dried thyme
Dry sherry

Have the fish boned and prepared for stuffing. Rub the inside with salt, pepper, and butter. Toast the almonds (page 96). Sauté the sliced onion and garlic in butter until soft. Combine them with the breadcrumbs, minced cucumber, and toasted almonds. Season with salt, pepper, and thyme and moisten with a little sherry. Stuff the fish and close the opening with wooden cocktail sticks or toothpicks. Salt and pepper the fish and bake in a well-greased dish at 350°F (180°C, mark 4) for 40–45 minutes, or until the fish flakes when tested with a fork. Baste with the pan juices.

Plain boiled or steamed potatoes and a salad of tomatoes and onions go especially well with this dish.

FINNAN FILLED PANCAKES

Cured haddock from Findon in Kincardineshire, known as Finnan Haddie, is cleaned and split before being smoked. Follow the recipe for pancakes on page 20, using 4 oz (100 g) flour and 8 fluid oz (225 ml) milk to 1 egg.

PREPARATION TIME: *20 min*
COOKING TIME: *30 min*
INGREDIENTS *(for 4):*
½ lb (225 g) cooked smoked finnan haddock or cod fillet
½ pint (300 ml) pancake batter (see above)
1 small onion
2 tablespoons chopped celery
4 oz (100 g) mushrooms
3½ oz (90 g) unsalted butter
14 or 16 oz (400 or 450 g) tinned tomatoes
Salt and black pepper*
Lemon juice
3–4 tablespoons grated Cheddar or Gruyère cheese
GARNISH:
Lemon wedges
Parsley sprigs

Make eight small thin pancakes from the batter and set them aside. Peel and finely chop the onion, and prepare the celery. Trim the mushrooms and slice them thinly.

Melt 1½ oz (40 g) of the butter and fry the onion, celery and mushrooms until soft. Add the tomatoes, and season with salt and freshly ground pepper. Simmer the contents of the pan, uncovered, until it has reduced to a thick purée.

Meanwhile, remove the skin from the haddock, and flake the flesh. Add the haddock to the onion and tomato mixture, sharpen to taste with lemon juice and adjust seasoning.

Spoon 2 tablespoons of the filling down the centre of each pancake and fold the sides over to form an envelope. Arrange the stuffed pancakes side by side in a shallow flameproof dish. Melt the remaining butter and pour it over the pancakes. Sprinkle generously with grated cheese and set the dish under a hot, pre-heated grill or in the oven until the cheese is bubbly brown.

Garnish the pancakes with lemon wedges and parsley sprigs and serve with buttered peas.

BRILL SOUFFLÉ

Brill is an ideal fish for pies and soufflés, served with a mousseline sauce. Any firm-fleshed white fish can be used.

PREPARATION TIME: *30 min*
COOKING TIME: *45 min*
INGREDIENTS *(for 4–6):*
1 lb (450 g) brill
Salt and black pepper*
1 small bay leaf
1 blade mace
¼ pint (150 ml) milk
3 oz (75 g) unsalted butter
3 oz (75 g) plain flour
Nutmeg
3 large eggs
MOUSSELINE SAUCE:
Juice of ½ large lemon
2 large egg yolks
4 oz (100 g) unsalted butter
Salt and black pepper*
4 tablespoons double cream

Wash the brill thoroughly and put it whole into a saucepan; cover with cold water. Add ½ teaspoon of salt, the bay leaf and mace to the fish, and cover the pan with a lid. Bring slowly to simmering point, turn off the heat and leave the pan to stand for 10 minutes. Lift out the fish, set aside ½ pint (300 ml) of the liquid and make it up to ¾ pint (425 ml) with milk.

Remove the skin and bones from the fish and flake the flesh roughly. Melt 3 oz (75 g) of the butter in a large saucepan and stir in the flour. Cook this roux over low heat for 2 minutes, stirring continuously, then gradually stir in the fish and milk liquid. Bring to the boil, still stirring, and cook for 2 minutes or until the mixture is thick and smooth. Season to taste with salt, freshly ground pepper and nutmeg. Carefully fold the flaked fish into the sauce. Separate the three eggs and beat the yolks into the fish mixture, one by one; whisk the egg whites until stiff then gently fold them in as well.

Spoon the mixture into a prepared 3 pint (1¾ litre) soufflé dish; cook in the centre of the oven preheated to 400°F (200°C, mark 6) for 45 minutes or until the soufflé is risen and golden brown on top.

For the sauce, put the lemon juice and 1 teaspoon of cold water in a basin. Beat the egg yolks lightly and stir them into the lemon juice. Stand the basin over a saucepan of gently simmering water, but do not allow the bottom of the basin to touch the water. Stir in ½ oz (10 g) of butter and whisk the mixture until it thickens.

Remove the basin from the heat and gradually whisk in the remaining butter, cut into small knobs. Whisk until the butter is completely absorbed before adding the next knob. Season to taste with salt and pepper. Whip the cream and fold it gently into the sauce. Heat the sauce in the basin over the pan of simmering water, whisking all the time.

Serve the soufflé immediately, and offer the mousseline sauce in a sauceboat. Boiled broccoli or cauliflower, or a green salad, could be served with the soufflé.

MEDITERRANEAN FISH SOUP

On a cold winter's evening, this thick soup serves almost as a meal in itself. It can be prepared well in advance and re-heated just before serving without losing any of its delicate flavour.

PREPARATION TIME: *35 min*
COOKING TIME: *45 min*
INGREDIENTS *(for 6–8):*
12 oz (350 g) each of grey or sea mullet, whiting and plaice
1 large onion
6 tablespoons olive oil
1 clove garlic
14 or 16 oz (400 or 450 g) tin tomatoes
2 level tablespoons tomato paste
1 heaped tablespoon chopped parsley
1½ pints (900 ml) fish stock (page 81) or water

BRILL SOUFFLÉ

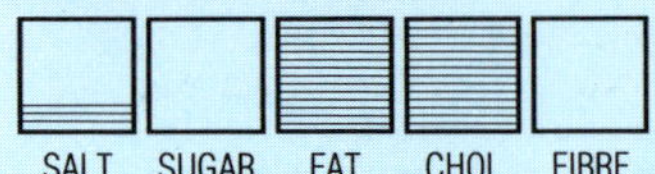

GLUTEN-FREE* WHOLEFOOD*
TOTAL CALORIES: ABOUT 3140

You can reduce the **fat** level (but not the **cholesterol**) in the soufflé itself to medium by halving the amount of butter and flour used to make the soufflé base. However, the mousseline sauce is very high in fat, which cannot easily be reduced. Instead, try serving the soufflé with a mixture of smetana, lemon juice and herbs, seasoned with black pepper and gently heated but *not* boiled. This gives a fairly low fat and cholesterol level. (Calories lost: up to 1255.) For an even lower cholesterol version, use only 1 egg yolk added to 3 egg whites for the soufflé. (Further calories lost: 140.)
Commercial **gluten-free** flour can be successfully used for the soufflé; so can potato flour, in about half the quantity.

Microwave: ✓ for cooking the fish.

MEDITERRANEAN FISH SOUP

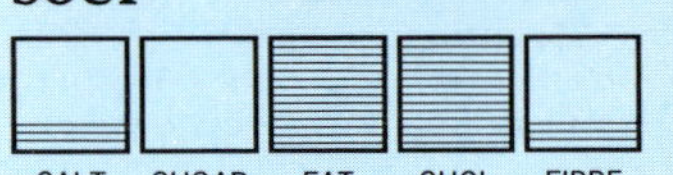

GLUTEN-FREE WHOLEFOOD
TOTAL CALORIES: ABOUT 2675

Remember that the **salt** level will only be low if the tomatoes and tomato paste used have no added salt.
To reduce levels of both **fat** and **cholesterol** to low, use only 1 tablespoon of oil to soften the

onion, and substitute low fat yogurt or smetana for the cream. The cream can even be omitted completely and you will still have a delicious soup. (Calories lost: up to 1288).
If cholesterol content only, and not fat, is your worry, there is no need to reduce the oil so drastically, and it does contribute to the taste of the soup. The prawns, which are rich in cholesterol, could be omitted, especially if all you can get are frozen prawns which have little taste anyway.

Freezing: √ up to 1 month.
Microwave: √

BREAM PLAKI

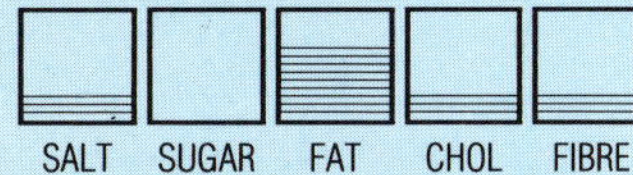

SALT SUGAR FAT CHOL FIBRE

GLUTEN-FREE WHOLEFOOD
TOTAL CALORIES: ABOUT 2025

This dish is almost ideal for whatever diet you may be following, except for the **fat**. Greek cooking tends to be generous with olive oil, and the amount given here can easily be reduced to only 1 tablespoon, making the dish low in fat. (Calories lost: up to 265.)
The only **cholesterol** comes from the fish, and this type is low in cholesterol. Sunflower or safflower oil can be substituted for the olive oil if you are on a diet which aims at actually lowering the level of blood cholesterol, but the taste of good fruity olive oil is part of the character of this dish.

Freezing: √ up to 1 month.
Microwave: √

¼ pint (150 ml) dry white wine
1 bay leaf
Large piece lemon peel
Salt and black pepper*
¼ pint (150 ml) double cream
GARNISH:
Prawns
Tomato slices

Clean, fillet and skin the fish (page 84); use the trimmings and bones as a base for the fish stock. Cut the fish fillets diagonally into 2 in (5 cm) pieces. Peel and finely chop the onion. Heat the oil in a heavy-based pan and cook the onion in this until soft, but not browned. Crush and add the garlic, fry for a minute or two before adding the tinned tomatoes with their juice, tomato paste and chopped parsley. Mix it all together and simmer slowly for 15 minutes. Add the fish, the stock, wine, bay leaf and lemon peel, bring back to the simmer, cover with a lid and cook slowly for 20 minutes. Discard the bay leaf and lemon peel. Season with salt and freshly ground pepper and leave the soup to cool slightly.

Remove one piece of fish for each serving and keep warm; liquidise the rest, along with the contents of the pan, until blended to a smooth creamy consistency.

Stir in the cream and re-heat the soup without bringing it to the boil. Place one piece of fish in each individual bowl and pour over the soup. Float slices of skinned tomatoes (page 97), garnished with a few peeled prawns, on top of each bowl.

BREAM PLAKI

Large fish such as bream, brill and John Dory are well suited to being cooked by this Greek method. The fish is baked whole in the oven, and tomatoes and lemon are traditional in a plaki.

PREPARATION TIME: *15 min*
COOKING TIME: *45 min*
INGREDIENTS *(for 4–6):*
2–3 lb (1–1½ kg) bream
1 large onion
1 large clove garlic
1 level teaspoon fennel or coriander seeds
3 tablespoons olive oil
Salt and black pepper*
1 large lemon
1–2 level tablespoons chopped parsley
14 or 16 oz (400 or 450 g) tin of tomatoes
4 fluid oz (100 ml) dry white wine

Peel and thinly slice the onion and peel the garlic. Crush the fennel or coriander seeds in a mortar or with a broad-bladed knife. Scale and clean the fish and place it whole in an oiled baking dish; sprinkle generously with salt, freshly ground pepper and the juice from half the lemon.

Heat the remaining oil in a pan and fry the onion and crushed garlic over medium heat, until soft and transparent. Stir in the tomatoes, with their juice; add the parsley, crushed seeds and wine. Cook this sauce for a few minutes until well blended, then season the sauce with salt and pepper.

Pour the sauce over the bream, topping up with a little water, if the baking dish is large. Cut the remaining lemon into thin slices and lay them on top of the fish. Cover the dish with foil or a lid, and bake in the centre of a preheated oven, at 375°F (190°C, mark 5), for about 45 minutes.

Serve the bream in the sauce, straight from the dish. Jacket or floury boiled potatoes will go especially well with this dish.

BAKED HALIBUT STEAKS

This is a good way to cook firm fish, such as halibut, grey mullet, cod, haddock or flounder.

PREPARATION TIME: *20 min*
COOKING TIME: *10–12 min*
INGREDIENTS *(for 4):*
2–2½ lb (about 1 kg) halibut, cut into 1 in (2½ cm) thick slices
4 tablespoons olive oil
2 large onions
4 cloves garlic
14 or 16 oz (400 or 450 g) tin of tomatoes
Juice of ½ lemon
1 large bunch parsley
2 bay leaves
Pinch of rosemary (optional)
Pinch of thyme (optional)
Salt and black pepper*
White wine (optional)
GARNISH:
Lemon wedges

Heat the olive oil in a heavy pan and sauté a few of the halibut slices at a time very briefly on each side to sear them. As they are seared, transfer them to an ovenproof baking dish large enough to hold the slices in one layer. Peel and slice the onion; peel the garlic. Add these to the pan and sauté them for about 10 minutes or until they are soft and slightly coloured.

Add the tomatoes, lemon juice, chopped parsley, bay leaves, and the rosemary and thyme (if used). Season generously with salt and freshly ground pepper. Stir well, then simmer very gently for about 10 minutes. If the mixture gets too thick as it cooks, add a little white wine or water.

Pour this sauce over the fish and bake in a pre-heated oven at 425°F (220°C, mark 7) for 10–12 minutes. Cover the top with a piece of cooking parchment or aluminium foil after the first 5 minutes of cooking time. Garnish with lemon wedges. This is also good served warm, rather than hot. Boiled potatoes and a green salad go well with it.

BAKED HALIBUT STEAKS

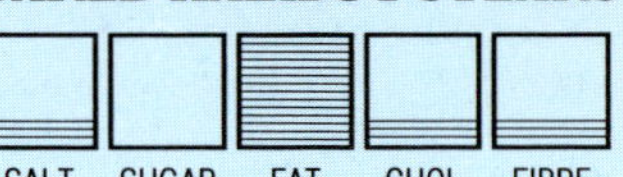

SALT SUGAR FAT CHOL FIBRE

GLUTEN-FREE WHOLEFOOD
TOTAL CALORIES: ABOUT 1855

Remember that this is only low in **salt** if the tomatoes used are unsalted.
The **fat** can be reduced to low by using only 2 teaspoons of oil to sauté the onions and garlic, and sealing the fish by placing it under a very hot grill for 30 seconds on each side. The only **cholesterol** comes from the fish, and this type has very little. (Calories lost: up to 400.)

Freezing: √ up to 1 month.
Microwave: √

CASSEROLE OF HALIBUT

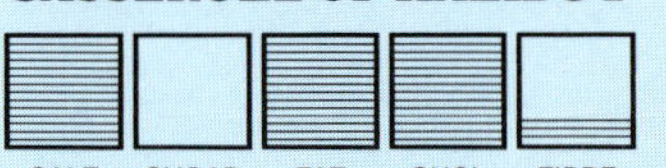

SALT SUGAR FAT CHOL FIBRE

GLUTEN-FREE* WHOLEFOOD*
TOTAL CALORIES: ABOUT 3080

Reduce **salt** to low by omitting the shrimps or using drained canned shrimps.
Reduce both **fat** and **cholesterol** to low by cooking the halibut in a dish that is oiled rather than buttered, and topping it with a mixture of smetana and low-fat soft cheese, diluted to the consistency of cream with dry white wine. Omitting the shrimps will reduce the cholesterol level to low when combined with these fat-cutting changes. Serve with tiny scones instead of high-fat puff pastry crescents, using the scone dough given for the Fisherman's Pie on page 12, with the low-fat variations

suggested, and bake in a pre-heated oven at 450°F (230°C, mark 8) for 7–8 minutes. The scones can be made in advance, frozen if necessary, and reheated in the oven with the fish. (Calories lost: up to 1000.) **Gluten-free** garnishes include piped toasted balls of mashed potato or slivers of raw carrot.

Freezing: ✓ up to 1 month.

Microwave: ✓

TURBOT WITH SWEET CORN

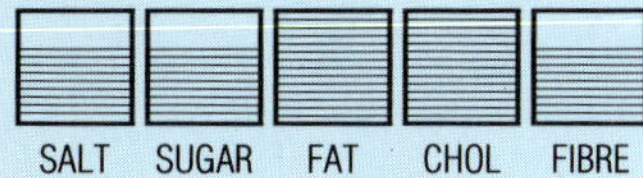

GLUTEN-FREE WHOLEFOOD
TOTAL CALORIES: ABOUT 3435

To reduce the **salt** and added **sugar** to low and none, use fresh or frozen sweet corn. You can reduce the **fat** and **cholesterol** to low (in the method for cooking the fish) by omitting all or most of the butter from the sweet corn, and lightly oiling the foil for cooking the fish instead of buttering it. However, sauce Béarnaise is by nature very high in fat and cholesterol. To reduce both to medium, try replacing the egg yolks and butter with 1 whole egg blended into ¼ pint (150 ml) of low-fat thick yogurt or smetana, then heating gently in a double boiler to thicken, and flavouring as in the main recipe with vinegar and onion. (Calories lost: up to 1160.)

Freezing: ✓ up to 1 month.

Microwave: ✓ for cooking the turbot.

CASSEROLE OF HALIBUT

This is a highly nutritious, easily prepared dish. A garnish of puff pastry crescents adds a touch of sophistication.

PREPARATION TIME: *15 min*
COOKING TIME: *50 min*
INGREDIENTS *(for 6):*
2 lb (900 g) piece halibut or flounder
2 oz (50 g) unsalted butter
1 heaped tablespoon finely chopped onion
½ pint (300 ml) double cream
Juice of half lemon
2 heaped teaspoons paprika
¼ lb (100 g) button mushrooms
3 oz (75 g) peeled shrimps
GARNISH:
Puff pastry crescents

Wipe and skin the halibut. Butter an ovenproof casserole dish, place the piece of halibut in this and cook for 15 minutes on the middle shelf of an oven pre-heated to 325°F (170°C, mark 3). Remove from the oven, sprinkle the onion over the fish, pour over the cream mixed with the lemon juice and dust with paprika.

Cover the dish with a lid or foil, return to the oven and cook for a further 20 minutes, basting twice with the cooking liquid. Trim and slice the mushrooms, and sprinkle them, with the shrimps, over the fish; cook for a further 15 minutes, again basting twice. Transfer the fish to a warm dish and pour over the liquid.

Garnish with puff pastry crescents and serve boiled new potatoes with the fish.

TURBOT WITH SWEET CORN

In this baked fish recipe, the delicate flavour of turbot is complemented by sweet corn and a Béarnaise sauce. The dish is also good made with flounder.

PREPARATION TIME: *15 min*
COOKING TIME: *25 min*
INGREDIENTS *(for 6):*
6 turbot steaks or fillets, 4–6 oz (about 150 g) each
2 teaspoons lemon juice
Black pepper
4 oz (100 g) unsalted butter
15 oz (425 g) tin sweet corn
½ pint (300 ml) Béarnaise sauce (page 83)

Wipe the turbot with a damp cloth. Butter two large sheets of kitchen foil and place the turbot steaks on one sheet. Sprinkle with lemon juice, grind over a little pepper and dot the fish with knobs of butter. Cover with the second piece of foil and seal tightly to form a loose parcel. Bake the turbot for 25 minutes on the centre shelf of an oven pre-heated to 350°F (180°C, mark 4).

Heat the sweet corn over moderate heat, then stir 2 oz (50 g) butter into it. Season with freshly ground pepper and spread the sweet corn over the base of a shallow serving dish. Arrange the turbot on the sweet corn, pour over the juices from the foil parcel, and coat each steak with Béarnaise sauce.

Serve with a green vegetable such as broccoli or spinach.

TURBOT DUGLÉRÉ

This classic French dish can also be made with halibut steaks or thick fillets of Dover sole, which should be folded over in two. For a first course, half quantities only are necessary. The fish should be flaked, mixed with Dugléré sauce (tomato, cream and parsley), and served in small dishes.

PREPARATION TIME: *15 min*
COOKING TIME: *35 min*
INGREDIENTS *(for 4):*
4 turbot steaks
Fish trimmings
1 oz (25 g) butter
Juice of a lemon
Salt and black pepper*
4 fluid oz (100 ml) dry white wine
SAUCE:
2–3 tomatoes
1 oz (25 g) butter
$1\frac{1}{2}$–2 level tablespoons plain flour
1 heaped tablespoon fresh chopped parsley
$2\frac{1}{2}$ fluid oz (65 ml) double cream
GARNISH:
Lemon twists (page 97) and parsley sprigs

Wash and trim the turbot steaks and put the trimmings in a pan of cold water to make a court bouillon (page 87).

Butter a shallow ovenproof dish thoroughly. Rub the steaks with lemon juice, place them in the dish and season with salt and freshly ground pepper. Add the wine and sufficient court bouillon to come to the top of the fish without covering it. Place a piece of buttered foil or greaseproof paper over the turbot and cook in the centre of a pre-heated oven, at 375°F (190°C, mark 5), for 25 minutes, or until a white curd appears on it: this is a sign that the turbot is sufficiently cooked.

Lift the turbot steaks on to a warm serving dish, and strain the cooking liquid.

While the fish is cooking, skin the tomatoes (page 97). Remove the pulp in the centre of the tomatoes with a teaspoon and rub it through a sieve to remove the seeds. Set the tomato liquid aside and cut the flesh into thin strips.

Melt the butter for the sauce in a small pan, remove from the heat and stir in sufficient flour to absorb all the butter. Blend in the tomato liquid and about $\frac{1}{2}$ pint (300 ml) of the reserved fish liquid. Return the pan to the heat and bring the sauce to simmering point, stirring continuously. Cook over low heat for 3–5 minutes. Add the tomato strips and the parsley, and then stir in the cream; do not let the sauce boil again. Adjust seasoning with salt, pepper and lemon juice and pour the sauce over the fish.

Garnish the turbot steaks with lemon twists and sprigs of parsley. Serve with creamed potatoes or with small moulds (timbales) of boiled and buttered rice.

SOLES AUX CRÊPES

The combination of buttered fillets of sole and featherlight strips of pancake is a speciality from Bayeux in northern France.

PREPARATION TIME: *15 min*
COOKING TIME: *25 min*
INGREDIENTS *(for 6):*
12 fillets of sole
Seasoned flour (page 100)
4 oz (100 g) clarified butter (page 95)
3 oz (75 g) unsalted butter
1 heaped tablespoon chopped parsley
BATTER:
2 oz (50 g) plain flour
$\frac{1}{4}$ level teaspoon salt
1 egg
$2\frac{1}{2}$ fluid oz (65 ml) milk
GARNISH:
Lemon wedges

Begin by making the batter so that it can rest while the fillets are being fried. Sift the flour and salt into a bowl, make a well in the centre and add the lightly beaten egg. Mix thoroughly and add 4 tablespoons water and milk gradually, beating well, until the batter is free from lumps and has the consistency of single cream. Add more water to the batter if necessary.

Wipe the sole fillets on a damp cloth, coat them with seasoned flour and shake off any surplus. Melt the clarified butter in a large pan and fry the fillets until golden brown on both sides, turning once. Arrange the fillets on a serving dish and keep them warm.

Butter a clean frying pan and fry three or four pancakes from the batter. Roll the pancakes up and cut them, crossways, into $\frac{1}{2}$ in (1 cm) strips. Melt the remaining butter and re-heat the pancake ribbons, turning them until they are hot and golden. Blend in the chopped parsley and pile the pancake strips over and among the sole fillets. Garnish with wedges of lemon.

A salad of chicory and orange would make a good accompaniment to the pancakes.

TURBOT DUGLÉRÉ

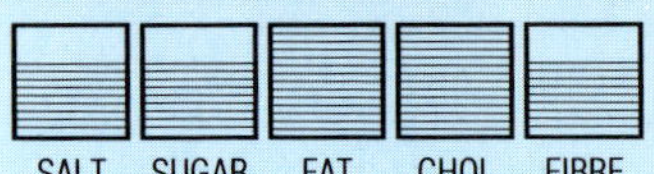

GLUTEN-FREE* WHOLEFOOD*
TOTAL CALORIES: ABOUT 1755

To reduce both **fat** and **cholesterol** to low, oil the dish and the covering for the fish sparingly, instead of using butter. Halve the amount of butter for the sauce and replace the double cream with smetana. (Calories lost: up to 400.)
For a **gluten-free** sauce, you can use cornflour, potato flour or brown rice flour, as well as commercial gluten-free flour.

Freezing: ✓ up to 1 month.

Microwave: ✓ for cooking the turbot.

SOLES AUX CRÊPES

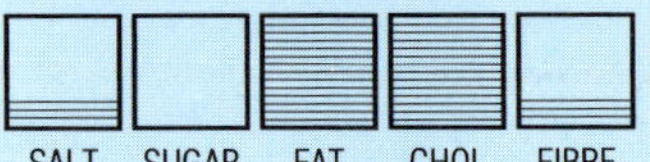

GLUTEN-FREE* WHOLEFOOD*
TOTAL CALORIES: ABOUT 2460

To reduce the **salt** further, and simultaneously reduce the **fat** to low, grill the sole fillets in a shallow baking dish with 1 tablespoon each of hot oil and hot butter (or use oil throughout): brush the pancake pan sparingly with oil rather than buttering it when making the crêpes, and brush again very lightly with oil and butter to brown the pancake strips. (Calories lost: up to 790.)
Using oil throughout and skim milk in the crêpe batter also keeps the **cholesterol** level low; to cut it even further, use only white of egg in the crêpe batter.

FILETS DE SOLE WALEWSKA

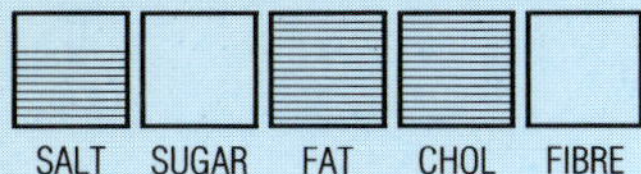

GLUTEN-FREE* WHOLEFOOD*
TOTAL CALORIES: ABOUT 3470

The **salt** content comes mainly from the crawfish and cheese: to reduce it to low, halve the amount of each.
To reduce both **fat** and **cholesterol** content to medium, omit the crawfish or replace it with scallops or monkfish; make the sauce with only 1 oz (25 g) of butter or vegetable margarine; use skim milk and replace the cream with smetana or thick low-fat unflavoured yogurt. Sauté the crawfish (or scallops or monkfish) in a pan lightly brushed with oil, or under a hot grill, brushing the fish lightly with oil. (Calories lost: up to 1745.)

Microwave: ✓ for cooking the sole.

FILETS DE SOLE WALEWSKA

This classic dish is named after the beautiful Polish Countess Maria Walewska, who was so devoted to Napoleon that she begged in vain to be allowed to accompany him into exile in Elba. It is composed of sole and crawfish (or langouste), garnished with slices of truffle. If truffles are too expensive, use small mushrooms.

PREPARATION TIME: *40 min*
COOKING TIME: *1¼ hours*
INGREDIENTS *(for 4):*
2 Dover sole, 1¼ lb (550 g) each
1 bay leaf
1 large parsley sprig
1 small onion
6 peppercorns
*Salt**
Juice of a large lemon
4 fluid oz (100 ml) dry white wine
4 cooked crawfish tails, each weighing 6 oz (175 g)
4 oz (100 g) unsalted butter
1½ oz (40 g) plain flour
¼ pint (150 ml) milk
3–4 oz (75–100 g) grated Cheddar or Gruyère cheese
2½ fluid oz (65 ml) double cream
Salt and black pepper*
GARNISH:
8 thin slices of truffle or 8 small flat mushrooms
Lemon slices
Parsley sprigs

Have each sole skinned and filleted and cut into four. Put the bones and skin into a pan with the bay leaf, parsley, peeled onion and whole peppercorns; cover with lightly salted water. Simmer over low heat for 20–30 minutes then strain this court bouillon and set it aside.

Wash and trim the fillets. Rub them with lemon juice to whiten them, then arrange them in a buttered shallow ovenproof dish. Pour over the wine and enough court bouillon just to cover the fillets. Cover the dish with lightly buttered greaseproof paper, and cook in the centre of a pre-heated oven, at 375°F (190°C, mark 5), for 20–25 minutes.

Meanwhile, remove the shells from the crawfish tails and take out the flesh in one piece. Cut each crawfish in half lengthways.

When the sole fillets are cooked, lift them out carefully with a perforated slice and keep them warm. Pour the liquid into a pan, boil over high heat for 5 minutes to reduce it, and strain off 8 fluid oz (225 ml).

Make a roux (page 82) with half the butter and all the flour. Gradually stir in the milk and bring this sauce to simmering point. Blend in the reserved fish liquid and cook for a further 5 minutes. Stir in the grated cheese until it has melted. Gradually add the cream. Season to taste with salt and freshly ground pepper. Cover the pan with a lid and keep the sauce warm without further cooking.

Heat the remaining butter and sauté the crawfish tails over high heat for about 3 minutes until they are just turning colour.

Arrange the sole fillets in a circle on a round, warm serving dish, with the tail ends towards the centre, and set the crawfish around the edge of the dish. Stir the sauce, which should now just coat a wooden spoon; otherwise thin it with a little fish liquid. Coat the fillets carefully with the sauce and put the dish under a hot grill for 1 minute to glaze it.

Garnish each fillet with a slice of truffle – if mushrooms are used, sauté them lightly in a little butter and place them, dark side uppermost, on the fillets. Decorate the dish with lemon twists (page 97) and tiny sprigs of parsley. Serve the fish with creamed potatoes and mange-tout peas.

GOUJONS OF SOLE WITH TARTARE SAUCE

In France, the small, smelt-like goujons or gudgeons are deep fried and served like whitebait. This recipe is adapted to Dover sole or plaice.

PREPARATION TIME: *20 min*
COOKING TIME: *2–3 min*
INGREDIENTS *(for 4):*
1 large Dover sole
Seasoned flour (page 100)
1 large egg
2 teaspoons olive oil
Golden breadcrumbs
Oil for frying
*Salt**
TARTARE SAUCE:
1 rounded tablespoon mayonnaise (page 83)
1 tablespoon double cream
1 rounded teaspoon each, chopped parsley, gherkins, capers
1½ rounded teaspoons chopped onion
GARNISH:
Lemon wedges

Have the sole skinned and filleted into four; rinse the fillets in cold water and pat them dry on a clean cloth. Making a slanting cut, slice each fillet in half and then cut each half lengthways into three or four narrow strips.

Coat the fish thoroughly with seasoned flour, shaking off any surplus. Beat the egg lightly and mix in the olive oil; dip the fish pieces in this mixture before rolling them in the breadcrumbs. Set the fish aside in a cool place.

For the sauce mix the mayonnaise, cream, parsley, gherkins, capers and onions together. Spoon into a serving dish and chill until required.

Heat the oil in a deep fryer until a small crumb of bread sizzles. Put the fish in the basket and lower it into the hot oil; fry for 2–3 minutes until crisp and golden brown. Remove from the heat and drain the fish on crumpled absorbent paper. Sprinkle with salt and pile the fish on to a hot serving dish. Garnish with wedges of lemon and offer the sauce separately.

A green salad and crusty bread could be served with the fillets.

GOUJONS OF SOLE WITH TARTARE SAUCE

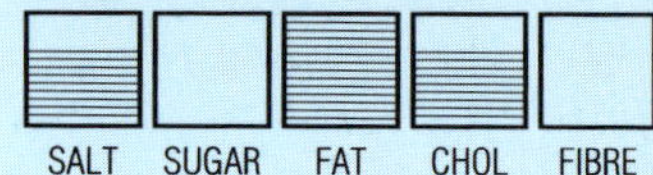

GLUTEN-FREE* WHOLEFOOD*
TOTAL CALORIES: ABOUT 1650

Reduce **salt** to low by using breadcrumbs made from unsalted flour.
To reduce **fat** to low, do not deep fry the fish but grill it on a heated shallow baking dish containing 1 tablespoon of hot oil. Turn by shaking the dish once a minute for 3–4 minutes until the fish is cooked. Instead of the tartare sauce, blend the chopped parsley, gherkin, capers and onion with 2 rounded tablespoons of smetana, low-fat curd cheese or thick low-fat yogurt. (Calories lost: up to 530.) This will give low **cholesterol** if you also omit the egg for coating the fish.
For a **gluten-free** dish, use cornflour or millet flakes for coating the fish. As an alternative to bread, try toasted baked potato skins.

Freezing: ☑ up to 1 month.

WINTER GARDEN PLAICE

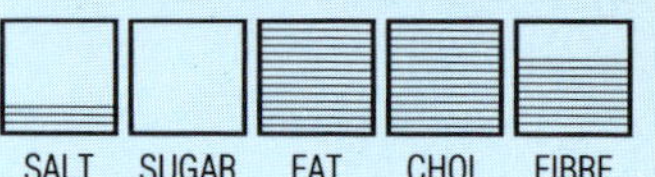

GLUTEN-FREE WHOLEFOOD
TOTAL CALORIES: ABOUT 1960

Reduce both **fat** and **cholesterol** to low by using only 2 teaspoons of butter and 3 tablespoons of stock in which to cook the vegetables; replace the cream with smetana or thick low-fat yogurt, taking care that the dish does not come back to

the boil. (Calories lost: up to 530.)
To cut cholesterol still further, replace all the butter with vegetable margarine or oil. Serve with unbuttered vegetables.

Freezing: ✓ up to 1 month.

Microwave: ✓ the vegetables and the fish can be cooked in a microwave, but the final reduction and thickening of the sauce must be done on the stove.

PLAICE WITH ORANGES

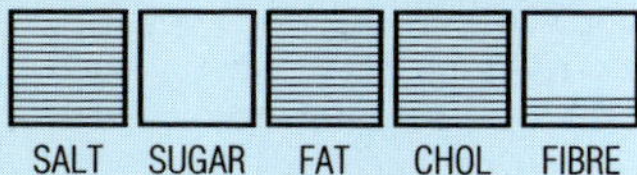

GLUTEN-FREE WHOLEFOOD
TOTAL CALORIES: ABOUT 1675

This will be low in **salt** if the anchovies are omitted; they could be replaced by some of the strips of red and green peppers. Remember to check that there is no salt in the seasoning, mayonnaise or French dressing.
Reduce the **fat** to moderate by using only half the amount of mayonnaise and mixing it with 4 tablespoons of low-fat curd cheese or plain yogurt (or a mixture of both). Reduce **cholesterol** by not buttering the fish before baking, and grease the dish and the greaseproof paper or foil very lightly by brushing with a little oil instead of butter. (Calories lost: up to 500.)

Microwave: ✓ for cooking the plaice fillets.

WINTER GARDEN PLAICE

The distinctive flavour of Jerusalem artichokes blended with leeks is an excellent combination with plaice or other white fish.

PREPARATION TIME: *25 min*
COOKING TIME: *50 min*
INGREDIENTS *(for 4)*:
2 plaice, 1¼ lb (550 g) each
1 lb (450 g) Jerusalem artichokes
½ lb (225 g) leeks
2 oz (50 g) butter
4 fluid oz (100 ml) cider or white wine
1 lemon
Salt and black pepper*
2½ fluid oz (65 ml) double cream

Have each fish skinned and filleted into four. Use the trimmings to make a court bouillon (page 87).

Peel and thinly slice the artichokes; wash and trim the leeks and slice them thinly. Melt the butter in a shallow flameproof casserole, add the vegetables, cover with a lid and cook gently for 5 minutes. Add the cider (or wine), the juice of half the lemon and strain in just enough court bouillon to cover the vegetables. Cover again and simmer gently for 30 minutes or until the artichokes are just tender.

Trim and wipe the fillets, season with salt, freshly ground pepper and lemon juice; fold them in half and place on top of the vegetables. Cover and cook over low heat for 15 minutes. Remove the fish to a warm plate; reduce the liquid in the pan slightly, then stir in the cream. Adjust seasoning and replace the fish; heat through.

Serve the plaice in the casserole, with buttered peas.

PLAICE WITH ORANGES

Cold poached plaice fillets coated in mayonnaise make a quick and simple meal. The rich sauce is balanced by an orange garnish in a sharp French dressing.

PREPARATION TIME: *20 min*
COOKING TIME: *20 min*
INGREDIENTS *(for 4–6)*:
12 fillets of plaice or lemon sole
Juice of half lemon
3 oranges
Salt and black pepper*
1½ oz (40 g) butter
¼ pint (150 ml) mayonnaise (page 83)
Paprika
Small tin anchovy fillets
2 tablespoons French dressing (page 83)

Sprinkle the fillets with the lemon juice and the juice of half an orange, then season with salt and freshly ground pepper. Finely grate the rind from one orange over the fish. Roll up the fillets; secure with wooden cocktail sticks or toothpicks. Lay them in a buttered ovenproof dish.

Squeeze the juice of half an orange over the fish. Dot with small pieces of butter and cover the dish with buttered greaseproof paper or foil. Bake in the centre of a pre-heated oven at 350°F (180°C, mark 4) for about 20 minutes, or until the fillets are tender, but still firm. Remove from the oven and leave to cool.

Lift the cold fillets carefully on to a shallow serving dish, and remove the toothpicks. Add the juice and grated rind of half an orange, drop by drop, to the mayonnaise and coat the fillets with it. Sprinkle with paprika and decorate with halved anchovies.

Peel the remaining oranges, removing all pith, and cut them into thin round slices. Dip them in the French dressing and serve as a garnish to the fillets.

Serve with a salad of blanched, sliced courgettes, strips of peppers and onion rings.

HERRINGS IN OATMEAL

For breakfast, herrings make a welcome change from bacon and eggs. They are equally suitable for both high tea and supper. In Scotland, small trout are often treated in the same way.

PREPARATION TIME: *15 min*
COOKING TIME: *20 min*
INGREDIENTS *(for 4)*:
4 small herrings
Salt and black pepper*
3–4 tablespoons milk
4 level tablespoons coarse oatmeal
4 oz (100 g) unsalted butter
GARNISH:
Lemon wedges

Scale, wash and clean the herrings (page 84); cut off the heads and carefully remove the backbones. Sprinkle a little salt and freshly ground pepper over the inside of each herring. Close the fish to their original shape, dip them in milk and coat evenly and firmly with the oatmeal.

Melt the butter in a heavy-based pan; fry the herrings over gentle heat for 10 minutes on each side. Lift the fish from the pan and arrange on individual serving plates; spoon a little of the butter over each herring and garnish with lemon wedges.

SOUSED HERRINGS

In Germany and Scandinavia, fresh, smoked or salted herrings are firm favourites as a first course. Fresh herrings are usually steeped in a spicy dressing, as in this recipe.

PREPARATION TIME: *35 min*
COOKING TIME: *15–20 min*
INGREDIENTS *(for 6)*:
6 large herrings
¾ pint (425 ml) cider vinegar
3 juniper berries
6 cloves
1 bay leaf
5 peppercorns
2 large onions
6 level teaspoons German mustard
2 dill-pickled cucumbers

Put the vinegar, ¾ pint (425 ml) of water, juniper berries, cloves, bay leaf and peppercorns in a saucepan and bring to the boil. Simmer this marinade for 10 minutes, then leave to cool.

Gut and clean the herrings (page 84); remove the heads and backbones but not the tails. Wash the herrings and dry them thoroughly on absorbent kitchen paper. Peel the onions, slice thinly and separate the slices into rings. Open the herrings out flat, and spread 1 teaspoon of mustard over the inside of each. Cut each cucumber into three slices lengthways and place a piece of cucumber crossways at the head end of each herring. Arrange a few of the smaller onion rings down the length of the body and roll each herring from head to tail, securing it with wooden cocktail sticks or toothpicks.

Arrange the herring rolls in an ovenproof dish and pour over the strained marinade. Sprinkle with

HERRINGS IN OATMEAL

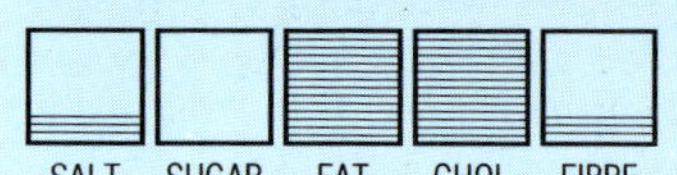

SALT SUGAR FAT CHOL FIBRE

WHOLEFOOD
TOTAL CALORIES: ABOUT 2905

The **fat** and **cholesterol** inherent in the herrings cannot be reduced, but these fish provide a high level of essential fatty acids and fat-soluble vitamins as well, so are worth eating. The total levels of fat and cholesterol in the dish can be kept to low if the butter is omitted and instead the herrings are grilled on a lightly-oiled baking sheet for about 5 minutes on each side. (Calories lost: up to 900.) If trout are substituted for herrings the fat level will be lower.
The **gluten** in oatmeal is not the same as that in wheat and is sometimes tolerated by those who cannot eat wheat. If not, millet flakes make a good gluten-free substitute, as could rice flakes or ground almonds. These last go particularly well with trout.

SOUSED HERRINGS

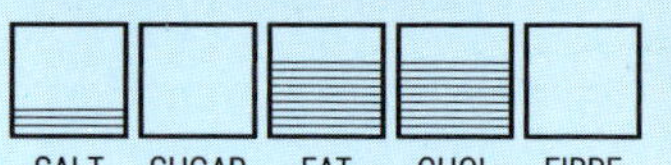

SALT SUGAR FAT CHOL FIBRE

GLUTEN-FREE WHOLEFOOD
TOTAL CALORIES: ABOUT 2400

The low **salt** level will depend on the amount of salt previously added to the pickled cucumbers, and on the amount in the mustard. You may prefer to substitute your own made-up mustard, remembering that mustard powder contains almost no salt.
The **fat** and **cholesterol** cannot

be reduced as they are inherent in herrings (see notes on the previous recipe).
Gluten-free if the mustard is gluten-free. Good German mustard should not contain gluten.

Microwave: ✓

BUCKLING WITH HORSERADISH CREAM

SALT SUGAR FAT CHOL FIBRE

GLUTEN-FREE WHOLEFOOD
TOTAL CALORIES: ABOUT 1315

All smoked fish is very high in **salt**. As a low-salt alternative, use well-flavoured fresh fish such as trout or monkfish, or mix smoked and fresh fish in the proportions of one part smoked to three parts fresh. Reduce **fat** and **cholesterol** levels to medium by replacing the double cream with low-fat unflavoured yogurt or low-fat curd cheese. Using trout in place of buckling will reduce the fat level to low. If, however, you are tempted to use sea trout, remember that it contains over twice as much natural salt as fresh-water trout. (Calories lost: up to 870.)

the remaining onion rings. Cover the dish with a lid or foil and bake the herrings for 15 minutes in the centre of an oven pre-heated to 350°F (180°C, mark 4). Leave them to cool in the marinade, before setting them to souse in the refrigerator for 2 days.

Remove the toothpicks and serve the herrings with thin slices of pumpernickel, wholemeal or coarse rye bread.

BUCKLING WITH HORSERADISH CREAM

Whole smoked herrings, known as buckling, are inexpensive appetisers. Alternatively, smoked trout or smoked mackerel can be used for this recipe.

PREPARATION TIME: *15 min*
INGREDIENTS *(for 4):*
2 large buckling
4 tablespoons double cream
2–3 teaspoons lemon juice
2 rounded teaspoons grated horseradish
1 teaspoon tarragon vinegar
Salt and black pepper*
½ cucumber
GARNISH:
Lemon slices

Fillet each buckling into two halves, carefully removing the roe, skin and all bones. Break the fillets up into bite-sized pieces.

Blend the cream with the lemon juice, horseradish and vinegar, and season to taste with salt and freshly ground pepper.

Cut the unpeeled cucumber into thin slices and use to line four deep scallop shells or individual shallow serving dishes. Mix the buckling carefully into the dressing and pile the mixture into the centre of the shells.

Top each portion with a lemon slice and serve with thin brown bread and butter.

MACKEREL WITH CUCUMBER

The cool, pale green look of young cucumber heralds summer. Its clean taste suits oily fish, such as mackerel and trout. The dish can be served hot or cold.

PREPARATION TIME: *25 min*
COOKING TIME: *35 min*
INGREDIENTS *(for 4):*
4 mackerel, about ½ lb (225 g) each
3 oz (75 g) butter
1 small cucumber
Salt and black pepper*
2 tablespoons white wine vinegar or dry white wine

Gut and clean the mackerel (page 84) and cut off the heads. Wash the fish and pat them dry on absorbent paper. Grease a large, shallow, ovenproof dish with 1 oz (25 g) of the butter. Wash and dry the cucumber and slice it thinly; put a layer of cucumber slices over the base of the dish. Place the mackerel on top and cover with the remaining cucumber slices. Season to taste with salt and freshly ground pepper.

Sprinkle the vinegar or wine over the fish and cucumber, and dot with 1 oz (25 g) of butter cut into small knobs. Cover the dish with a lid or foil and bake on the centre shelf of an oven pre-heated to 400°F (200°C, mark 6) for 30 minutes.

Remove the dish from the oven and transfer the fish and cucumber to a serving dish. Keep it warm if the mackerel is to be served hot. Strain the juices from the fish through a fine sieve into a saucepan. Bring to the boil and continue boiling briskly, adding the remaining butter in bits and stirring occasionally. When the liquid has reduced by about half and looks thick and shiny, pour it over the mackerel and serve at once or leave to cool.

For a hot main course, serve with potatoes and young peas. Served cold, a green salad and mashed potatoes flavoured with cooked garlic could complement the dish.

MACKEREL IN CIDER

It is essential to cook mackerel as soon as possible after catching it. The recipe given here comes from Somerset.

PREPARATION TIME: *20 min*
COOKING TIME: *35 min*
INGREDIENTS *(for 4):*
4 mackerel
Salt and black pepper*
2 dessert apples
1 small onion
7 oz (200 g) Cheddar cheese
2–3 oz (50–75 g) butter
2 oz (50 g) fresh breadcrumbs
3–4 tablespoons dry cider
GARNISH:
Lemon wedges
Freshly chopped parsley

Prepare the mackerel as in the previous recipe and season them with salt and pepper.

Peel and coarsely grate the apples, onion and 3 oz (75 g) of the cheese. Melt the butter in a small pan over low heat. Mix the grated apple, onion, cheese and the breadcrumbs together in a bowl and bind with 1 tablespoon of the melted butter. Stuff the mackerel with this mixture and secure the opening of each with two or three wooden skewers.

Grate the remaining cheese finely. Place the mackerel side by side in a fireproof dish and sprinkle 1 tablespoon of grated cheese over each. Pour over the remaining melted butter and enough cider to cover the base of the dish. Lay a piece of buttered kitchen foil or greaseproof paper loosely over the dish and place in the centre of a pre-heated oven, at 350°F (180°C, mark 4). Bake for 25–35 minutes, or until the mackerel are cooked through

MACKEREL WITH CUCUMBER

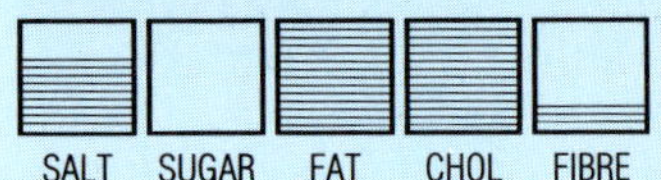

GLUTEN-FREE WHOLEFOOD
TOTAL CALORIES: ABOUT 1665

Mackerel is fairly high in **salt**. Compensate for the lack of added salt with up to 1 teaspoon of lightly crushed dill seeds.
To reduce the **fat** and **cholesterol** to moderate, use this dish in late winter, when mackerel have least fat. Grease the baking dish with a very little oil and sprinkle the fish with a little more. The only way to reduce the fat to low is to use another kind of fish, such as trout. (Calories lost: up to 500 if mackerel is used, up to 660 if you use trout.)

Microwave: ✓ for the fish.

MACKEREL IN CIDER

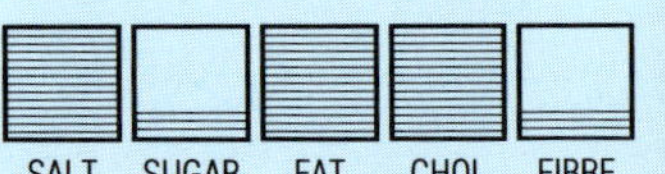

GLUTEN-FREE* WHOLEFOOD*
TOTAL CALORIES: ABOUT 2735

For medium **salt**, use only 3 oz (75 g) cheese, unsalted butter and crumbs from unsalted bread.
To reduce **fat** and **cholesterol** to moderate, use mackerel in late winter when they are least oily, halve the amount of cheese (use low-fat Cheddar if you can find it) and bind the mixture with milk instead of the butter. Omit the butter poured over the fish and brush the fish covering sparingly with a little oil. (Calories lost: up to 1100.)

Microwave: ✓

MACKEREL WITH GOOSEBERRY SAUCE

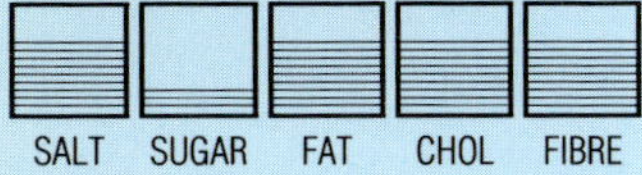

GLUTEN-FREE* WHOLEFOOD*
TOTAL CALORIES: ABOUT 1835

To reduce **salt** in this dish, use crumbs from unsalted bread, replace mackerel with trout, or serve smaller portions.
For low **fat**, use trout or make in late winter when mackerel has much less oil. Do not brush the fish with oil, but make slits in their sides and brush the grill very lightly with oil. The oil from the fish will quickly provide all that is needed. For lower **cholesterol** omit butter from gooseberries. (Calories lost: up to 660.)
Wholefood: sweeten with 1 tablespoon of honey.

MACKEREL WITH TOMATOES

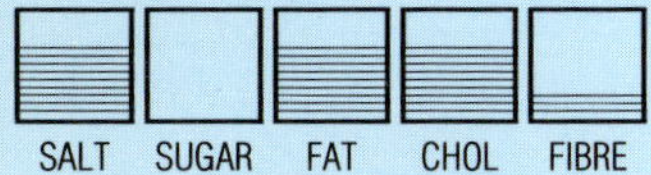

GLUTEN FREE* WHOLEFOOD*
TOTAL CALORIES: ABOUT 2245

To reduce **salt** to low, use small portions, with extra garlic and parsley to compensate for the lack of added salt.
For low **fat** and **cholesterol**, reduce the portions or substitute almost any white fish or fresh water trout. Grill the fish. Use only 1–2 teaspoons oil to cook the onions and mushrooms, and garnish with uncooked or grilled tomatoes. (Calories lost: up to 730.)

Freezing: ☑ up to 1 month.
Microwave: ☑

and golden brown in colour.

Serve the mackerel straight from the dish, garnished with lemon wedges and parsley.

Potatoes in their jackets make a perfect addition to this dish.

MACKEREL WITH GOOSEBERRY SAUCE

The tart taste of gooseberries contrasts well with mackerel. If gooseberries are not available, rhubarb can be used instead.

PREPARATION TIME: *15 min*
COOKING TIME: *16 min*
INGREDIENTS *(for 4):*
4 mackerel
4 heaped tablespoons breadcrumbs
1 level tablespoon chopped parsley
Grated rind of a lemon
1 egg
Grated nutmeg
Salt and black pepper*
Melted butter
GOOSEBERRY SAUCE:
½ lb (225 g) gooseberries
2 level tablespoons caster sugar
1 oz (25 g) butter
1 tablespoon fresh chopped fennel or 1 teaspoon ground fennel

Make a stuffing by mixing the breadcrumbs, parsley and lemon peel. Bind with the lightly beaten egg and season with nutmeg, salt and pepper. Secure the stuffed mackerel with cocktail sticks. Brush lightly with melted butter and grill under moderate heat for about 8 minutes on each side.

To make the sauce, put the gooseberries in 3 fluid oz (75 ml) water with the sugar, butter and fennel. Bring to the boil and simmer until the gooseberries pop open. Serve the sauce in a bowl, with the mackerel.

MACKEREL WITH TOMATOES

Mackerel is sometimes known as the poor man's trout – unjustly so; although both are oily fish, their flavours are quite distinct. Mackerel makes an excellent and economical main course.

PREPARATION TIME: *30 min*
COOKING TIME: *20 min*
INGREDIENTS *(for 4–6):*
6 medium mackerel
Seasoned flour (page 100)
3 tablespoons cooking or olive oil
1 onion
2 oz (50 g) mushrooms
1 clove garlic
¾ lb (350 g) firm tomatoes
1 oz (25 g) butter
Salt and black pepper*
1 rounded teaspoon chopped parsley
2 teaspoons wine vinegar

Clean and fillet the mackerel (page 84). Wash the fillets, wipe them dry on a clean cloth and coat them with seasoned flour, shaking off any surplus. Heat 2 tablespoons of the oil in a heavy-based frying pan and, when hot, fry the fillets for about 10 minutes, or until golden brown, turning once.

While the mackerel is frying, peel the onion and garlic, and wipe and trim the mushrooms. Finely chop the onion and mushrooms, and crush the garlic. Skin the tomatoes (page 97) and slice them thinly. Heat the remaining oil in a clean pan and fry the onion for a few minutes over moderate heat. Add the mushrooms and garlic, and cook very slowly for a further 5 minutes. Season to taste with salt and freshly ground pepper, and stir in the parsley and vinegar. Fry the tomato slices for 3 minutes in the butter, using a separate pan over gentle heat.

To serve, arrange the warm mackerel fillets on a serving dish, put the tomatoes between them and spoon a little of the onion mixture on to each fillet. Serve with new potatoes and a salad.

SALMON KEDGEREE

In the 19th century, kedgeree, of Indian origin, was an established country house breakfast dish. Nowadays it is more often served for a light lunch or supper.

PREPARATION TIME: *5 min*
COOKING TIME: *30 min*
INGREDIENTS *(for 4–6):*
8 oz (225 g) cooked salmon
Salt, black pepper and cayenne*
6 oz (175 g) long grain rice
1 onion
2 oz (50 g) butter
2 hardboiled eggs
GARNISH:
Chopped parsley

Remove any skin and bones from the salmon, and flake it carefully. Bring 1 pint (570 ml) of water to the boil in a large saucepan, adding a pinch each of salt, pepper and cayenne. Add the rice, cover tightly with a lid or foil, and cook over low heat for about 25 minutes, or until all the water is absorbed and the rice is fluffy.

While the rice is cooking, peel and finely chop the onion. Melt a little of the butter in a pan and fry the onion until soft and transparent. Set aside. Roughly chop the whites of the hardboiled eggs, and press the yolks through a sieve.

Cut the remaining butter into small knobs and stir into the cooked rice, with the flaked salmon, onion and egg whites. Season to taste and heat the mixture through gently.

To serve, pile the kedgeree up on a warmed flat dish and decorate with the sieved egg yolks, arranged in a star or cross pattern. Sprinkle generously with chopped parsley. You could serve the kedgeree with hot buttered toast fingers.

SALMON TROUT IN JELLY

This makes an excellent and attractive centrepiece for a special dinner occasion or a cold buffet. It also has the advantage that it can be prepared well in advance.

PREPARATION TIME: *30 min*
COOKING TIME: *1–1½ hours*
INGREDIENTS *(for 8):*
1 salmon trout, approx. 2½–3 lb (1·1–1·4 kg)
1 tablespoon gelatine
1 tablespoon white wine vinegar
3 fluid oz (75 ml) dry sherry
2 egg whites
STOCK:
1 carrot
1 onion
Bouquet garni (page 99)
4 peppercorns
1½ tablespoons wine vinegar
½ level teaspoon salt
GARNISH:
4 oz (100 g) peeled prawns
Watercress

Begin by making the stock, putting all the ingredients, with 1 pint (570 ml) of water, in a pan. Bring to the boil, cover the pan with a lid and simmer for 20 minutes. Strain the stock through muslin.

Remove the fins and gills from the salmon trout, if not already done by the fishmonger, and cut a 1 in (2½ cm) deep inverted V out of the tail to make it resemble a mermaid's tail. Wash the fish thoroughly to remove all traces of blood, and put it in a fish kettle, or large flameproof dish. Pour over the warm stock and cover with a lid or foil. Cook the fish for 25–30 minutes on top of the stove, or for 50 minutes in a pre-heated oven at

SALMON KEDGEREE

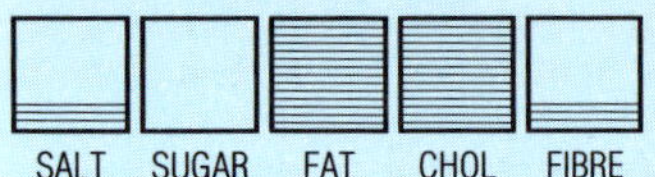

GLUTEN-FREE WHOLEFOOD
TOTAL CALORIES: ABOUT 1690

You can reduce the **fat** level of this recipe to low by using only 1 teaspoon of butter to turn the rice. The mixture will not be dry, as salmon is an oily fish. This will give a moderate **cholesterol** level: to reduce it to low, omit the eggs or use the whites only. (Calories lost: up to 580.)
White rice provides only about 1 gram of **fibre** per person in this dish (making 4 servings). Using brown rice would provide about twice as much – still not high, but $\frac{1}{15}$th of a day's target intake. It also makes the dish **wholefood**, but will require to be cooked in about 2¼ times its own volume of water for about 40–45 minutes. In this way all the water is absorbed, recouping any minerals and vitamins leached into the water.

SALMON TROUT IN JELLY

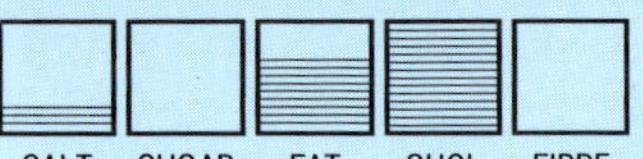

GLUTEN-FREE WHOLEFOOD
TOTAL CALORIES: ABOUT 2875

The **fat** in this recipe comes almost entirely from the salmon, averaging 13% fat. However, this is still lower than much meat and is a less saturated type of fat. The **cholesterol** in salmon is medium, but high in the prawn garnish. To avoid this, replace the prawns with the traditional cucumber and watercress and, if liked, skinned pistachio nuts. (Calories lost: up to 120.)

Microwave: √ this is perfectly suitable for microwave cooking, but few microwaves are big enough to take a whole salmon trout, so you will probably have to cut it into chunks.

SWEET-SOUR SALMON

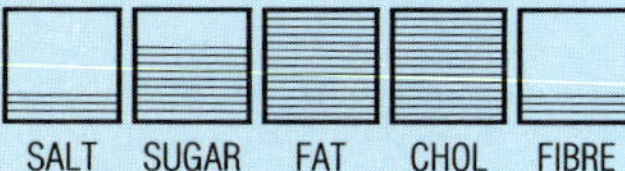

SALT SUGAR FAT CHOL FIBRE

GLUTEN-FREE WHOLEFOOD
TOTAL CALORIES: ABOUT 1795

The **fat** and **cholesterol** content of salmon is moderate, and the fat of a less saturated kind than in most meat. Because of the richness of the fish, the other elements pushing up the fat and cholesterol – the egg yolk and cream sauce – can be changed without spoiling the recipe. Replace with smetana, low-fat curd cheese or thick low-fat plain yogurt, flavoured with the same cooking juices but not cooked: reduce the juice on its own. (Calories lost: up to 270.)

Microwave: √ for cooking the fish.

350°F (180°C, mark 4), basting with the stock.

Leave the fish to cool in the liquid. When quite cold, snip the skin near the head with a pair of scissors and peel it carefully off, leaving the head and tail intact. Split the fish along the backbone with a sharp knife and snip the bone below the head and above the tail. Ease the backbone out carefully without breaking the salmon trout.

Strain the fish liquid, through muslin, into a saucepan. Dissolve the gelatine in a small cupful of the liquid, and heat the remainder over moderate heat, whisking steadily until the liquid is hot. Stir in the dissolved gelatine, the vinegar, sherry and the egg whites; whisk steadily until the mixture comes to the boil. Draw the pan off the heat at once and leave the liquid to settle for 5 minutes. Bring to the boil again, draw it off the heat and leave it to settle once more. The liquid should now look clear; otherwise repeat the boiling process again. Strain the liquid through a clean cloth and set aside to cool.

Spoon a little of the cool jelly over the base of a serving dish and leave it to set. Lift the salmon trout carefully on top of the jelly. Garnish the fish with the prawns and spoon over a little of the jelly. When the prawns have set, spoon jelly over the whole salmon and leave to set.

Serve the salmon trout garnished with sprigs of watercress and the remaining chopped jelly.

SWEET-SOUR SALMON

In German cookery, a sweet-sour sauce is frequently served with fish and with braised meat. It is often served hot, but the flavour improves when chilled.

PREPARATION TIME: *10 min*
COOKING TIME: *35–40 min*
CHILLING TIME: *2–3 hours*
INGREDIENTS *(for 4):*
4 salmon steaks
Salt and black pepper*
2 large onions
2 tablespoons white wine vinegar
2 rounded tablespoons soft light-brown sugar
Juice of 2 lemons
2 egg yolks
2½ fluid oz (75 ml) double cream
GARNISH:
Cucumber slices

Wash and dry the salmon steaks. Season with salt and freshly ground pepper and arrange in a shallow ovenproof dish. Cover with peeled and sliced onions.

Pour boiling, lightly salted water over the fish just to cover it. Seal the dish with foil and bake in the centre of a pre-heated oven at 325°F (170°C, mark 3) for 20–25 minutes, or until cooked. Lift the steaks carefully with a slotted spoon and arrange on a serving dish.

Strain the cooking liquid through muslin and measure ½ pint (300 ml) into a saucepan; add the vinegar, brown sugar and lemon juice. Simmer over low heat until the liquid has reduced slightly. Beat yolks and cream together in a bowl and stir in a tablespoon of the reduced liquid; blend thoroughly and gradually add all the liquid. Set the bowl over a pan of simmering water, and stir the sauce continuously until it thickens to a coating consistency.

Pour the sauce over the salmon and cool before chilling for at least 2 hours in the refrigerator.

Garnish the salmon steaks with thin slices of unpeeled cucumber and serve with boiled potatoes and a crisp green salad.

COULIBIAC

This traditional Russian fish pie is usually served hot, with soured cream, but also makes an exceptionally good buffet choice.

PREPARATION TIME: *2 hours*
COOKING TIME: *30 min*
INGREDIENTS *(for 8–10):*
8 oz (225 g) tapioca
2 onions
¾ lb (350 g) button mushrooms
2 oz (50 g) unsalted butter
Salt and black pepper*
2 slices middle-cut salmon, each 1 in (2½ cm) thick
½ pint (300 ml) dry white wine
3 hardboiled eggs
6 thin pancakes (page 20: use 4–5 fluid oz (approx 125 ml) milk, leaving the other ingredients as they are)
1 lb (450 g) prepared puff pastry
1 egg for glazing
½ pint (300 ml) soured cream

Bring a pan of salted water to the boil, sprinkle in the tapioca, stirring all the time. Bring to the boil and simmer gently for 30 minutes, after which the tapioca should be transparent. Drain through a fine sieve and rinse under cold water to remove excess starch. Set aside.

Meanwhile, peel and finely chop the onions; wipe, trim and finely chop the mushrooms. Melt the butter in a large frying pan and add the onions; cover with a lid and cook over low heat for 5 minutes until the onions are soft, but not brown. Increase the heat and add the mushrooms. Season with salt and freshly ground pepper and cook, stirring continuously, for 5 minutes. Remove the pan from the heat, stir in the tapioca; correct seasoning if necessary and leave the mixture to cool.

Wipe the salmon pieces and put them in a saucepan together with the wine and a pinch of salt and pepper. Simmer the salmon gently for about 10 minutes; draw the pan off the heat and let the salmon cool in the liquid. Drain; remove skin and bones from the salmon and flake the flesh.

When ready to assemble the coulibiac, heat the mushroom and tapioca mixture slightly to soften. If necessary warm the pancakes over a pan of boiling water to unstick them. Slice the eggs into rounds. Roll out the puff pastry to a rectangle no more than ¼ in (½ cm) thick and approximately 16 in (40 cm) long by 9 in (23 cm) wide. Cut the edges straight and reserve the trimmings for decoration. Brush the pastry with the lightly beaten egg to within 1 in (2½ cm) of the edges.

Brush three of the pancakes with egg and lay them in a single line down the pastry. Spoon a quarter of the mushroom mixture in a neat strip, 2–3 in (5–8 cm) wide and to within 2 in (5 cm) of the shorter pastry edges, over the pancakes. Top with half the flaked salmon and then with another layer of mushroom and all the egg slices. Spoon a further quarter of mushrooms on before the remaining salmon and then the last of the mushrooms. Top with the remaining pancakes, brush with egg and wrap the pancakes round the filling.

Fold the sides of the pastry up and over the top of the filling so that the edges overlap. Brush thoroughly with egg to seal the edges. Fold the pastry ends over the top and seal with egg. Place the coulibiac on a wet baking tray with the sealed edges underneath. Brush the top with egg.

Roll out the pastry trimmings and use for decoration. Cut a small hole in the centre of the pastry and insert a chimney of greaseproof paper.

Place the baking tray on the centre shelf of a pre-heated oven. Bake at 425°F (220°C, mark 7) for about 30 minutes or until the pastry is golden brown.

Serve the coulibiac with a separate bowl of soured cream.

COULIBIAC

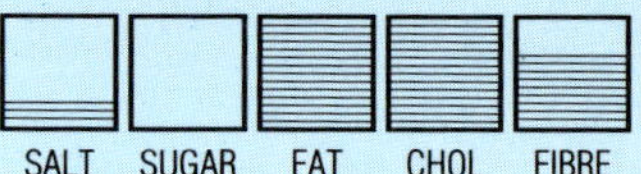

SALT SUGAR FAT CHOL FIBRE

GLUTEN-FREE*
TOTAL CALORIES: ABOUT 6110

The **salt** content is low only if there is no added salt in either the pastry or the pancakes.
To reduce both **fat** and **cholesterol** to low, use only ½ oz (10 g) butter or 1 tablespoon of oil to cook the onions and mushrooms; use only 1 yolk, with whites of other eggs if wished; make the pancakes with skim milk; and reduce the amount of soured cream (or substitute smetana, cultured buttermilk or thick low-fat yogurt). Puff pastry is very high in fat and usually in cholesterol, and attempts to adapt it are not really satisfactory; instead, use either bought phyllo pastry or a yeast dough (this is in fact more traditional than puff pastry). (Calories lost: up to 1060.)
For a **wholefood** coulibiac, use wholemeal flour for the pancakes and for a yeast dough to wrap it in; substitute brown rice for the tapioca, cooking it as suggested in the alternatives to the salmon kedgeree on page 28. This will also increase the **fibre** content considerably.

PICKLED SALMON

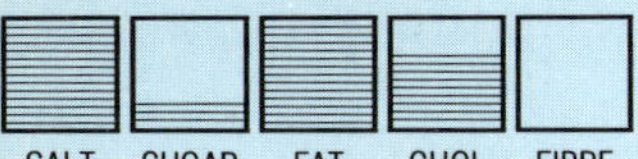

SALT SUGAR FAT CHOL FIBRE

GLUTEN-FREE* WHOLEFOOD*
TOTAL CALORIES: ABOUT 2485

The **salt** content of this recipe cannot be reduced, as it provides the pickling agent. However, you can avoid the full content of sugar in the sauce by adding a smaller amount, say half a tablespoon, of honey (which is sweeter, especially when eaten cold).
The **fat** content of salmon is moderate, but of a less saturated type than in most meat. Reduce the fat content of the total dish to moderate by making sauce with a base of smetana or thick low-fat yogurt – both traditional to Scandinavia – rather than using oil and egg yolk. This will also reduce the **cholesterol** to low. (Calories lost: up to 650.)
Gluten-free: there will only be gluten in this dish if there is any in the mustard, and possibly in the white pepper. Check the list of ingredients.

PICKLED SALMON

This Scandinavian dish (*gravad lax*) traditionally uses fresh dill, but it can also be made with dried dillweed. The pickling adds a subtle flavour to fresh salmon.

PREPARATION TIME: *30 min*
INGREDIENTS *(for 6)*:
1½ lb (700 g) salmon tailpiece
PICKLE:
1 heaped tablespoon sea salt
1 rounded tablespoon granulated sugar
1 teaspoon crushed black peppercorns
1 tablespoon brandy (optional)
1 rounded tablespoon fresh dill or 1 level tablespoon dried dillweed
SAUCE:
2 rounded tablespoons made French or German mustard
1 rounded tablespoon granulated sugar
1 large egg yolk
7 tablespoons olive oil
2 tablespoons wine vinegar
1 rounded teaspoon fresh dill or 1 level teaspoon dried dillweed
Salt and white pepper*

Have the salmon filleted into two triangles. Mix all the pickling ingredients together and spread a quarter of this mixture over the base of a flat dish. Lay the first piece of salmon, skin down, on top of the mixture and spread half of the remaining pickle over the cut side. Place the other piece of salmon, skin side up, over the first. Spread the top with the remaining mixture, rubbing it well into the skin. Cover the salmon with a piece of foil and a board weighed down with a couple of tins.

Leave the salmon to press in a cool place or the refrigerator for anything up to 5 days, but not less than 12 hours, turning the salmon once a day.

Before serving, slice the salmon thinly, either parallel to the skin as with smoked salmon or obliquely to the skin.

For the sauce, beat the mustard with the sugar and egg yolk until smooth. Gradually add the oil and vinegar, mixing well between each addition. Season to taste with dill, salt and pepper.

Arrange the slices of salmon on individual plates, and serve buttered rye bread and the sauce separately in a bowl.

TROUT WITH BRETON SAUCE

Breton sauce is reminiscent of mayonnaise, but is easier to make and less oily, more like a Béarnaise sauce (page 83) flavoured with mustard and herbs. The sharp flavour of the sauce makes it a perfect foil for fish dishes. It goes exceptionally well with cold trout, mackerel or herring as well as salmon or sea trout.

PREPARATION TIME: *25 min*
COOKING TIME: *25–30 min*
INGREDIENTS *(for 4–6):*

4 large trout
1 tablespoon olive oil
SAUCE:
2 level tablespoons Dijon mustard
2 egg yolks
2 teaspoons wine, cider or tarragon vinegar
Salt and black pepper*
3 oz (75 g) unsalted butter
2 tablespoons chopped fresh parsley and chives
GARNISH:
½ cucumber

Wash and clean the trout thoroughly; cut off the heads and dry the fish on a clean cloth. Wrap each trout in a piece of oiled aluminium foil and put them in a fireproof dish. Bake in the centre of a pre-heated oven at 325°F (170°C, mark 3) for about 25–30 minutes or until they are cooked through.

Remove the dish from the oven and open the foil packets to allow the trout to cool slightly. Split each fish along the belly and, with a pointed knife, carefully loosen the backbone; ease it out gently so that most of the small bones come away with it (see page 85 for illustrated instructions on how to do this). Set the trout aside to cool.

To make the sauce, beat the mustard, egg yolks and vinegar together until well blended; season to taste with salt and freshly ground pepper. Put the butter in a bowl over a pan of hot water and stir until it has softened, but not melted. Gradually add the butter to the egg mixture, beating all the time, until the sauce has the consistency of thick cream. Stir in the finely chopped herbs.

Before serving, gently peel the skin from the cold trout, cut each into two fillets and arrange on a serving dish. Pour the sauce over. Peel the cucumber, cut it in half lengthways and scrape out the seeds with a pointed teaspoon. Dice the flesh and sprinkle it over the trout.

Serve with crusty bread and butter and lightly cooked broccoli or spinach for a main course or, in small quantities and on its own or with wholemeal bread, as a starter for a dinner party.

SMOKED TROUT MOUSSE

This mousse, which has a creamy texture and smoky flavour, makes an attractive first course. The cottage cheese helps to counter the richness of the fish. Smoked mackerel and smoked salmon (the bits left over from slicing a whole side are ideal and not too expensive) are also suitable. It can be prepared a day in advance and kept in the refrigerator until required.

PREPARATION TIME: *15 min*
CHILLING TIME: *1 hour*
INGREDIENTS *(for 4–6):*
¾ lb (350 g) smoked trout
4 oz (100 g) cottage cheese
5 fluid oz (150 ml) soured cream
Juice of half lemon
Salt and black pepper*
GARNISH:
Finely chopped parsley

Remove the skin and bones from the flesh of the trout, and flake the meat into a liquidiser. Sieve the cottage cheese and add, with the soured cream, to the flaked fish. Blend the mixture until smooth. Alternatively, pound the flaked fish to a smooth paste with a mortar and pestle, before mixing in the sieved cottage cheese and the soured cream. Season to taste with the lemon juice, salt and pepper.

Spoon the mousse into individual ramekin dishes and leave to chill in the refrigerator.

Sprinkle finely chopped parsley in a neat border round the edge of each dish. Serve with fingers or triangles of hot brown toast and butter. You could, if you wished, serve it with hot pita bread or French bread for a more substantial course.

TROUT WITH BRETON SAUCE

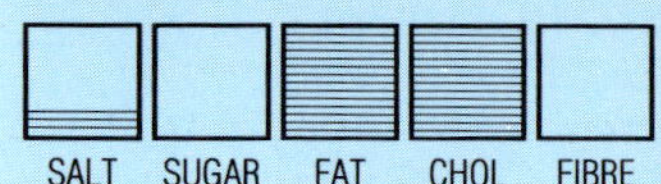

GLUTEN-FREE* WHOLEFOOD
TOTAL CALORIES: ABOUT 1625

To keep **salt** level low, look for a mustard with little or no added salt. Mustard itself is very low in sodium.
To reduce the **fat** and **cholesterol** to low, base the sauce on smetana, low-fat curd cheese or thick low-fat yogurt rather than butter and egg yolks. Use about 4 fluid oz (125 ml) and flavour with the mustard, vinegar, seasoning and herbs. Heat gently but do not let it boil. Chill before serving. (Calories lost: up to 750.)
Gluten-free if there is no gluten in the mustard; check the ingredients list.

Microwave: ☑ for cooking the trout.

SMOKED TROUT MOUSSE

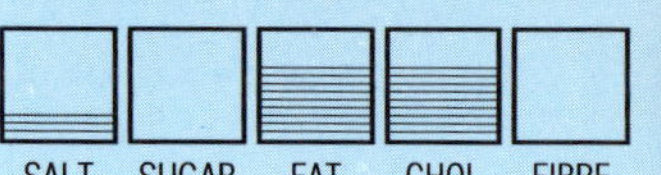

GLUTEN-FREE WHOLEFOOD
TOTAL CALORIES: ABOUT 700

Smoked fish is very salty. The only way to reduce the **salt** level of this dish is to mix a small amount of smoked trout with fresh, poached trout, in the proportions, say, of one part smoked trout to two parts fresh. This will give a moderate salt level.
To reduce **fat** and **cholesterol** to low, replace the soured cream with smetana, low-fat

curd cheese or thick low-fat unflavoured yogurt. (Calories lost: up to 200.)

Food processor: ✓ very useful for blending the mixture to a smooth paste.

TROUT WITH MUSHROOMS

GLUTEN-FREE* WHOLEFOOD*
TOTAL CALORIES: ABOUT 2615

To reduce levels of both **fat** and **cholesterol** to low, grill the trout on a baking sheet lightly brushed with butter or fat, and brush the fish itself very lightly with oil or butter before coating it with flour. Trout is a moist, slightly oily fish so it will not get dry provided it is not cooked too long. Grill the mushrooms and garlic on the same baking sheet after the fish have been removed; if necessary, add a very little more fat, shaking the sheet to coat the vegetables. Transfer the mixture to a saucepan and continue with the recipe. Reduce the sauce to the consistency of cream before stirring in smetana or thick low-fat yogurt (instead of cream), off the heat, just before serving. (Calories lost: up to 1225.) Alternatives for coating which are both **gluten-free** and **wholefood** include brown rice flour, potato flour and chick pea flour.

Microwave: ✓ for cooking the trout.

TROUT WITH MUSHROOMS

This recipe from the Pyrenees combines fresh river trout with button mushrooms, served in a Pernod sauce.

PREPARATION TIME: *10 min*
COOKING TIME: *15 min*
INGREDIENTS *(for 4)*:
4 trout, 6–8 oz (about 200 g) each
Seasoned flour (page 100)
3–4 oz (75–100 g) clarified butter (page 95)
8 oz (225 g) button mushrooms
1 clove garlic
2–3 tablespoons Pernod or Pastis
¼ pint (150 ml) double cream
*Salt**
Black pepper

Wipe the trout lightly with a damp cloth, but do not remove the blue-grey outer coating. Slit the trout along the belly and remove the entrails. Coat each trout with seasoned flour, shaking off any excess. Melt the clarified butter in a large, heavy-based pan and fry the trout over moderate heat for 5 minutes on each side, or until golden brown and crisp.

Meanwhile, trim the mushrooms and slice them thinly. Peel and crush the garlic. Lift the trout on to a serving dish and keep them warm. Fry the mushrooms and garlic in the trout juices, over low heat, for 3–4 minutes. Stir in the Pernod and let the liquid bubble rapidly for a few minutes. Add the cream, stirring continuously until the sauce has reduced to the consistency of thick cream. Season to taste with salt, freshly ground pepper, and a little more Pernod if necessary. Pour the sauce over the trout.

Serve immediately, with boiled buttered potatoes and a crisp green salad or some green vegetables.

LOBSTER AND AVOCADO BRISTOL FASHION

Scarlet lobster and green avocados make an attractive starter for a special occasion. Avocados should be prepared at the last minute, otherwise the delicate green flesh turns brown. If you do have to prepare it a little bit in advance, sprinkle well with lemon juice and this will help to stop it discolouring.

PREPARATION TIME: *25 min*
INGREDIENTS *(for 4):*
1 medium-sized lobster
2 large avocado pears
3 fluid oz (75 ml) double cream
2 teaspoons lemon juice
Cayenne pepper
*Salt**
Paprika

Have the cooked lobster split into two halves. Remove the grey sac in each half of the head and the black intestinal tubes. Prise out all the lobster meat from the body, tail and claws, and set the thin scarlet crawler claws aside for garnish.

Chop the lobster meat finely, put it in a basin and stir in the cream and lemon juice. Season to taste with cayenne pepper.

Cut the pears in half lengthways and remove the stones. Scoop out some of the avocado flesh, leaving about ½ in (1 cm) lining to hold the shape of each half shell.

Dice the flesh finely and fold it into the lobster mixture. Season with salt if necessary.

Pile the lobster mixture into the avocado shells and sprinkle with a little paprika. Arrange the claws on top in a decorative pattern.

LOBSTER THERMIDOR

Lobster is the most expensive of all shellfish, but is also regarded by gourmets as the most delicious. This classic French recipe comes from the famous Café de Paris.

PREPARATION TIME: *50 min*
COOKING TIME: *1½ hours*
INGREDIENTS *(for 6):*
3 cooked lobsters, 1¼–1½ lb (550–700 g) each
½ pint (300 ml) fish stock (page 81)
¼ pint (150 ml) dry white wine
1 onion
4 peppercorns
1 bay leaf
1 sprig thyme
Salt and black pepper*
¾ pint (425 ml) milk
4 oz (100 g) unsalted butter
2 oz (50 g) plain flour
1 level teaspoon Dijon mustard
2 large egg yolks
¼ pint (150 ml) single cream
1 teaspoon lemon juice
3 oz (75 g) Parmesan cheese
2 oz (50 g) browned breadcrumbs
GARNISH:
Lettuce

Pour the fish stock and white wine into a saucepan, bring to the boil and boil briskly until the liquid has reduced to ¼ pint (150 ml). Peel the onion, cut it into quarters and put it in another saucepan with the peppercorns, bay leaf, thyme, a pinch of salt and the milk. Bring to the boil, remove the pan from the heat, cover with a lid and leave the milk to infuse for 30 minutes.

Meanwhile, remove the claws from the lobsters (page 88); split each body in half lengthways, through the head and tail and

LOBSTER WITH AVOCADO BRISTOL FASHION

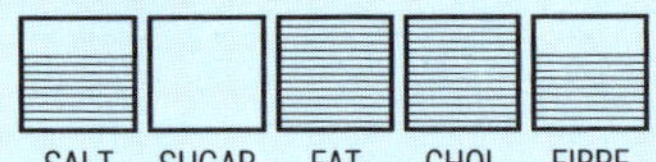

SALT SUGAR FAT CHOL FIBRE

GLUTEN-FREE WHOLEFOOD
TOTAL CALORIES: ABOUT 1265

Lobster is naturally fairly high in **salt** and the exact salt level will therefore depend on the size of the lobster; if each portion has less than 4 oz (100 g) lobster, the total salt will only be about 375 mg, in other words moderate.
Lobster is also relatively high in **cholesterol**, although low in **fat**. However, the amount in 4 oz (100 g) is less than in 1 egg. To reduce fat, use thick low-fat unflavoured yogurt or low-fat curd cheese instead of double cream. But the total fat in this recipe will still be at best moderate, since avocado pears are high in oil, ranging from 11 to 39% according to season. (Calories lost: up to 300.)

LOBSTER THERMIDOR

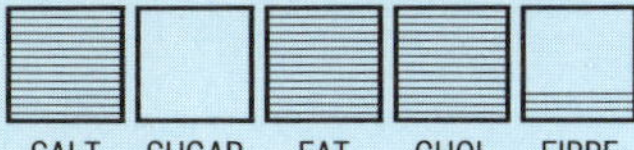

SALT SUGAR FAT CHOL FIBRE

GLUTEN-FREE* WHOLEFOOD*
TOTAL CALORIES: ABOUT 3350

Lobster is naturally higher than most natural foods in **salt**, while being much lower than cheese or bacon, for instance. However, the total salt content can be reduced to moderate by using less Parmesan cheese and using breadcrumbs from bread made without salt. Choose a mustard without added salt. To limit the **fat** to the low level naturally present in the lobster, use skim milk and make the sauce by blending flour and a little of the infused milk to a smooth paste, then gradually working in the remaining milk and stirring gently over a low heat. Add 1 teaspoon of butter and simmer for 5–6 minutes. Omit the egg yolks and cream from sauce, replacing with 5 oz (150 g) low-fat curd cheese, after which the sauce should not be boiled again. Use 2 teaspoons butter or oil to brush the pan in which you will sauté the lobster meat. This dish remains medium in **cholesterol**, which is fairly high in lobster. (Calories lost: up to 1330.)

along the centre line of the shell. Set the shells aside, with the feeler claws intact. Discard the grey sac in the head and the black intestinal tube in the body.

Rub any loose coral (or spawn) through a fine sieve. Remove the meat from the shells and the claws and cut it carefully into $\frac{3}{4}$ in (2 cm) cubes. Melt 2 oz (50 g) of the butter in a shallow, heavy-based pan and gently fry the lobster meat, turning it frequently, for 3–4 minutes. Remove the pan from the heat and set aside.

Melt the remaining butter in a saucepan, stir in the flour and cook gently for 2 minutes; remove the pan from the heat. Strain the infused milk through a fine sieve and gradually stir this and the reduced fish stock into the roux. Bring this sauce to the boil, stirring continuously, and cook gently for 3 minutes, until the sauce thickens. Leave to cool for 2 minutes, then stir in the mustard, egg yolks, sieved coral and the cream. Season with salt and pepper, and stir in the lemon juice.

Coat the inside of the empty lobster shells with a little of the sauce. Stir half the remaining sauce into the lobster in the pan and carefully spoon the mixture into the shells. Cover with the remaining sauce; grate the Parmesan cheese, mix it with the breadcrumbs and sprinkle over the lobsters. Place the shells under a high grill and cook until the topping is golden brown.

Serve the lobster on a bed of lettuce, with crisp French bread and a tossed green salad.

CRAB TART

Most savoury tarts or flans are baked blind – that is the pastry is partly cooked before the filling is added. They are ideal for summer fare, since they are quick to make and equally tasty served either hot or cold.

PREPARATION TIME: *20–30 min*
COOKING TIME: *30 min*
INGREDIENTS *(for 4–6):*
PASTRY:
8 oz (225 g) plain flour
*¼ level teaspoon salt**
¼ level teaspoon cayenne pepper
2 oz (50 g) butter
2 oz (50 g) lard
1 oz (25 g) Cheddar cheese
1 egg yolk
FILLING:
½–¾ lb (225–350 g) crab meat
3 eggs
2 teaspoons lemon juice
½ teaspoon Worcestershire sauce
4 fluid oz (100 ml) double cream
*Salt**

For the pastry, sift the flour, salt and cayenne pepper into a mixing bowl. Rub in the butter and lard, cut into knobs, until the mixture is crumbly. Grate in the cheese; bind the pastry with the egg yolk and a little cold water. Leave the pastry to rest for 30 minutes.

Roll this shortcrust pastry out on a lightly floured surface, and use to line a 9 in (23 cm) flan ring. Prick the base of the pastry and bake it in the pre-heated oven at 400°F (200°C, mark 6) for 10 minutes or until golden.

Extract the meat from the crab (page 87) and flake it finely into a bowl. Beat the eggs lightly with the lemon juice and Worcestershire sauce and stir it into the crab meat before blending in the cream. Add salt to taste.

Spoon the crab mixture into the pastry case and bake in a pre-heated oven at 375°F (190°C, mark 5) for 25–30 minutes.

Serve the tart, hot or cold, cut into wedges, and with crusty bread and a mixed salad, for a light lunch. Lemon wedges would be used to garnish.

HOT CRAB SOUFFLÉ

The French invented the soufflé, which is basically a sauce and a savoury or sweet purée blended with stiffly beaten egg whites. It should emerge from the oven light, fluffy and golden.

PREPARATION TIME: *20 min*
COOKING TIME: *35–40 min*
INGREDIENTS *(for 4):*
6 oz (175 g) crabmeat, fresh, tinned or frozen
1 oz (25 g) butter
1 oz (25 g) plain flour
½ pint (300 ml) milk, less 2 tablespoons
Salt and black pepper*
Cayenne pepper
2 oz (50 g) grated Cheddar cheese
4 eggs

Melt the butter in a saucepan; stir in the flour and cook over low heat for a few minutes. Gradually beat in the milk, stirring continuously until the sauce thickens and comes to the boil. Season to taste with salt, freshly ground pepper and cayenne. Stir in the cheese and leave the sauce to cool for 5 minutes.

Separate the eggs and beat the yolks, one at a time, into the cheese sauce. Flake the prepared crabmeat finely and blend it into the sauce. Correct seasoning if necessary. Whisk the egg whites until stiff, then add to the crab mixture; fold them in gently with a metal spoon.

Pour into a buttered 1½ pint (900 ml) soufflé dish and level the top. Bake in the centre of an oven pre-heated to 375°F (190°C, mark 5), for 35–40 minutes, until well risen and golden brown. Serve immediately; a green salad could also be served.

CRAB TART

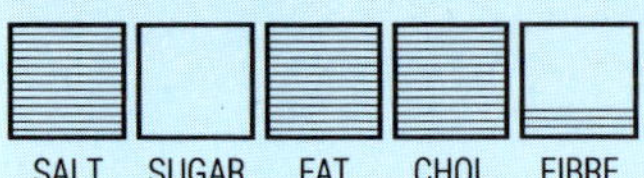

GLUTEN-FREE* WHOLEFOOD*
TOTAL CALORIES: ABOUT 3185

It is difficult to reduce the **salt** in this dish, as most comes from the crab naturally, but you can omit the Worcestershire sauce and halve the amount of cheese. The **fat** level is also difficult to reduce unless you replace the shortcrust pastry with scone dough pastry (see page 12). The cream in the filling can be replaced with full cream milk or soured cream, and the number of eggs reduced to 2. (Calories lost: up to 1140.)
The levels of salt, fat and **cholesterol** (from the crab and eggs) will remain medium-high.

Food processor ✓ for pastry.

HOT CRAB SOUFFLÉ

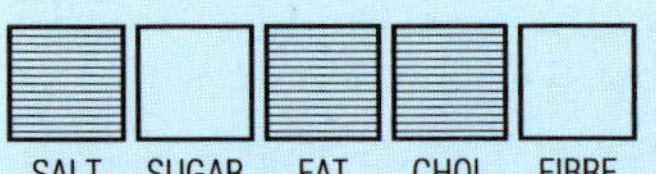

GLUTEN-FREE* WHOLEFOOD*
TOTAL CALORIES: ABOUT 1330

To reduce the **salt** to medium, replace the cheese with 1 oz (25 g) Parmesan and mix the crabmeat half and half with flaked fresh cooked white fish. To reduce **fat** and **cholesterol**, use skim milk; use 3 yolks and 4 whites in the soufflé, and make the soufflé base with vegetable margarine instead of butter. However the levels of both will remain moderate to high. (Calories lost: up to 160.) Potato flour is a good **gluten-free** flour for soufflés, but only half the quantity given is needed.

CRAB WITH MUSHROOMS

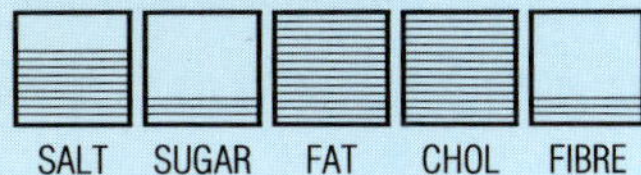

SALT SUGAR FAT CHOL FIBRE

GLUTEN-FREE WHOLEFOOD
TOTAL CALORIES: ABOUT 1775

To reduce **salt**, replace the olives in the garnish by, for instance, slices of pepper or fennel which are lower in salt. As crab contains a substantial amount of salt, a version moderate in salt would be obtained by mixing crab half and half with poached flaked white fish or scallops.
This would also reduce the **cholesterol** level (which in crab, as in most shellfish, is fairly high) to moderate.
To reduce the **fat** level to low, substitute thick low-fat yogurt, smetana or low-fat curd cheese for the oil and double cream. (Calories lost: up to 900.)

CUCUMBER CUPS WITH PRAWNS

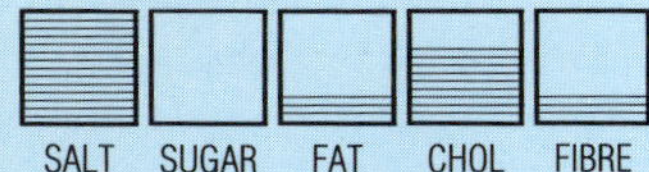

SALT SUGAR FAT CHOL FIBRE

GLUTEN-FREE WHOLEFOOD
TOTAL CALORIES: ABOUT 375

Prawns are high in **salt** and the only way of reducing salt to a moderate level in this dish is to mix them half and half with poached flaked white fish. Monkfish is particularly good as its firm texture is not unlike that of prawns.
The **cholesterol** also comes from the prawns, so would be reduced to low by the same alteration. (Calories lost: up to 60.)

CRAB WITH MUSHROOMS

This combination of mushrooms and crabmeat, frozen or tinned, makes a good main course. The dish can also be served as a starter, and shrimps can be substituted for crab.

PREPARATION TIME: *10 min*
CHILLING TIME: *1 hour*
INGREDIENTS *(for 4–6):*
8 oz (225 g) crabmeat
½ lb (225 g) button mushrooms
2 cloves garlic
Juice of half lemon
Tabasco sauce
6 tablespoons olive oil
¼ level teaspoon caster sugar
Salt and black pepper*
¼ pint (150 ml) double cream
GARNISH:
3 oz (75 g) black olives
Chopped parsley

Trim and finely slice the mushrooms into a deep bowl. Crush the garlic and add to the mushrooms, together with the strained lemon juice, a few drops of Tabasco and the olive oil. Season to taste with sugar, salt and freshly ground pepper. Blend all the ingredients thoroughly; spoon them into a shallow serving dish; leave to chill for 1 hour.

Just before serving, blend the flaked crabmeat with the cream and stir this mixture into the mushrooms.

Garnish the crab and mushrooms with olives and finely chopped parsley. Serve with warm crusty bread and butter. A salad of green peppers, endive and Florence fennel tossed in a garlic dressing would also go well with the crab.

CUCUMBER CUPS WITH PRAWNS

Few ingredients combine so well for flavour and eye-appeal as cucumber and shellfish.

PREPARATION TIME: *15 min*
CHILLING TIME: *30 min*
INGREDIENTS *(for 6–8):*
1 large plump cucumber
1 tablespoon finely chopped fresh mint or 1 teaspoon dried mint leaves
2 tinned pimentoes
5 fluid oz (150 ml) natural yogurt
½ lb (225 g) small peeled prawns
Salt and pepper*
Paprika

Chop off the stalk end of the cucumber and cut the remainder into eight equal pieces. Drain and chop the pimentoes. Stand the cucumber sections upright on a serving dish and, with a pointed spoon, hollow out the centres to form cup shapes. Leave about ¼ in (½ cm) around the sides and base.

Add the chopped mint and pimento to the yogurt and fold in the prawns. Season with salt and pepper. Spoon the mixture into the cucumber cups and sprinkle with a little paprika. Chill for 30 minutes and serve with slices of wholemeal bread.

PRAWNS IN COCONUT CREAM, MALAY STYLE

It is worth making the amount of garam masala given here, as although only a little is needed in this recipe, any surplus can be stored in an airtight jar and will keep for up to a month. It is an essential ingredient of curry dishes. The Indian cook will blend spices each day according to his own choice, but the following recipe is a suitable one for most curries.

PREPARATION TIME: *10 min*
COOKING TIME: *20 min*
INGREDIENTS *(for 4):*
2 large onions
2–3 tablespoons ghee (page 95)
1 rounded teaspoon garam masala
1 green pepper
12–16 cooked, unshelled large prawns
*Salt**
½ pint (300 ml) coconut cream (see below)
GARAM MASALA:
2 oz (50 g) coriander seeds
2 oz (50 g) black peppercorns
1½ oz (40 g) cumin seeds
20 peeled cardamom seeds
4 teaspoons whole cloves
2 level tablespoons ground cinnamon

First make the garam masala. Grind the whole seeds, peppercorns and cloves in a coffee grinder and blend the ground mixture with the cinnamon.

Finely chop the onions and fry them over low heat in the ghee until soft and pale golden. Add the teaspoon of garam masala and cook for a further 2–3 minutes. Blend in the sliced pepper, cover and simmer for 10 minutes. Add the prawns, season with salt and cook over low heat for 1 minute.

Keeping the heat as low as possible, stir in the coconut cream and simmer until the prawns and the sauce are heated through. Do not let the sauce boil.

Coconut cream and milk
Fresh or processed coconut yields both cream and milk which are used in many soups and sauces.

Drill two or three holes at the top of a fresh coconut and shake out the colourless liquid. Saw the coconut in half and scrape out the flesh. Shred it finely, pour over ¼ pint (150 ml) boiling water and leave for 20 minutes. Squeeze through muslin to produce cream.

For coconut milk, put the squeezed coconut and ¼ pint (150 ml) cold water in a pan and bring to the boil. Remove from the heat, leave for 20 minutes and squeeze through muslin again. Coconut cream and milk can also be made in a liquidiser.

Failing a fresh coconut, the product known as creamed coconut is very easy to grate and gives excellent results. For coconut cream, use equal quantities of grated creamed coconut and hot water; for coconut milk, double or treble the amount of water. Whether or not you use a blender, always strain before using.

Desiccated coconut produces an acceptable milk if treated in the same way, but it does not produce a very satisfactory cream.

SCAMPI PROVENÇALE

In cooking, 'Provençale' always implies the use of garlic and tomatoes. This recipe can be used as a first course or as a light lunch or supper dish.

PREPARATION TIME: *15 min*
COOKING TIME: *15 min*
INGREDIENTS *(for 4):*
12–16 oz (350–450 g) shelled scampi
1 onion
1 clove garlic
2 tablespoons oil
14 or 16 oz (400–450 g) tin of tomatoes
3 tablespoons dry white wine
Salt and black pepper*
1 rounded teaspoon cornflour
1 rounded tablespoon chopped parsley

Rinse the scampi under cold running water and pat them dry on absorbent paper. Peel and finely chop the onion and garlic. Heat the oil in a large, heavy-based pan, add the onion and fry over low heat for about 5 minutes or until soft, but not browned. Add the garlic and scampi and fry for a further 3 minutes, before blending in the tomatoes and the wine; season to taste with salt and freshly ground pepper. Bring to the boil and simmer for about 6 minutes.

Blend the cornflour with 1 tablespoon of water and stir into the scampi. Cook for a few minutes, stirring until the sauce has thickened. Remove from the heat and add the parsley.

As a first course the scampi could be served within a ring of plain boiled rice. For a lunch or supper dish, buttered French beans would also be suitable.

PRAWNS IN COCONUT CREAM, MALAY STYLE

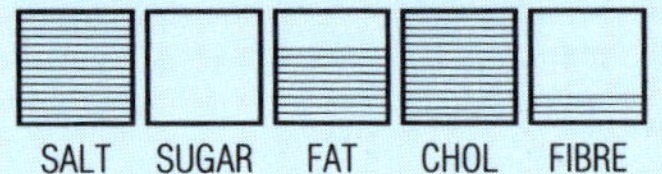

GLUTEN-FREE WHOLEFOOD
TOTAL CALORIES: ABOUT 1000

The **salt** content is in the prawns and the coconut cream. As in the previous recipe, monkfish may be substituted for some or all of the prawns, and the coconut cream may be mixed half and half with water, which will reduce the salt level to low.
For a low **fat** level, use only 1 tablespoon of ghee (or clarified butter or oil) to fry the onions and spices. For low **cholesterol**, substitute monkfish as above, and use oil instead of ghee. Coconut cream and milk contain no cholesterol. (Calories lost: up to 300.)

Microwave: ☑

SCAMPI PROVENÇALE

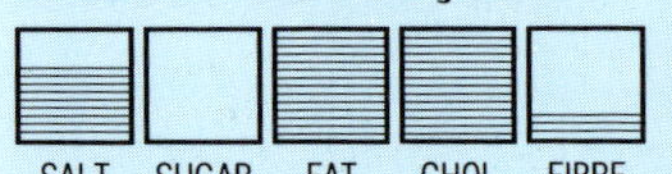

GLUTEN-FREE WHOLEFOOD
TOTAL CALORIES: ABOUT 1000

To limit the **salt** to the amount naturally present in scampi, choose tomatoes canned without added salt.
To reduce the **fat** level to low, cook the onions and scampi in a pan which has been brushed lightly with oil, using a tightly fitting lid to prevent the mixture drying out. (Calories lost: up to 200.)
Scampi naturally contain a significant amount of **cholesterol** but are lower in it

than many shellfish. For moderate to low cholesterol, replace half the scampi with monkfish, halibut or cod. Serving with brown rice will add **fibre** as well as being **wholefood**.

Freezing: ✓ up to 1 month.

Microwave: ✓

MOULES À LA POULETTE

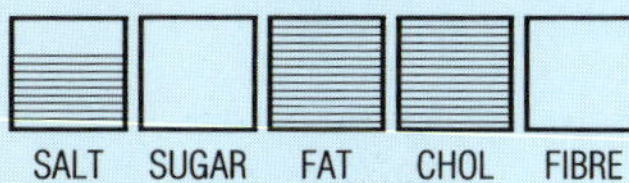

SALT SUGAR FAT CHOL FIBRE

GLUTEN-FREE WHOLEFOOD
TOTAL CALORIES: ABOUT 1400

The **salt** comes mainly from the mussels themselves, which also contain a significant amount of **cholesterol**, neither of which can therefore be substantially altered.
However, the total **fat** level can be reduced to very low, and the cholesterol to medium, if the mussel cooking liquid is thickened by blending a tablespoon of cornstarch or arrowroot with a little of the liquid to a smooth paste, then adding this back to the remaining liquid. Simmer together for at least 1 minute, then remove from the heat and stir in $\frac{1}{4}$ pint (150 ml) smetana or thick low-fat yogurt. Do not boil again. Using this method, the egg yolks and cream are omitted. (Total calories lost: up to 680.)

MOULES À LA POULETTE

In France, the mussels in this classic dish are served in their half shells and eaten with the fingers. Alternatively, remove the mussels entirely from the shells and serve them in the sauce as a soup.

PREPARATION TIME: *30 min*
COOKING TIME: *10 min*
INGREDIENTS *(for 6–8):*
8 pints (3½ kg) mussels
1 bay leaf
1 parsley sprig
1 shallot
6 black peppercorns
¾ pint (425 ml) dry white wine
¼ pint (150 ml) double cream
2 egg yolks
2 tablespoons chopped parsley
Black pepper
Lemon juice

Clean the mussels (page 89) thoroughly, discarding any with broken or open shells. Scrape away all grit and remove the beards. Put the mussels in a large, heavy-based saucepan with the bay leaf, parsley, peeled and finely chopped shallot and the peppercorns. Pour over the wine, cover the pan with a lid and cook the mussels over high heat until the shells open.

As the shells open, remove the mussels from the pan, throw away the empty top halves and place the mussels in their half shells in a warmed casserole. Cover them with a clean cloth to prevent them drying out, and to keep them warm. Strain the cooking liquid through muslin.

Mix the cream and egg yolks together in a bowl and blend in a few tablespoons of the mussel liquid. Add to the remaining liquid, together with the chopped parsley. Season to taste with freshly ground pepper and lemon juice. Re-heat the liquid, without boiling, until it has thickened slightly.

Serve the mussels in individual deep soup plates, with the sauce poured over them. Set a finger bowl with a slice of lemon by each plate. Offer plenty of crusty bread to mop up the sauce and provide a spare bowl or plates for the empty mussel shells.

SCALLOPS IN THE SHELL

Scallops, with their firm white flesh and coral-red tongues, are at their best in the winter months. In this recipe, they are used for a main course, served in the deep rounded shells which afterwards make useful hors d'oeuvre dishes.

PREPARATION TIME: *20 min*
COOKING TIME: *35 min*
INGREDIENTS *(for 2–4):*
4 large scallops
4 oz (100 g) button mushrooms
¼ pint (150 ml) dry white wine or dry cider
1 slice lemon
1 bay leaf
1 lb (450 g) potatoes
1 oz (25 g) butter
SAUCE:
1 oz (25 g) butter
1 oz (25 g) plain flour
Salt and black pepper*
1 egg yolk
2 tablespoons double cream
GARNISH:
Chopped parsley

Slide the scallops (page 89) off the shells, wash them well under running cold water and remove the black beards and intestines. Cut each scallop into four or six slices. Wipe and thinly slice the mushrooms. Put the scallops and mushrooms in a pan, with ½ pint (300 ml) of water, the wine (or cider), lemon slice and bay leaf. Bring to the boil, cover with a lid and simmer gently for 15–20 minutes. Strain through a colander and set aside ½ pint (300 ml) of the fish liquid for the sauce. Remove the lemon slice and bay leaf, and keep the scallops and mushrooms hot.

Meanwhile, put the peeled potatoes on to boil and make the sauce. Melt the butter in a saucepan over low heat, stir in the flour and cook gently for a few minutes. Gradually mix in the reserved fish liquid, stirring continuously until the sauce is smooth. Bring to the boil and simmer gently for 2–3 minutes. Add the mushrooms and scallops; season to taste with salt and freshly ground pepper; re-heat gently. Lightly mix the egg yolk and cream, remove the pan from the heat and stir the egg into the fish mixture.

Mash and season the potatoes. Using a large piping bag, fitted with a rosette nozzle, pipe a border of mashed potato around the edges of the deep scallop shells. Brush the potato border with 1 oz (25 g) melted butter and place the shells under a hot grill for a few minutes until the potatoes are golden brown.

Spoon the scallops into the centre of each shell and sprinkle them with chopped parsley. Serve with a tossed green salad for a main course, or on their own as a first course for a dinner party.

SCALLOPS IN THE SHELL

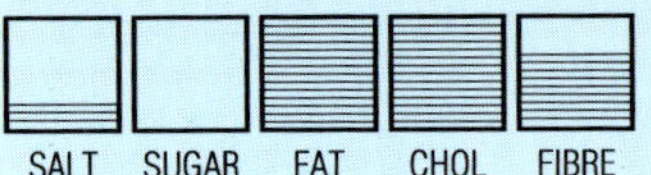

GLUTEN-FREE* WHOLEFOOD*
TOTAL CALORIES: ABOUT 1510

To reduce **fat** and **cholesterol** levels to low, mash and glaze the potatoes with milk in place of butter and enrich the fish mixture with a few tablespoons of smetana or low-fat curd cheese in place of the egg yolk and cream.
This leaves only the cholesterol in the low-fat scallops – lower than in most molluscs – and in the butter used to make the sauce. The latter can be partly or wholly exchanged for vegetable margarine. (Calories lost: up to 150.)
Potato flour or cornflour, both **gluten-free**, can be used for the sauce.

Freezing: ☑ up to 1 month.

Microwave: ☑ for cooking the scallops. It could be used for cooking the whole dish if you use special microwave dishes instead of the scallop shells.

SCALLOP CHOWDER

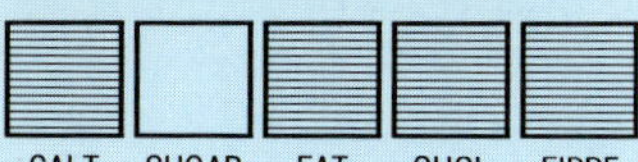

GLUTEN-FREE* WHOLEFOOD*
TOTAL CALORIES: ABOUT 2725

Reduce the level of **salt** to the moderate amount provided by the scallops by omitting the pork. Use 2 teaspoons of fat and a little stock in which to cook the vegetables.
To reduce **fat** to low, omit the pork as above, use skim milk and avoid the need to thicken the chowder with flour and butter, either by simmering a little longer, or by adding 2 tablespoons rolled oats to the chowder with the milk. (Calories lost: up to 1260.)
Scallops contain a significant amount of **cholesterol**, but less than most molluscs. Replacing half the scallops with monkfish will reduce the cholesterol level to moderate.
Millet flakes can be used as an alternative to **gluten-free** flour for thickening the soup.

Freezing: ✓ up to 1 month.

SCALLOP CHOWDER

Chowder is derived from the French *chaudière*, meaning cauldron, in which this thick soup was traditionally cooked.

PREPARATION TIME: *15 min*
COOKING TIME: *1 hour*
INGREDIENTS *(for 4–6)*:
12 scallops
Juice of a lemon
½ pint (300 ml) fish stock
1 large onion
6 oz (175 g) belly pork
4 potatoes
1 carrot
1 parsnip
1 green pepper
2 sticks celery
1 pint (570 ml) milk
Salt and black pepper*
Juice of an orange
1 level tablespoon plain flour
1 oz (25 g) butter
GARNISH:
Paprika

Slide the scallops (page 89) from their shells, and discard the beards and any black threads. Wash the scallops under cold running water, sprinkle with lemon juice and allow to stand for 15 minutes. Cut each scallop into four pieces and put them in a saucepan with the fish stock. Bring to the boil, cover the pan and simmer for 10 minutes.

Peel and thinly slice the onion. Put the belly pork in a sauté pan and cook over low heat until the fat runs. Remove the pork and add the onion to the pan, cooking it in the pork fat until transparent. Peel and dice the potatoes, carrot and parsnip. Cut the pepper in half, remove the stem, seeds and white midribs, and slice the flesh. Add these vegetables, with the cleaned and roughly chopped celery, to the onion.

Pour the milk into the pan and bring to simmering point. Season with salt and freshly ground pepper. Add the orange juice; return the belly pork to the pan, and simmer, covered, until the vegetables are tender.

Lift out the pork and dice it finely. Stir the scallops, the stock and the pork into the chowder.

If necessary, make a beurre manié (page 82) from the flour and butter and use it to thicken the chowder.

Serve the chowder in individual bowls, sprinkled with paprika.

CHICKEN AND ALMOND SOUP

Feather Fowlie is the true name of this traditional Scottish soup. By adding cream to the soup, it was given a French touch to please Mary, Queen of Scots.

PREPARATION TIME: *30 min*
COOKING TIME: *about 3½ hours*
INGREDIENTS *(for 6)*:
1 boiling fowl, 4–5 lb (about 2 kg)
1 lb (450 g) mixed root vegetables (onions, carrots and turnips)
3 sticks celery
10 black peppercorns
*½ level teaspoon salt**
Bouquet garni (page 99)
2 oz (50 g) ground almonds
3 rounded tablespoons fresh breadcrumbs
¼ pint (150 ml) double cream
GARNISH:
Chopped parsley or chives
Bread croûtons (page 96)

Peel and roughly chop the vegetables. Put the cleaned chicken in a large saucepan, together with the vegetables, peppercorns, salt and bouquet garni. Cover with cold water and bring to the boil over high heat. Remove any scum from the surface, lower the heat and cover the pan with a lid. Simmer for 2–3 hours or until the fowl is sufficiently tender.

Lift the chicken from the stock; let it cool slightly before removing the skin and cutting all the flesh off the carcass. Put the meat in the liquidiser, with the vegetables.

Put the purée in a large clean pan, mix in the almonds and breadcrumbs and stir in about 2 pints (1·2 litres) of the chicken stock, strained through a sieve. Bring the soup to the boil and simmer over low heat for 30 minutes, stirring frequently.

Before serving, blend half a cup of hot soup with the cream and stir this mixture back into the soup.

Correct seasoning and serve the soup garnished with finely chopped parsley or chives and with bread croûtons.

CHICKEN YOGURT SOUP

In the Middle East, yogurt is often used instead of cream. It gives a refreshing tang to a soup.

PREPARATION TIME: *15 min*
COOKING TIME: *20 min*
INGREDIENTS *(for 6)*:
15–16 fluid oz (425–450 ml) natural yogurt
1½ level teaspoons cornflour
1½ pints (900 ml) chicken stock
5 egg yolks
3 level tablespoons ground almonds
Salt and black pepper*
2 level tablespoons chopped mint
½ oz (10 g) unsalted butter

Stabilise the yogurt before cooking, by blending the cornflour with a little water, and gradually beating it into the yogurt. Pour into a saucepan and bring slowly to the boil over moderate heat, stirring continuously. Simmer gently for 10 minutes or until thickened.

Meanwhile, bring the chicken stock to the boil in another pan. Remove from the heat, let it cool slightly, while lightly beating the egg yolks. Spoon a little of the stock into the eggs and blend thoroughly, before stirring this mixture into the stock. Heat over low heat until just simmering – if brought to boiling point, the eggs will curdle – stirring all the time until the stock thickens. Gradually, stir the yogurt into the chicken stock.

Blend the ground almonds into the soup, and correct seasoning if necessary. Sauté the chopped mint for 1–2 minutes in a little butter and blend into the soup just before serving.

CHICKEN AND ALMOND SOUP

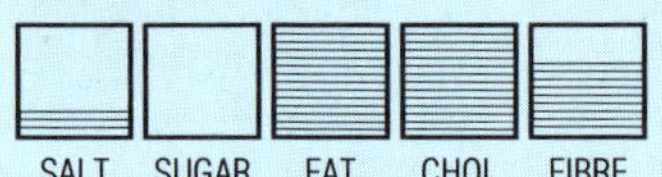

GLUTEN-FREE* WHOLEFOOD*
TOTAL CALORIES: ABOUT 2400

To reduce both **fat** and **cholesterol** to low, skin the chicken before cooking. Cook it well ahead of time to give the stock time to cool, and remove all the fat which will have congealed on the top. Smetana can be substituted for the cream and is, to some tastes, an improvement. Toast or bake the bread croûtons instead of frying them.
For very low fat, halve the amount of almonds used, or substitute chestnut flour or ground hazelnuts, both of which are less fatty than almonds and also go especially well with chicken. (Calories lost: up to 550.)
If you have no **gluten-free** bread to hand, omit the breadcrumbs and add a large potato to the other vegetables in order to thicken the soup. Omit the garnish of croûtons.

Pressure cooker: ✓

Freezing: ✓ up to 6 months.

CHICKEN YOGURT SOUP

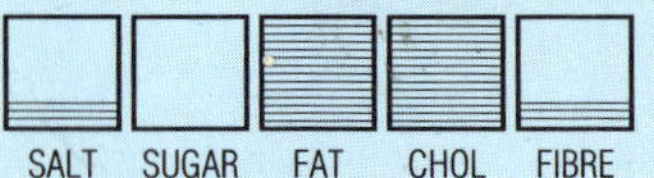

GLUTEN-FREE WHOLEFOOD
TOTAL CALORIES: ABOUT 1020

To reduce the **fat** to fairly low and the **cholesterol** to moderate, use low-fat yogurt and substitute 2 whole eggs for the egg yolks. It is not

necessary to sauté the chopped mint in butter before stirring it in. As in the previous recipe, remove all fat from the stock and, if you like, replace the almonds with hazelnuts. (Calories lost: up to 350.)
This soup can also be made with no eggs at all and will then be very low in both fat and cholesterol. (Further calories lost: 400.)
Without the eggs it will serve 4 people rather than 6.

COCK-A-LEEKIE SOUP

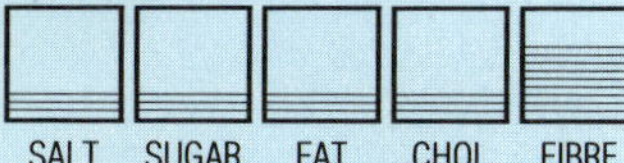

SALT SUGAR FAT CHOL FIBRE

GLUTEN-FREE WHOLEFOOD
TOTAL CALORIES: ABOUT 1120

Although the **salt** content is low if none is added, this is a soup that many people would find unpalatable without salt, so that omitting it simply creates other problems. Try adding the finely grated rind of half a lemon, season well with freshly ground black pepper and be generous with the chopped parsley.
Dried mushrooms also add flavour; ½–1 oz (15–25 g) should be enough. Soak them for half an hour in a little warm water. Strain this liquid into the soup, rinse the mushrooms, chop them roughly and add them to the soup with the prunes.
To ensure very low levels of both **fat** and **cholesterol**, cook the chicken ahead of time, as in the previous recipes, and scrupulously remove all fat from the surface when the stock has cooled. Make sure also that all the skin is removed.

Pressure cooker: ✓

Freezing: ✓ up to 6 months.

COCK-A-LEEKIE SOUP

Legend has it that this traditional Scottish soup originated in the days when cockfighting was a favourite sport. The loser was then thrown into the stock pot together with leeks; prunes were a later addition for extra flavour.

PREPARATION TIME: *10–15 min*
COOKING TIME: *2 hours*
INGREDIENTS *(for 6)*:
1 chicken, about 3 lb (1·4 kg)
*1 level tablespoon salt**
6 peppercorns
6 leeks
6 prunes
GARNISH:
Chopped parsley

Soak the prunes for 6 hours in cold water. Wipe the trussed chicken, rinse the giblets and place both in a deep saucepan. Pour over cold water to cover the chicken (if necessary, split the bird in half so that it remains submerged). Add the salt and peppercorns and bring to the boil. Remove any scum from the surface, cover with a tight-fitting lid and simmer for about 1½ hours.

Meanwhile, trim the coarse leaves off the leeks to within 2 in (5 cm) of the top of the white stems and cut off the roots. Split the leeks lengthways, wash them well under running cold water, then cut them into 1 in (2½ cm) pieces. Skim the soup again; add the leeks and the soaked prunes, which may be stoned or left whole. Simmer for another 30 minutes.

Lift the chicken and giblets from the soup; remove skin and bones from the chicken flesh. Reserve the best breast pieces for another recipe, and cut the remaining meat into small pieces. Add these pieces to the soup and correct the seasoning according to taste.

Just before serving the hot soup, sprinkle finely chopped parsley over it.

GARDENER'S CHICKEN

A casserole of chicken and vegetables makes a change from roast chicken. Once in the oven, the casserole can be left to cook.

PREPARATION TIME: *40 min*
COOKING TIME: *1½ hours*
INGREDIENTS *(for 4–6):*
1 chicken, approx. 3 lb (1·4 kg)
2 oz (50 g) streaky bacon
2 large onions
2 sticks celery
¼ lb (100 g) mushrooms
2–3 oz (50–75 g) unsalted butter
1 lb (450 g) new potatoes
½ lb (225 g) turnips
14 or 16 oz (400 or 450 g) tin of tomatoes
1 bouquet garni (page 99)
Salt and black pepper*
GARNISH:
Fresh parsley and orange rind

Joint the chicken (page 91) into four or six pieces, and wipe clean. Dice the bacon, after first removing the rind. Peel and thinly slice the onions; scrub and coarsely chop the celery; clean and slice the mushrooms. Melt the butter in a large, heavy-based pan and fry the bacon, onions, mushrooms and celery for 5 minutes. Tip the frying pan to drain the butter to one side, remove the vegetables with a perforated spoon and spread over the base of a large casserole.

Fry the chicken joints in the butter residue, adding a little more if necessary, until they are golden brown. Remove from the pan and place on the bed of vegetables. Scrape the potatoes, peel and slice the turnips and add these, together with the tomatoes and bouquet garni, to the casserole. Season with salt and freshly ground pepper, and cover the casserole with kitchen foil, before securing the lid so that no steam can escape. Cook on the middle shelf of the oven heated to 300°F (150°C, mark 2) for about 1½ hours or until tender.

Immediately before serving, sprinkle chopped parsley, mixed with the finely chopped rind of half an orange, over the casserole. No additional vegetables are needed.

GARDENER'S CHICKEN

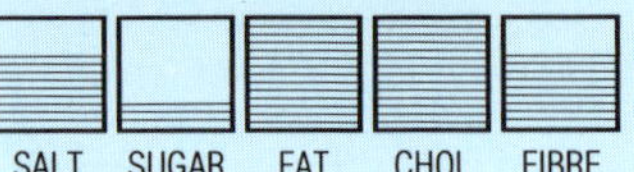

SALT SUGAR FAT CHOL FIBRE

GLUTEN-FREE WHOLEFOOD
TOTAL CALORIES: ABOUT 2400

This is low in **salt** if the bacon is omitted and unsalted tomatoes used. You can compensate by adding a clove or two of garlic, chopped, to the onions, celery and mushrooms.
To reduce the **fat** and **cholesterol** to moderate, use lean bacon rather than streaky, and use only half the quantity (or omit it entirely). Skin the chicken joints before cooking them. There is no need to fry the skinned chicken joints. (Calories lost: up to 700.)

Pressure cooker: √

Freezing: √ up to 4 months.

ROAST CHICKEN WITH WATERCRESS STUFFING

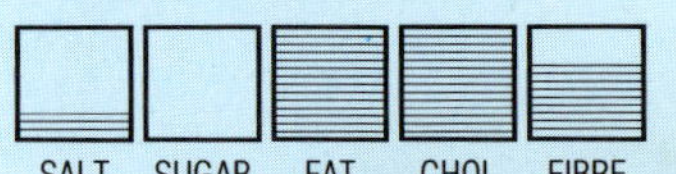

SALT SUGAR FAT CHOL FIBRE

GLUTEN-FREE* WHOLEFOOD*
TOTAL CALORIES: ABOUT 2520

Reduce both **fat** and **cholesterol** to moderate by using only 1 oz (25 g) butter or 2 tablespoons oil to sauté the onion and celery. Omit the bread sautéed in butter, and use instead 2 oz (50 g) brown rice, previously cooked in twice its volume of water for 30 minutes. Do not rub the chicken with butter before cooking it, and stand it on a grid so that the fat can drain. (Calories lost: up to 1200.)
Roast chicken does not really adapt to a very low-fat version

as skinning it would rather defeat the object. However, this is an ideal dish to serve if some but not all of the guests are on a low-fat diet: those who are will want to avoid the skin while the others can have double helpings. The brown rice suggested above also makes an excellent **gluten-free** and **wholefood** alternative to breadcrumbs.

CHICKEN LIVERS WITH GRAPES

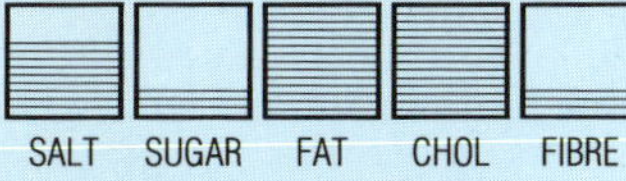

GLUTEN-FREE* WHOLEFOOD*
TOTAL CALORIES: ABOUT 3295

The **salt** can be reduced to fairly low if the bread used contains no salt. It cannot go below this, however, as chicken livers themselves contain a fair amount of sodium.
To limit **fat** to the moderate level naturally present in chicken livers, toast, bake or grill the bread (which can be lightly brushed with melted butter if you wish) instead of frying it; or replace it with a bed of plain rice or noodles. Cook the livers in a heavy pan lightly brushed with oil and omit the remaining oil and all the butter. Cover the livers when cooking so that they do not stick and the cooking juices are retained instead of drying on the pan. (Calories lost: up to 440.)
Chicken livers, like other organ meats, are high in **cholesterol**, but could be eaten occasionally if the rest of the food that day is very low in cholesterol.
Gluten-free alternatives are rice, as above, or potato. Cut thick slices from cold baked potatoes and grill them on both sides until well heated through.

ROAST CHICKEN WITH WATERCRESS STUFFING

A combination of watercress, onions, and celery is a welcome change from the usual stuffings for poultry.

PREPARATION TIME: *40 min*
COOKING TIME: *$1\frac{1}{4}$ hours*
INGREDIENTS *(for 4):*
1 medium onion
3 sticks celery
6 oz (175 g) unsalted butter
1 bunch watercress
4 oz (100 g) diced, day-old bread
1 roasting chicken, $3\frac{1}{2}$ lb ($1\frac{1}{2}$ kg)

Peel the onion, scrub the celery and dice both finely. Wash and drain the watercress, press out as much water as possible and chop it finely. Sauté the onion and celery in 2 oz (50 g) of the butter until soft. Add the watercress and cook until all the liquids have evaporated. In another pan sauté the bread in 2 oz (50 g) of the butter until lightly browned, and add to the vegetable mixture.

Stuff the chicken with this mixture. Truss the chicken (page 90), sprinkle it with salt and pepper, and rub it all over with the remaining butter. Place the chicken on its side in a roasting pan in a pre-heated oven at 425°F (220°C, mark 7) and roast for 20 minutes, basting once with the drippings. Turn the chicken on its other side and roast for another 20 minutes, basting once. Turn it on its back and continue to roast about 35 minutes more, basting about every 5 minutes. When the chicken is done, the juices will run clear at the thigh when it is pierced with the point of a knife.

Serve with jacket potatoes and a green vegetable or salad.

CHICKEN LIVERS WITH GRAPES

Chicken livers are readily available, either fresh or frozen, and usually at bargain prices. They make a good lunch or supper dish, served in a wine sauce delicately flavoured with grapes.

PREPARATION TIME: *25 min*
COOKING TIME: *10–12 min*
INGREDIENTS *(for 6):*
$1\frac{1}{2}$ lb (700 g) chicken livers
*Salt**
$\frac{3}{4}$ lb (350 g) large green grapes
6 slices bread
6 oz (175 g) unsalted butter
2 tablespoons cooking oil
3–4 fluid oz (75–100 ml) madeira, port or sweet sherry
Black pepper

Rinse the chicken livers in cold water and pat them dry. Cut away the white, stringy pieces and any discoloured parts which may have been in contact with the gall bladder – they add a bitter flavour if left in.

Season the livers with salt and freshly ground pepper and set them aside.

Peel and pip the grapes (page 96). Remove the crusts from the bread slices. Melt 4 oz (100 g) of the butter in a pan, together with the oil; when hot, fry the bread golden brown on both sides. Stand the fried bread upright on a baking tray and keep warm in the oven.

Melt the remaining butter and cook the livers for 3–5 minutes on each side; they should be slightly pink in the centre. Remove from the pan and keep warm. Stir the wine into the pan juices and reduce by rapid boiling until the sauce has thickened to a syrupy consistency. Add the grapes to the sauce and let them heat through.

To serve, arrange the hot bread on a serving dish, top with chicken livers and spoon the grapes on top. Serve immediately, before the sauce soaks into the fried bread.

CHICKEN BREASTS WITH SAGE

In Italy, where this dish originated, chicken breasts (*petti di pollo*) are usually cooked with a strong flavouring of herbs.

PREPARATION TIME: *10 min*
COOKING TIME: *45 min*
INGREDIENTS *(for 6):*
3 chicken breast portions
Seasoned flour (page 100)
1 tablespoon olive oil
1 tablespoon butter
2 oz (50 g) thin gammon rashers
$\frac{1}{4}$ pint (150 ml) dry white wine
$\frac{1}{4}$ pint (150 ml) chicken stock
12 sage leaves
Salt and black pepper*

Remove the skin from the chicken portions and cut off the wings. Slice the breast away from the bones and cut each portion into halves, lengthways. Coat the chicken with seasoned flour. Heat the oil and butter in a sauté pan over moderate heat and lightly brown the chicken.

Cut the gammon into narrow strips and add to the chicken. When the chicken is golden brown, pour in the wine and enough stock to come about two-thirds up the chicken breasts. Add the roughly chopped sage.

Cover the pan with a lid and simmer the chicken over moderate heat for 15–20 minutes. Remove to a serving dish and keep it warm. Increase the heat and rapidly boil the liquid until it has reduced to a thin coating consistency. Season to taste with salt and freshly ground pepper.

Pour the sauce over the chicken fillets and serve at once with fresh bread and a green vegetable.

POULET À LA CRÈME

This recipe for a casserole of chicken in a rich cream and calvados sauce comes from Normandy. It loses nothing of its flavour if any leftovers are reheated later.

PREPARATION TIME: *10 min*
COOKING TIME: *$1\frac{1}{4}$–$1\frac{1}{2}$ hours*
INGREDIENTS *(for 4–6):*

1 chicken weighing 3–4 lb (1·4–1·8 kg)
1 Spanish onion
2 oz (50 g) cooked ham or lean bacon
Salt and black pepper*
$2\frac{1}{2}$ oz (65 g) butter
4 tablespoons calvados or brandy
2 teaspoons chopped celery leaves
$\frac{1}{2}$ pint (300 ml) dry still cider or unsweetened apple juice
2 large egg yolks
$\frac{1}{4}$ pint (150 ml) double cream
GARNISH:
2 dessert apples
1 oz (25 g) unsalted butter

Peel and finely chop the onion, and dice the ham or bacon after removing the rind. Wipe the trussed chicken inside and out with a clean damp cloth and set the giblets aside. Season the chicken with salt and pepper.

Melt the butter in a pan over moderate heat and cook the onion until soft and transparent. Stir in the ham or bacon and cook for another 2–3 minutes. Brown the chicken lightly all over in the butter. Warm the calvados or brandy in a small pan and set alight (calvados will produce a fair amount of flame). While the spirit is still flaming, pour it over the chicken. Shake the pan gently until the flames die out.

Add the chicken neck, gizzard and heart to the pan, but omit the liver. Sprinkle in the chopped celery leaves and pour over the cider or apple juice; let it come to the boil, then simmer for a few minutes. Turn the chicken on its side and cover the pan closely with foil and then a lid. Cook over low heat. (If necessary, put the contents in a casserole and cook at 325°F (170°C, mark 3) in the centre of the oven.)

After 20–25 minutes cooking, turn the chicken over on the other side and cook for a similar period, still covered. Finally, turn the chicken breast upwards, cover and cook for a further 10 minutes.

Lift the chicken on to a warm serving dish and keep hot. Strain the liquid, and reduce slightly by fast boiling. Remove the pan from the heat. Beat together the egg yolks and the cream; mix in a few spoonfuls of the warm liquid, and whisk into the pan juices. Stir over low heat until the sauce has thickened.

While the chicken is cooking, peel and core the apples. Cut them into $\frac{1}{4}$ in ($\frac{1}{2}$ cm) thick rings. Fry the apple rings in butter until golden brown.

Just before serving, pour the hot sauce over the chicken and garnish with the apple slices. Little more than a green salad is needed, but boiled potatoes could also be served.

CHICKEN BREASTS WITH SAGE

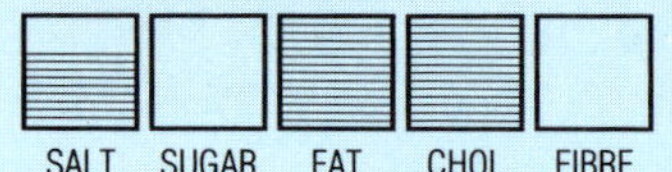

GLUTEN-FREE* WHOLEFOOD*
TOTAL CALORIES: ABOUT 1365

To reduce levels of **salt**, **fat** and **cholesterol** to low, omit the gammon (or use only half a rasher for flavour); omit the butter and seal the chicken on a lightly oiled baking sheet under the grill rather than sautéing it in oil. Make sure the chicken breasts are thoroughly skinned and that all fat has been removed from the stock. (Calories lost: up to 300.)

POULET À LA CRÈME

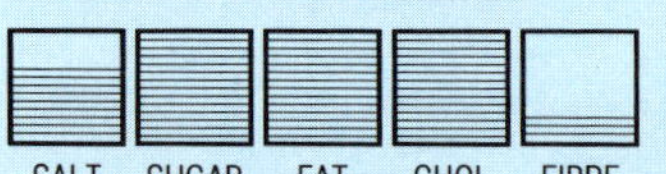

GLUTEN-FREE WHOLEFOOD
TOTAL CALORIES: ABOUT 2910

The **salt** level can be reduced to low by using only half a rasher of bacon or $\frac{1}{2}$ oz (10 g) ham, preferably unsmoked.
To ensure low levels of both **fat** and **cholesterol**, reduce the bacon or ham as above; skin the chicken and seal it in a pan brushed lightly with oil. The butter can then be omitted. Use one whole egg instead of 2 yolks for thickening the sauce.
Replace the double cream with smetana: it may not be authentically Norman but it is very good. For the garnish, soften the apple rings by simmering them in a little cider or apple juice for a few minutes. (Calories lost: up to 1340.)

Freezing: √ up to 4 months.

BANGKOK CHICKEN AND RICE

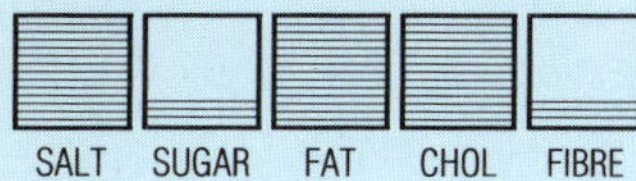

GLUTEN-FREE WHOLEFOOD*
TOTAL CALORIES: ABOUT 3560

The main sources of **salt** here are the ham and prawns, and to some extent the peanut butter. To reduce the level to moderate, grind the peanuts without adding any salt and replace the ham with a chopped green or red pepper: the prawns can be replaced with less salty seafood, such as mussels or monkfish.
These adaptations also reduce the levels of **fat** and **cholesterol**; to reduce them still further, to low, halve the amount of peanut butter and use only 1 egg, chopped in smaller pieces. Skin the chicken before cooking and trim off any surplus fat. Cook it ahead of time and let the stock get cold enough for all the fat to be removed easily. Use only 2 tablespoons oil to fry the onion.
Side dishes served with the chicken are not traditionally dressed, but served plain. Banana should be tossed in lemon juice to avoid it browning, but not fried. Coconut is very high in saturated fat and could be replaced with other oriental side dishes, such as chopped spring onions. If you wish to serve a side dish of nuts, hazelnuts are lower in fat than almonds or cashews. Other alternatives include chopped cucumber with chopped mint, or slices of mango. (Calories lost: up to 300.)

Pressure cooker: ☑ for cooking the chicken.
Freezing: ☑ up to 2 months.

BANGKOK CHICKEN AND RICE

In spite of its name, this is one of the great dishes from the famous Indonesian *rijstafel*. It makes an attractive centrepiece for a buffet, surrounded by small dishes of colourful fresh vegetables and fruit to which guests can help themselves.

PREPARATION TIME: *35 min*
COOKING TIME: *$2\frac{3}{4}$ hours*
INGREDIENTS *(for 6–8)*:
1 small boiling chicken, approx. $3\frac{1}{2}$ lb ($1\frac{1}{2}$ kg)
1 lb (450 g) onions
1 bay leaf
1 sprig parsley
Salt and black pepper*
1 lb (450 g) long grain rice
3 tablespoons olive or vegetable oil
2 level tablespoons peanut butter
$\frac{1}{2}$ level teaspoon chili powder
4 oz (100 g) peeled prawns
4 oz (100 g) diced cooked ham
1 level teaspoon cumin seeds
$1\frac{1}{2}$ level teaspoons coriander seeds
1 clove garlic
Pinch ground mace
GARNISH:
Half a cucumber
2 hardboiled eggs
8–12 unpeeled prawns

Put the chicken in a large pan, with one whole peeled onion, the bay leaf and parsley sprig. Add a seasoning of salt and freshly ground pepper and enough cold water to cover the chicken. Bring to the boil, remove any scum from the surface, then cover the pan with a lid and simmer over gentle heat for about 2 hours or until the chicken is tender.

Lift out the chicken and leave to cool slightly. Strain the stock through a fine sieve and use it to cook the rice until just tender. Drain the rice through a colander and cover it with a dry cloth.

Remove the skin from the chicken and cut the meat into small pieces. Peel and thinly slice the remaining onions. Heat the oil in a large pan, and fry the onions over low heat until they begin to colour. Stir in the peanut butter and chili powder. Add the peeled prawns, diced ham and the chicken and finally the rice, which should now be dry and fluffy. Continue frying over low heat, stirring frequently until the rice is slightly brown. Crush the cumin and coriander seeds and the peeled garlic, and stir them, with the mace, into the rice. Season to taste with salt.

Pile the rice and chicken mixture on to a hot serving dish and garnish with thin slices of unpeeled cucumber, wedges of hardboiled egg and large prawns.

Arrange a number of small side dishes or bowls round the chicken. A suitable selection might include apricot and mango chutney; sliced tomatoes, dressed with sugar and lemon juice; peeled, sliced oranges; and sliced green and red pepper with raw onion rings, both in a vinaigrette sauce (page 83). Other bowls could contain small wedges of fresh pineapple; fried sliced bananas with lemon juice; and fresh shredded and toasted coconut. Shelled almonds or cashew nuts fried in a little butter are also frequently served with this dish.

CHICKEN WITH FORTY CLOVES OF GARLIC

The long cooking gives the garlic a subtle taste and in spite of the quantity it is not overpowering.

PREPARATION TIME: *15 min*
COOKING TIME: *1½ hours*
INGREDIENTS *(for 8):*
8 chicken legs and thighs
40 cloves garlic
4 sticks celery
¼ pint (150 ml) olive oil
6 sprigs parsley
1 tablespoon dried tarragon
4 fluid oz (100 ml) dry vermouth
¼ teaspoon pepper
Dash of nutmeg
*2½ teaspoons salt**

Rinse the chicken in cold water and pat dry with paper towels. Peel the garlic, leaving the cloves whole. Cut the celery into thin slices.

Pour the oil into a shallow dish or a plate and turn all the chicken pieces in the oil so that they are coated on all sides. Put the celery slices in the bottom of a heavy casserole with a tight-fitting cover. Add the parsley and tarragon. Lay the chicken pieces on top and sprinkle with the vermouth, pepper, nutmeg, and 1 teaspoon of the salt.

Pour the remaining oil in the plate into the casserole. Add the garlic cloves; sprinkle with the remaining salt. Over the top of the casserole lay a piece of aluminium foil large enough to extend 1 inch (2½ cm) over the edge all around. Cover with the lid of the casserole to make a tight seal. Alternatively, make a thick flour and water paste and spread it with the fingers all around the edge of the casserole where the cover and casserole meet, to make an air-tight seal. Put a layer of foil around the lid to cover the circle of flour paste.

Bake at 375°F (190°C, mark 5) for 1½ hours. Do not remove the lid during the cooking period. Serve from the casserole, with hot toast or thin slices of pumpernickel on which to spread the softened garlic cloves.

CHICKEN LIVER PÂTÉ

Frozen chicken livers are readily available and are excellent for pâtés and terrines.

PREPARATION TIME: *15 min*
COOKING TIME: *10 min*
CHILLING TIME: *2–3 hours*
INGREDIENTS *(for 6):*
1 lb (450 g) chicken livers
2 oz (50 g) butter
1 small onion
2 bay leaves
Dried thyme
Salt and black pepper*
2 tablespoons brandy

Melt the butter and fry the peeled and finely chopped onion, the bay leaves and a good pinch of thyme for 2–3 minutes. Trim away any green bits of gall bladder, and cut the chicken livers into small pieces; add to the pan. Cook over low heat for 5 minutes or until the livers are cooked. Discard the bay leaves and put the liver mixture in a liquidiser until smooth, or mince the liver twice.

Season to taste with salt and freshly ground pepper and stir in the brandy. Pour the pâté into a jar and leave to chill in the refrigerator for several hours.

CHICKEN MARYLAND

A favourite dish on the American dinner table, chicken Maryland is traditionally accompanied by corn fritters. These batter cakes are, like all the other ingredients in this dish, fried until golden.

PREPARATION TIME: *25 min*
COOKING TIME: *45 min*
INGREDIENTS *(for 6):*
3 lb (1·4 kg) chicken, jointed into 8 pieces, or 6 chicken joints
Seasoned flour (page 100)
1 egg
3–4 oz (75–100 g) fresh breadcrumbs
4–5 oz (100–150 g) unsalted butter
8 lean bacon rashers
3 bananas
1 tablespoon olive or corn oil
CORN FRITTERS:
4 oz (100 g) plain flour
1 egg
¼ pint (150 ml) milk
11 oz (300 g) tin creamed sweet corn
Salt and black pepper*
GARNISH:
Watercress

Remove the skin from the chicken pieces and coat them with seasoned flour. Lightly beat the egg and dip the chicken portions in this before coating them with breadcrumbs. Shake off any loose crumbs. Melt about 2 oz (50 g) of the butter in a large frying pan and fry the chicken pieces for about 10 minutes, until brown on both sides. Turn down the heat, cover the pan with a lid or tight-fitting foil and cook gently, turning the chicken once, for 25–30 minutes. If cooked in the oven, allow 40 minutes at 400°F (200°C, mark 6).

CHICKEN WITH FORTY CLOVES OF GARLIC

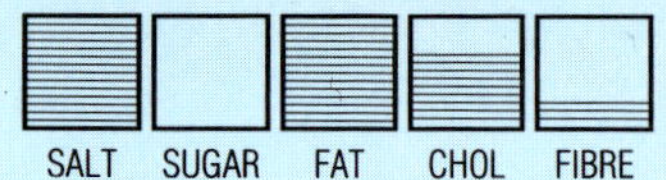

GLUTEN-FREE WHOLEFOOD
TOTAL CALORIES: ABOUT 3255

The **salt** content is very high, but omitting it will alter the taste of the dish. This is one occasion when a salt substitute might be worth considering, if your diet allows it.
To reduce the **fat** to moderate, first skin the chicken pieces. This also reduces the **cholesterol** to low. 4–6 tablespoons of oil will be enough to cook the chicken. (Calories lost: up to 600.) If you can use good olive oil it is well worth it as the taste will come through, but if you are actually on a cholesterol-lowering diet use sunflower oil instead.

CHICKEN LIVER PÂTÉ

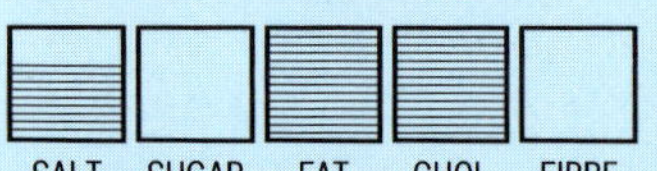

GLUTEN-FREE WHOLEFOOD
TOTAL CALORIES: ABOUT 000

The **salt** level cannot be less than moderate, even if unsalted butter is used, as chicken livers are high in sodium, but this should not be a problem as pâté is not normally eaten in vast quantities.
The **fat** content becomes moderate if only half the quantity of butter is used. It could be reduced still further, to about a quarter, if you do not mind losing a certain softness and richness of texture. (Calories lost: up to 000.) Substituting sunflower oil or other vegetable fat for the

butter will help to lower the **cholesterol**, but as the livers are high in it anyway this remains something to be eaten only on occasion.

Food processor: ☑ for blending to a smooth purée.
Freezing: ☑ up to 2 months.

Microwave: ☑ Very suitable for this recipe, as the livers can be cooked in a covered container using less fat.

CHICKEN MARYLAND

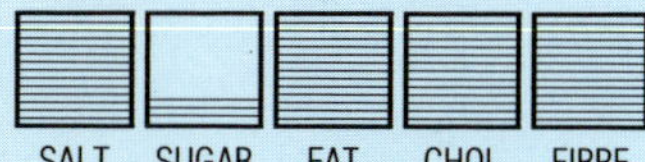

SALT SUGAR FAT CHOL FIBRE

GLUTEN-FREE* WHOLEFOOD*
TOTAL CALORIES: ABOUT 4680

The high level of **salt** in this dish comes mainly from the bacon, followed by the breadcrumbs, with possibly some in the creamed sweet corn. To reduce it to low, omit the bacon. Use fresh or frozen sweet corn kernels, or buy unsalted sweet corn and purée it yourself.
The **fat** level can be reduced, and the **cholesterol** limited to the low amount in the chicken itself, by cooking the chicken in the oven with 2 oz (50 g) olive or peanut oil instead of butter. The bananas and corn fritters can also be cooked in a pan lightly brushed with oil and well heated, rather than using butter. Use skim milk and egg white only in the fritters, and serve with plain rice. (Calories lost: up to 720.)
Gluten-free alternatives are cornflour or millet flakes for coating the chicken, and corn fritters made with fine cornmeal (or a mixture of cornmeal and potato flour) instead of flour.

Cut the rind from the bacon and stretch each rasher with the flat blade of a knife. Cut each rasher in half, roll them up and thread them on two skewers. Peel and halve the bananas lengthways; coat them evenly in seasoned flour, ready for frying.

Sift the flour for the fritters into a mixing bowl, make a well in the centre and add the egg and milk. Using a wooden spoon, mix from the centre, gradually drawing in the flour from around the sides of the bowl. Beat to make a smooth batter. Stir in the sweet corn and season to taste with salt and freshly ground pepper.

When the chicken pieces are tender, transfer them to a serving dish and keep them warm. Melt 1 oz (25 g) of butter in the pan, add the bananas and fry over low heat.

Heat the remaining butter and the oil in a second frying pan. When hot, add tablespoons of the corn fritter batter, cook until golden brown on the underside, then turn each fritter and fry on the other side. Fry the fritters a few at a time – they take 1–2 minutes to cook; keep the fritters warm in the oven while frying the next batch.

While the last fritters are cooking, put the skewers with bacon rolls under a high grill for about 2 minutes.

Serve the chicken pieces garnished with the corn fritters, bacon rolls and fried bananas and sprigs of watercress. A tossed green salad goes well with this dish.

CHICKEN IN MUSHROOM SAUCE

This method of cooking chicken produces a light, easily digestible meal, particularly suitable for invalids. Any remains of the chicken and mushroom sauce can be made into soup.

PREPARATION TIME: *25 min*
COOKING TIME: *$1\frac{1}{2}$ hours*
INGREDIENTS *(for 6):*
1 chicken, approx. $3\frac{1}{2}$ lb ($1\frac{1}{2}$ kg)
2 onions
2 sticks celery
$1\frac{1}{2}$ oz (40 g) unsalted butter
Salt and black pepper*
1 bay leaf
12–16 button mushrooms
Worcestershire sauce
1 level tablespoon plain flour
$2\frac{1}{2}$ fluid oz (75 ml) double cream
GARNISH:
1 tablespoon finely chopped parsley

Peel and finely chop the onions; scrub the celery and chop finely. Melt 1 oz (25 g) of the butter in a large, heavy-based pan over low heat; cook the onion and celery until soft and just beginning to colour.

Meanwhile, wash and wipe the chicken, inside and out; clean the giblets and liver. Put the chicken, giblets and liver in the pan with the onion and celery, with enough water to cover the chicken. Bring to the boil, remove any scum and add salt, freshly ground pepper and the bay leaf. Cover the pan with a lid and simmer gently for about $1\frac{1}{2}$ hours, or until the chicken is tender. Lift the chicken on to a warm dish and keep it hot. Strain the cooking liquid and set aside.

Trim and thinly slice the mushrooms. Melt the remaining butter in a small pan and cook the mushrooms over low heat for 2–3 minutes. Add a few drops of Worcestershire sauce and sprinkle the flour over the mushrooms. Cook, stirring continuously, until all the fat has been absorbed into the flour. Gradually blend in about $\frac{1}{4}$ pint (150 ml) of the strained chicken liquid, to make a smooth sauce. Correct seasoning if necessary. Stir in the cream and heat the sauce through.

Carve the chicken and arrange the slices and joints in a deep serving dish. Pour the mushroom sauce over it and garnish with chopped parsley. Serve with broccoli spears and plain potatoes, or buttered rice.

COQ AU VIN

Burgundy is the home of this classic method of cooking a cockerel (or chicken), and wine from the same region is the obvious choice to cook it in, although any reasonably good red wine can be used.

PREPARATION TIME: *40 min*
COOKING TIME: *about $1\frac{1}{4}$ hours*
INGREDIENTS *(for 4):*
1 chicken, 3–$3\frac{1}{2}$ lb (about $1\frac{1}{2}$ kg)
Bouquet garni (page 99)
Salt and black pepper*
4 oz (100 g) pickled belly pork or green streaky bacon
4 oz (100 g) button onions
1 large clove garlic
4 oz (100 g) button mushrooms
2 oz (50 g) unsalted butter
1 tablespoon olive oil
2 tablespoons brandy
1 pint (570 ml) red wine
$\frac{1}{2}$ pint (300 ml) stock
Beurre manié (page 82)
GARNISH:
4 oz (100 g) button onions
2 oz (50 g) button mushrooms
1 level tablespoon chopped parsley

Clean and truss the bird. Use the giblets with the bouquet garni, a little salt and freshly ground pepper to make stock. Dice the pickled pork or bacon having first removed the rind and gristle. Peel the onions and garlic and trim and slice the mushrooms.

Heat the butter and oil in a flameproof casserole dish or pan and fry the pork or bacon until the fat runs. Remove from the casserole. Brown the bird all over in the hot fat, then spoon off any surplus fat. Warm the brandy in a spoon or small pan, set it alight and pour it flaming over the bird. As soon as the flames subside, pour in the wine and add the pork, onions, mushrooms and crushed garlic. Pour over enough stock to make the liquid come halfway up the bird. Cover with a lid and cook over low heat on top of the stove or in the oven, at 300°F (150°C, mark 2), for 1 hour or until the bird is tender, turning it from time to time.

Remove the bird and divide it into joints; keep these warm on a serving dish. Lift out the onions, bacon and mushrooms with a perforated spoon and arrange them over the chicken. Reduce the cooking liquid by brisk boiling, then lower the heat and gradually whisk in pieces of beurre manié until the sauce has thickened. Correct seasoning and pour the sauce over the chicken.

Serve garnished with glazed button onions, fried or grilled button mushrooms and freshly chopped parsley.

CHICKEN IN MUSHROOM SAUCE

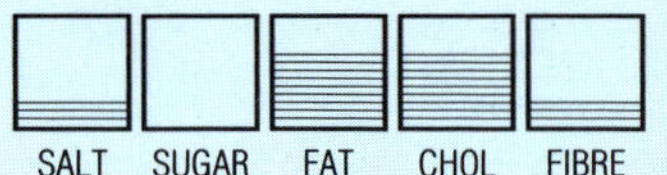

GLUTEN-FREE* WHOLEFOOD*
TOTAL CALORIES: ABOUT 1905

To reduce the **fat** and **cholesterol** to low, first of all skin the chicken. This is most easily done after it has been simmered. Try to do this a little ahead of time so that the stock will have time to cool and the fat to solidify on top of it. Remove all the fat before using the stock to make the sauce. Use smetana instead of the double cream, and do not boil the sauce after working it in. Soften the vegetables in a heavy pan lightly brushed with oil instead of butter and do the same for the mushrooms. (Calories lost: up to 400.)
Use cornflour or potato flour as **gluten-free** alternatives in the mushroom sauce.

Pressure cooker: ✓ for cooking the chicken.
Freezing: ✓ up to 4 months.

COQ AU VIN

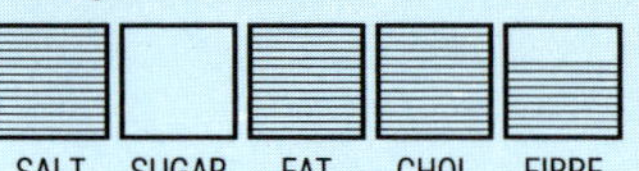

GLUTEN-FREE WHOLEFOOD
TOTAL CALORIES: ABOUT 2985

To reduce the **salt** to moderate, use sweet cured bacon and only half the amount; to reduce it to low, the pork or bacon can be omitted completely. Compensate by adding an extra clove or two of garlic and $\frac{1}{2}$ oz (10–15 g) dried mushrooms, soaked for half an hour in a little warm water. (Their

soaking juice, strained, can be added to the stock.)
For low to moderate **fat** and **cholesterol**, skin the chicken, preferably before cooking, although it is easier to do so after it is cooked. Fry only half the amount of pork or bacon in its own fat, omitting the butter. Skim as much fat as possible off the stock. Instead of the beurre manié, thicken with ½ tablespoon of cornflour or arrowroot (see page 82). (Calories lost: up to 1050.)

Freezing: ✓ up to 4 months.

CHICKEN CHAUD-FROID

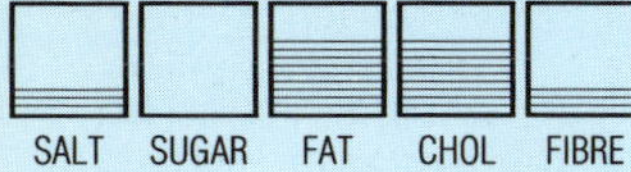

GLUTEN-FREE* WHOLEFOOD*
TOTAL CALORIES: ABOUT 1700

The **fat** in this recipe can be reduced to low if the milk is replaced with skim milk, chicken stock or a mixture of the two. If you are using chicken stock make sure it has cooled enough for the fat to rise to the surface so that it can be skimmed off easily. (Calories lost: up to 80.)
Cholesterol can be reduced to very low by using vegetable oil or margarine in place of butter, and skim milk or stock as above.
Use cornflour or potato flour as a **gluten-free** alternative to flour.
Potato flour is also **wholefood**. You can make a wholefood aspic jelly by using 2 teaspoons gelatine or 1 teaspoon agar agar to set ½ pint (300 ml) chicken or vegetable stock.

Pressure cooker: ✓ for cooking the chicken joints.

CHICKEN CHAUD-FROID

This is a classic French dish of whole cooked chicken, coated with aspic sauce (chaud-froid sauce) and elaborately garnished. Individual chicken joints are however easier to coat than a whole chicken.

PREPARATION TIME: *1 hour*
COOKING TIME: *1½–1¾ hours*
INGREDIENTS *(for 6):*
6 chicken portions
1 large onion
1 sprig thyme
1 small bay leaf
1 small carrot
6 parsley stalks
6 peppercorns
*¼ level teaspoon salt**
½ pint (300 ml) milk
1 oz (25 g) unsalted butter
1 oz (25 g) plain flour
Salt and black pepper*
½ pint (300 ml) aspic jelly
2 level teaspoons powdered gelatine
GARNISH:
Cucumber peel
1 large tomato
1 small green pepper
Peel of a small lemon

Wipe the chicken portions and put them in a large saucepan. Peel the onion, cut off a 1 in (2½ cm) slice and add the larger piece to the pan together with the thyme, bay leaf and enough cold water to cover the chicken. Bring slowly to the boil, remove the scum and cover the pan with a lid. Simmer for 1–1¼ hours or until tender. Lift out the chicken portions and drain.

Scrape the carrot, leaving it whole, and put it in a saucepan with the onion slice, parsley stalks, peppercorns, salt and milk. Bring slowly to the boil, then turn off the heat and leave the milk to infuse for 30 minutes.

Melt the butter in a saucepan, stir in the flour and cook for 2 minutes; strain the infused milk and gradually stir into the butter and flour mixture. Bring the sauce to the boil over low heat, stirring continuously, and cook gently for 2 minutes. Season to taste with salt and freshly ground pepper.

Make up the aspic jelly as directed on the packet, adding the gelatine. Allow the jelly to stand until almost set, then gradually add half to the white sauce, stirring until thick but not set.

Remove the skin carefully from the chicken portions, pat them dry and place on a wire rack. Coat each portion carefully with the aspic sauce, allowing any excess to run off. Leave for 15 minutes to set.

Cut a 1 in (2½ cm) piece of cucumber peel, the tomato, pepper and lemon peel into narrow strips, dip them in the remaining aspic jelly and arrange them in decorative patterns on the chicken pieces. Allow the decorations to set before spooning over the remaining aspic jelly; leave the chicken in a cool place to set completely.

Salads, crusty bread or new potatoes could be served as side dishes with the chicken.

DUCK BREASTS EN CROÛTE

A little duck goes a long way and still constitutes a festive dish for a special occasion. The preparation of this dish can be done well in advance.

PREPARATION TIME: *1½ hours*
COOKING TIME: *25 min*
INGREDIENTS *(for 12):*
3 ducklings
4 tablespoons lean chopped bacon
2 chopped duck livers
4 tablespoons finely chopped onion
Rind of an orange
1 oz (25 g) butter
3 tablespoons chopped green olives
1 tablespoon brandy
1½ lb (700 g) prepared puff pastry
1 large beaten egg

Roast the ducklings in the centre of the oven for 45–60 minutes, at 400°F (200°C, mark 6). Set aside to cool.

Sauté the bacon, duck livers, onions and orange rind in the butter. Add the olives moistened with the brandy and cook this mixture over moderate heat for about 5 minutes.

Skin the ducklings and carve the breasts off each in two whole slices; cut each breast into two equal portions (set the duck carcasses aside for a pâté to be made the following day). Roll out the puff pastry, ¼ in (½ cm) thick, and divide into 12 pieces. Lay a portion of duck breast on each pastry square, spread a little of the bacon and onion mixture over the duck and wrap the pastry round each to form an envelope.

Seal the joins with egg and place the envelopes, seams up, on a moist, floured baking tray. Brush with egg and bake in a preheated oven at 400°F (200°C, mark 6) for about 25 minutes.

Serve with croquette potatoes and mushroom caps filled with green peas.

DUCK PÂTÉ

The rest of the duck meat and liver from the preceding recipe can be used to make a savoury pâté.

PREPARATION TIME: *15 min*
COOKING TIME: *1¼ hours*
INGREDIENTS *(for 8–10):*
3 duck carcasses (see above)
1 duck liver
½ lb (225 g) minced veal
2 oz (50 g) breadcrumbs
2 tablespoons finely chopped onion
1 tablespoon chopped chervil
3 tablespoons chopped parsley
Salt and pepper*
Grated rind of an orange
2 tablespoons brandy or dry sherry
2 eggs
4 oz (100 g) thin streaky bacon

Cut the meat from the duck carcasses and mince it coarsely, together with the remaining duck liver. Mix with the minced veal, breadcrumbs, finely chopped onion, chervil and parsley. Season to taste. Stir in the grated orange rind and the brandy or dry sherry. Beat the eggs lightly and mix them in to bind the pâté.

Spoon into a buttered terrine and cover with the bacon. Put into a roasting tin half filled with boiling water and bake in the centre of an oven pre-heated to 325°F (170°C, mark 3) for 1¼ hours.

When cool, cover and store in the refrigerator for a day or two before serving.

DUCK BREASTS EN CROÛTE

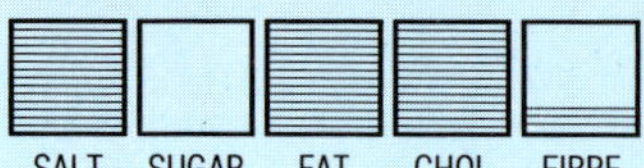

SALT SUGAR FAT CHOL FIBRE

TOTAL CALORIES: ABOUT 6330

For a **low-salt** version, replace the bacon and olives in the stuffing with chunks of apple and pieces of cooked dried apricot, mango or fennel; or use the stuffing suggested below. The **fat** and **cholesterol** cannot be reduced to less than moderate, unless you can substitute wild duck (which is much leaner) or pheasant. To reduce them as much as possible, roast the birds on a rack, first pricking them all over so that as much fat as possible drains off. Skinning the birds before cooking will also help. Yeast pastry, or bought phyllo pastry, are both good low-fat alternatives to puff pastry. (Calories lost: up to 800.) Serve with baked potatoes, scooped out and mashed with a little skim milk and the grated rind of an orange.

Neither **gluten-free** nor **wholemeal** puff pastry is very successful. Try a yeast dough instead, made if necessary with a special gluten-free mix.

ALTERNATIVE STUFFING:
Use only 1 tablespoon bacon and add ½ oz (10–15 g) dried mushrooms (soaked in warm water for half an hour and drained), and 4 tablespoons very finely chopped celery; omit the duck livers. This is low in both salt and cholesterol.

DUCK PÂTÉ

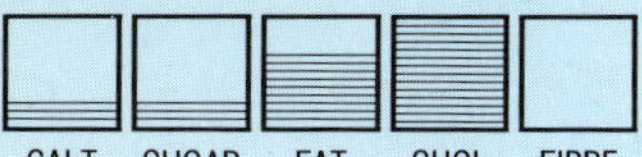

SALT SUGAR FAT CHOL FIBRE

GLUTEN-FREE* WHOLEFOOD*
TOTAL CALORIES: ABOUT 2415

To reduce the **salt** even further, use breadcrumbs from a loaf made without added salt, and use spinach leaves to wrap the pâté in instead of the terrine lining of streaky bacon. The spinach leaves also help to lower **cholesterol** content although this will still be high.
To reduce the **fat** content, the duck should be cooked as in the notes on previous recipe and the minced veal should be lean: to be certain of this, buy lean meat and mince it yourself at home. Use spinach leaves instead of bacon as above. Even so the fat content will be between low and moderate. (Calories lost: up to 1000.)

Food processor: ✓ for mincing and chopping.

Freezing: ✓ up to 1 month.

DUCKLING WITH ORANGE

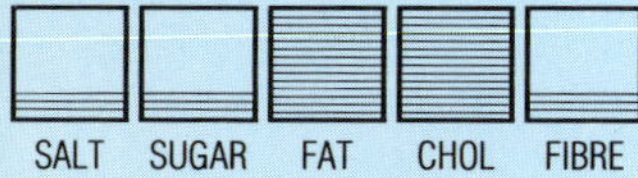

SALT SUGAR FAT CHOL FIBRE

GLUTEN-FREE WHOLEFOOD
TOTAL CALORIES: ABOUT 2030

To reduce **fat** and **cholesterol**, skin the ducks before roasting; roast on a rack so that the fat can drain off, and do not baste. Even so the levels of both fat and cholesterol will be moderate; the meat alone averages 10% fat when cooked: with the skin, this can be 29%!

DUCKLING WITH ORANGE

This classic dish is easy to cook and makes a good choice for a dinner party. It can also be made in advance and kept hot over low heat.

PREPARATION TIME: *45 min*
COOKING TIME: *1¾ hours*
INGREDIENTS *(for 4–6):*
2 ducks, each 4–5 lb (about 2 kg)
4 oranges
1 level tablespoon caster sugar
4 fluid oz (100 ml) red wine vinegar
10 fluid oz (300 ml) giblet stock
Juice of half lemon
1 level tablespoon arrowroot
3 tablespoons Curaçao

Peel the oranges over a plate to catch the juice. Remove all pith and divide the oranges into segments. Cut the rind into strips and boil them for 10 minutes in a little water. Drain them and set aside, with the orange segments, for garnishing.

Pre-heat the oven to 400°F (200°C, mark 6) and place the trussed ducks on their sides in a greased roasting tin. Cook for 40 minutes, then turn the ducks on to the other side and cook for 30 minutes. Finally place the ducks on their backs and cook for 30 minutes. Baste frequently.

Boil the sugar and vinegar until reduced to a light caramel. Add the stock, reserved orange and the lemon juice and boil for 5 minutes. Thicken the sauce with diluted arrowroot and stir until shiny. Strain the sauce, then stir in the Curaçao and pour over the duck.

Serve with new potatoes, green peas and perhaps a chicory and watercress salad.

DUCK PAPRIKA

The Hungarians traditionally flavour many of their poultry and meat dishes with paprika. This recipe makes a change from plain roast duck and is a good main course for a dinner party.

PREPARATION TIME: *15 min*
COOKING TIME: *1¼–1½ hours*
INGREDIENTS *(for 4–6):*
1 5–6 lb (about 2½ kg) duck
2 onions
1 clove garlic
1½ oz (40 g) unsalted butter
1 oz (25 g) plain flour
2 level teaspoons paprika
⅓ pint (200 ml) red wine
Salt and black pepper*
4–5 tomatoes
Chicken or duck stock (page 81)
1 rounded teaspoon arrowroot

Wipe the duck inside and out with a damp cloth, pat it thoroughly dry and truss it neatly (page 90). Peel and finely chop the onions and garlic. Melt the butter in a large flameproof casserole or sauté dish, and cook the onions and garlic for a few minutes until transparent. Add the duck, and brown on all sides. Lift the duck from the pan, sprinkle in the flour and paprika and cook for a few minutes. Pour in the wine and stir until this is a smooth sauce. Season to taste with salt and freshly ground pepper. Return the duck to the pan.

Skin and roughly chop the tomatoes (page 97) and add them to the duck, thinning with a little stock if necessary.

Cover the dish with a lid and simmer over low heat for about 1¼ hours or until the duck is tender. If necessary add more stock.

Remove the duck and carve it into six to eight portions; arrange these on a serving dish and keep hot. Skim any fat off the sauce; if necessary, blend a little arrowroot with cold water and stir into the sauce to thicken it. Spoon the sauce over the duck and serve with boiled rice.

WILD DUCK WITH MANDARINS

The largest wild duck is the mallard, which usually provides three or four servings; teal and widgeon are even smaller. As the meat is tough, wild duck are best roasted continental style with liquid in the roasting pan, and should be served with a fruit-flavoured sauce. The recipe is also successful for domestic duck.

PREPARATION TIME: *35–40 min*
COOKING TIME: *1 hour*
INGREDIENTS *(for 3–4):*
1 large mallard
Bouquet garni (page 99)
4 oz (100 g) cooked noodles
1 onion
2 teaspoons fresh chopped parsley
½ level teaspoon dried thyme
Pinch nutmeg
2½ tablespoons honey
2 tablespoons beer
2 egg yolks
2½ fluid oz (65 ml) double cream
3 mandarin oranges
2 fluid oz (50 ml) port
Lemon juice
Salt and black pepper*
GARNISH:
Mandarin slices and watercress

Clean the duck giblets and put them in a saucepan with water to cover; add salt, freshly ground pepper and the bouquet garni. Cover the pan with a lid and cook for about 25 minutes or until the giblets are tender. Strain and set the cooking liquid aside. Skin the gizzard and chop this, the heart and the liver finely.

Chop the drained noodles roughly and mix in the giblets, chopped onion, herbs and nutmeg. Mix half the honey and half

DUCK PAPRIKA

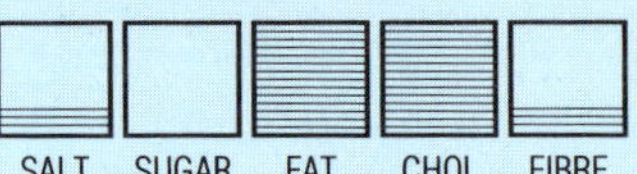

GLUTEN-FREE* WHOLEFOOD*
TOTAL CALORIES: ABOUT 2360

The **fat** and **cholesterol** can be reduced to medium if the duck is skinned before cooking and if it is then browned with the onions in the fat which it produces itself, without adding any butter. Skim the fat from the cooking juices; one way of doing this is to put the juices in a narrow jug and add a few ice cubes. The fat will solidify quickly on the ice, which can then be lifted out. (Calories lost: up to 500.)

Freezing: ✓ up to 2 months.

WILD DUCK WITH MANDARINS

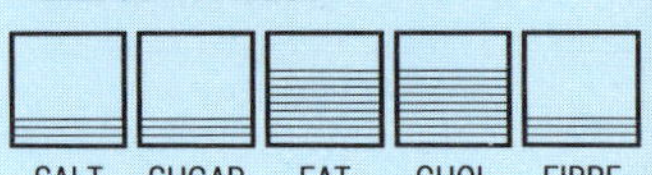

GLUTEN-FREE WHOLEFOOD
TOTAL CALORIES: ABOUT 2920

Wild duck has much less **fat** than duck bred for the table. Removing the skin will reduce the fat level to some extent, but is not really necessary unless you need a very low-fat diet. The fat in the rest of the recipe can be reduced by omitting the egg yolks and cream from the noodle stuffing and stirring in 4 tablespoons of low-fat curd cheese or smetana instead. Roast the duck on a rack throughout, and skim the pan juices before adding the oranges and other flavourings. Doing all this will result in low fat and medium **cholesterol**. (Calories lost: up to 375.)

This recipe is very sweet, and you may prefer to use half the amount of honey.
A **gluten-free** alternative to the noodles would be rice. Brown rice will also be **wholefood**. Use about 1 oz (25 g) uncooked brown rice if you have none ready cooked.

Pressure cooker: ✓ for stock.

SALMI OF WILD DUCK

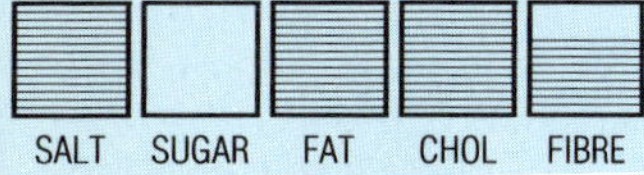

GLUTEN-FREE* WHOLEFOOD*
TOTAL CALORIES: ABOUT 3370

To reduce the **salt** to low, omit the bacon rashers and olives. If you are substituting a domestic, or farmed, duck, you will not need the bacon anyway. Make sure the stock is made without salt, and omit the ketchup unless it is salt-free.
For low **fat** and medium **cholesterol**, omit the bacon. Even wild duck has enough fat to keep it moist while cooking. If you fear it is getting dry, cover with foil or a lid. Make sure both the stock and the pan juices are well skimmed of fat, and thicken the sauce without using butter. This can be done by adding a tablespoon of arrowroot, slaked with water to a smooth consistency, and boiling for a few minutes; or simply by puréeing the onions and carrots in a blender and adding the purée back to the mixture. (Calories lost: up to 680.)
Either of these methods of thickening the sauce will make the recipe **gluten-free**, if there is no gluten in the ketchup.

Pressure cooker: ✓ for stock.

Freezing: ✓ up to 2 months.

the beer with the egg yolks and cream and stir this into the noodle mixture. Open the vent and remove any knobs of fat from the duck, spoon in the stuffing and close the opening.

Put the duck in a roasting pan, breast downwards, and pour water into the pan to a depth of ½ in (1 cm). Roast in the centre of a pre-heated oven, at 375°F (190°C, mark 5), for 20 minutes, basting occasionally. Remove the duck from the roasting pan, put in a wire rack and replace the duck, breast upwards. Pour the remaining honey and beer over the duck and continue roasting for a further 30 minutes, or until the duck is crisp and golden and the legs are tender when tested with a skewer.

Meanwhile grate the rind from the mandarin oranges and set aside. Remove the pith and pips and put the fruit in the liquidiser.

When the duck is ready, lift it on to a warm serving dish. Add the mandarin pulp and rind to the pan, together with the port and ½ pint (300 ml) of the reserved giblet stock. Boil on top of the stove over high heat until the gravy has reduced and thickened slightly. Sharpen with lemon juice and adjust seasoning. Strain the gravy into a warm sauce boat.

Garnish the duck with watercress sprigs and thin slices of unpeeled mandarin. Serve with roast or mashed potatoes and buttered green beans.

SALMI OF WILD DUCK

Salmi – a French cookery term – means a rich brown stew or casserole of game. It is a suitable method for making a party dish out of wild duck towards the end of their season.

PREPARATION TIME: *1 hour*
COOKING TIME: *40–45 min*
INGREDIENTS *(for 6):*

2 wild duck
Coarse salt
3 carrots
2 large onions
4 rashers streaky bacon
1 bay leaf
SAUCE:
1 pint (570 ml) duck stock
2 oz (50 g) butter
1½ oz (40 g) plain flour
1 tablespoon mushroom ketchup (optional)
3–4 tablespoons medium dry sherry or port
*Salt**
Squeeze lemon juice
6–8 stoned green olives
Black pepper

Wipe the ducks inside and out, and rub the skin with coarse salt. Peel and thinly slice a carrot and an onion and put them in a saucepan, together with the duck giblets. Pour over about 1½ pints (900 ml) of cold water, cover with a lid, bring to the boil and simmer for 30 minutes to make the stock.

Meanwhile, cut the rind off the bacon and cover the breast of the ducks with the rashers. Peel and slice the remaining carrots and onion and use them to cover the base of a lightly greased roasting pan. Add the bay leaf, place the birds on the bed of vegetables and roast for 30 minutes only, in the centre of the oven pre-heated to 375°F (190°C, mark 5). Remove the birds, discarding the bacon; carve each duck into four portions and put in a casserole.

Strain the fat from the roasting pan, but retain the vegetables. Pour 1 pint (570 ml) of strained duck stock into the pan and stir over moderate heat until boiling. Simmer gently until it has reduced by about one-third. Meanwhile, melt the butter in a saucepan over low heat. Stir in the flour and cook gently for 5–10 minutes, stirring occasionally until the mixture is nutty brown. Remove from the heat and stir in the hot reduced duck stock. Return the pan to the heat; stir until boiling, then add the mushroom ketchup (if used), sherry or port, a squeeze of lemon and salt and pepper to taste. Strain the sauce over the ducks in the casserole, cover with a lid and place in the centre of the oven preheated to 350°F (180°C, mark 4). Cook for 40–50 minutes or until the ducks are tender (if the juices that come out, when a meat skewer is gently pushed into the thigh, are clear, the ducks are cooked). Add the olives and allow to heat through for a few moments.

Serve creamed potatoes and broccoli with the salmi.

ROAST GOOSE WITH GERMAN-STYLE SWEET STUFFING

Goose is a much-neglected bird, yet it has endless possibilities. It is not only an excellent choice for holidays but makes a festive dinner any time of the year.

PREPARATION TIME: *30 min*
COOKING TIME: *2½–3 hours*
INGREDIENTS *(for 6–8):*
1 goose, fresh or frozen, 8–10 lb (3½–4½ kg)
STUFFING:
12 oz (350 g) day-old bread, cut into cubes
4 apples
6 oz (175 g) raisins
4 oz (100 g) sugar
*1 teaspoon salt**
1 teaspoon cinnamon
½ teaspoon allspice
4 fluid oz (100 ml) water
2 oz (50 g) melted butter

If the goose is frozen, place it, still in its original wrap, on a tray in the refrigerator for 1–1½ days to thaw. The goose may be thawed in 4 or 5 hours if it is placed, unwrapped, in a sink with cool or cold water. Change the water often to hasten thawing. To thaw at room temperature in 6–10 hours, leave the goose in its original wrap and place it in a brown paper bag, or wrap in 2 or 3 layers of newspaper and place on a tray.

Cook immediately after thawing, or refrigerate until ready to cook. Remove the neck and giblets from the body cavity; cook them immediately in enough salted water to cover and reserve for another use. Remove the excess fat from the body cavity and neck skin. Reserve this fat and render it (page 100) for use in other cooking. Rinse the bird inside and out, and drain well.

The wings may be removed at the second joint or tied flat against the body with a cord around each wing and across the back. If two end pieces of wings are removed, cook them with the neck and giblets.

To make the stuffing, chop the apples and combine them with the bread cubes and raisins in a large bowl. Mix the sugar with the salt, cinnamon, and allspice; sprinkle this over the bread mixture and toss well. Stir in the water and butter. Fill the neck and the body cavity loosely with the stuffing. Fasten the neck skin to the back of the goose with a skewer. Tie the legs together with string, or tuck the legs in the band of skin at the tail, if it is present. It is not necessary to truss the bird.

Place the goose, breast side up, on a rack in a roasting pan. Insert a meat thermometer deep into the inside thigh muscle without touching the bone. Roast, uncovered, for 1 hour in a pre-heated oven at 400°F (200°C, mark 6). Do not baste. During roasting, spoon or siphon off accumulated fat and reserve it for use in other cooking. This should be done at half-hour intervals to stop the fat browning excessively.

After roasting for 1 hour, reduce the oven temperature to 325°F (170°C, mark 3) and continue cooking for 1½–2 hours, or until thermometer registers 180°–185°F (82°–85°C). Stuffing temperature should also be checked and should register 165°F (75°C). If a thermometer is not used, press the meaty part of the leg between protected fingers. It should feel very soft. Also, prick the thigh with a fork. The juices running out should be beige in colour, not pink.

Serve with braised red cabbage or with Brussels sprouts.

GOOSE IN CIDER

This recipe adapts well for wild goose, should you ever have to cope with one. As wild goose is very lean, it will need plenty of butter added to the stuffing and should be rubbed with more butter and barded with bacon.

PREPARATION TIME: *15 min*
COOKING TIME: *3¼ hours*
INGREDIENTS *(for 4–6):*
1 goose, 8 lb (3½ kg)
18 fluid oz (500 ml) stock (page 81)
1 onion
6 cloves
½ orange
Salt and black pepper*
1 pint (570 ml) dry cider or white wine
2 tablespoons calvados or brandy (optional)
GARNISH:
Game chips (potato crisps)
Thick slices of bacon
Watercress
Oranges

Wipe the goose thoroughly inside and out with a damp cloth. Use the giblets to make stock.

Put the peeled onion, stuck with the cloves, and half an orange inside the goose. Sew up the vent or secure it with small skewers. Rub the skin with salt and freshly ground pepper and prick the breast with a fork so that the fat can drain out.

Place the goose, breast side up,

ROAST GOOSE WITH GERMAN-STYLE SWEET STUFFING

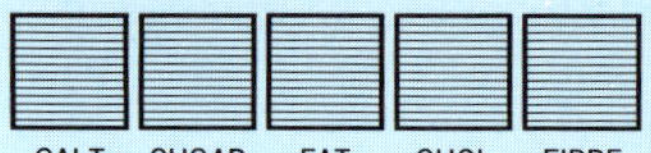

SALT SUGAR FAT CHOL FIBRE

GLUTEN-FREE* WHOLEFOOD*
TOTAL CALORIES: ABOUT 5910

Reduce the **salt** to low by using crumbs from bread made without added salt.
Goose is naturally a fatty bird (about 22% fat when roasted) and the levels of both **fat** and **cholesterol** will be high, unless you can acquire a wild goose, which is much leaner. Reduce both fat and cholesterol as far as possible (if you have managed to find a wild goose, the fat will be much lower anyway) by omitting the butter in the stuffing and being meticulous in removing as much of the goose fat as possible. (Calories lost: up to 450.)
Rice is a good **gluten-free** alternative to breadcrumbs in the stuffing. If you use white rice, wash about 1 lb (450 g) well to remove the starch. Measure the same volume of water as rice into a pan and bring it to the boil. Add the rice, cover tightly, turn down the heat and let it just simmer for 20 minutes. All the water should be absorbed. If it looks like drying out while cooking, add a little more cold water up to half as much again.
This method of cooking rice ensures that all the vitamins and minerals stay in it and do not leach out into the cooking water to be thrown away.
The same method can be used for brown rice, which makes an excellent stuffing and is of course **wholefood**. It needs more water, about 2¼ times the volume of the rice, and a longer cooking time, about 35–40

minutes (although this is not crucial, as it will continue to cook in the oven with the goose).

GOOSE IN CIDER

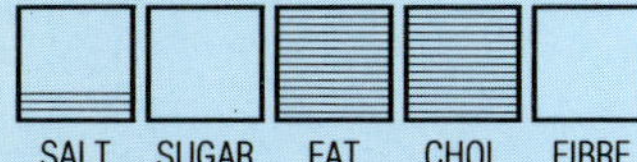

SALT SUGAR FAT CHOL FIBRE

GLUTEN-FREE WHOLEFOOD
TOTAL CALORIES: ABOUT 3930

For **fat** and **cholesterol** levels, see the notes on the previous recipe. To avoid any extra fat, skim the pan juices and stock meticulously, and garnish with plain potatoes, rice or toast snippets, omitting the chips and bacon.
This recipe is particularly good for wild duck, with its gamey taste. Wild duck needs constant basting while cooking.

Pressure cooker: ✓ The result will be more like a casserole, but is good, and time is saved. Be sure to skim off all the fat.

in a large roasting pan. Pour in half the cider and all the stock and roast the goose in the lower half of a pre-heated oven at 450°F (230°C, mark 8) for 15 minutes. Baste with more cider and reduce the heat to 350°F (180°C, mark 4). Continue roasting for about 3 hours, removing fat as it accumulates in the pan. Baste occasionally with cider.

Remove the roasting pan from the oven and skim as much fat as possible from the pan juices. Pour the warmed calvados over the goose and set it alight. As soon as the flames die down, transfer the goose to a serving dish and keep it warm while making the gravy.

Pour the pan juices into a saucepan and boil them briskly until they have reduced to a thin gravy.

Serve the goose garnished with game chips (potato crisps), thick slices of bacon cooked crisp, sprigs of watercress, and small halved oranges.

Red cabbage cooked with apple and vinegar is an excellent accompaniment. Serve the gravy separately.

GOOSE WITH BLACK PUDDING

In France, the main Christmas meal, the *réveillon*, is served after Midnight Mass on Christmas Eve. Whatever other glories it may include, there is always a dish of black pudding. This Norman recipe combines traditional ingredients: goose and black pudding, garnished with small red apples.

PREPARATION TIME: *25 min*
COOKING TIME: *$2\frac{3}{4}$ hours*
INGREDIENTS *(for 6–8):*
1 goose, about 10 lb ($4\frac{1}{2}$ kg)
1 lb (450 g) black pudding
1 clove garlic
2 large dessert apples
$2\frac{1}{2}$ fluid oz (65 ml) port
Salt and black pepper*

Peel and grate the apples; crush the garlic. Skin the black pudding and pound it smooth with the goose liver and garlic. Blend in the apples and bind the stuffing with the wine. Stuff the goose with this mixture. Prick the skin all over with a skewer, and rub it thoroughly with salt and pepper.

Place the goose in a roasting tin and cover with foil. Roast on the lowest shelf of an oven, preheated to 400°F (200°C, mark 6), and allow 15 minutes to the pound, plus 15 minutes. After 1 hour, drain the fat from the pan and pour 4 fluid oz (100 ml) cold water over the goose. Remove the foil 30 minutes before cooking is complete, and baste the goose every 10 minutes with the pan juices.

Serve the goose on a thick bed of unsweetened apple purée and garnish with polished apples set on cocktail sticks.

BLANQUETTE OF TURKEY

After Boxing Day, cold turkey tends to lose its charms; even so, the last left-overs may be turned into a savoury main course, and an excellent stock can be made from the carcass.

PREPARATION TIME: *20 min*
COOKING TIME: *30 min*
INGREDIENTS *(for 4–6):*
$1\frac{1}{2}$ lb (700 g) cooked turkey meat
1 large onion
3 oz (75 g) unsalted butter
2 oz (50 g) plain flour
1 pint (570 ml) turkey or chicken stock
1 small tin pimentoes
2 oz (50 g) button mushrooms
1 clove garlic
Pinch each of powdered mace and nutmeg
2 egg yolks
4 tablespoons double cream
1 tablespoon lemon juice
Salt and black pepper*

Cut the turkey meat into small pieces and peel and thinly slice the onion. Melt the butter in a large frying pan and cook the onion over low heat until soft and transparent. Mix in the flour and cook this roux for 3 minutes. Gradually stir in the stock, and simmer the sauce until the sauce thickens.

Meanwhile, slice the drained pimentoes thinly, trim and slice the mushrooms and peel and crush the garlic. Add these ingredients to the sauce, with the turkey; season to taste with salt, freshly ground pepper, mace and nutmeg. Heat the mixture through and then remove from the heat. Beat the egg yolks, cream and lemon juice until the mixture has the consistency of thin cream. Blend this slowly into the turkey mixture and return the pan to the heat. Heat through over low heat, but do not let the mixture boil.

Spoon the turkey into a warm serving dish, and serve with Brussels sprouts tossed in a little butter, soft brown sugar and allspice.

TURKEY OR CHICKEN TOASTS

This quick recipe provides another solution to the problem of what to do with Christmas leftovers from turkey, and cooked vegetables such as cauliflower, carrots, or broccoli.

PREPARATION TIME: *15 min*
COOKING TIME: *5 min*
INGREDIENTS *(for 4):*
8 thin slices turkey or chicken (skinned)
$\frac{1}{4}$ pint (150 ml) thick white sauce (page 82)
*Salt**
Dried tarragon
4 slices bread
Butter
$\frac{1}{2}$ lb (225 g) cooked, chopped vegetables
2 oz (50 g) grated Cheddar cheese
Black pepper

Make the white sauce and season with salt, freshly ground pepper and tarragon. Toast the bread, trim off the crusts and spread with butter. Arrange the turkey on the toast, cover with the vegetables and spoon over the sauce.

Sprinkle the toasts with the cheese and brown under a hot grill until the cheese has melted and is golden brown on top. Serve at once.

GOOSE WITH BLACK PUDDING

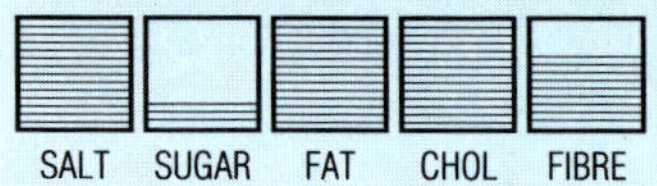

SALT SUGAR FAT CHOL FIBRE

GLUTEN-FREE* WHOLEFOOD
TOTAL CALORIES: ABOUT 5800

The only reduction in **salt** possible for this dish is using less black pudding.
This will also limit the fat to some extent, but levels of both **fat** and **cholesterol** will remain high unless you can use wild goose (see notes on the two preceding recipes). Use a roasting rack and do not baste.
This recipe is **gluten-free** if there is no gluten in the black pudding. Some black puddings contain wheat, but most contain oatmeal, which can be tolerated by some but not all people on gluten-free diets.

Food processor: ✓ for making the stuffing.

BLANQUETTE OF TURKEY

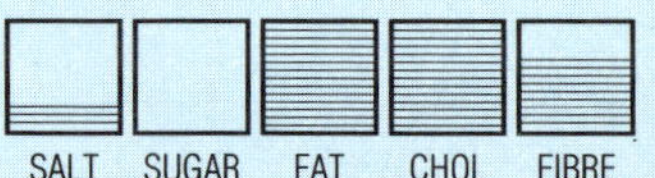

SALT SUGAR FAT CHOL FIBRE

GLUTEN-FREE* WHOLEFOOD*
TOTAL CALORIES: ABOUT 2780

To reduce **fat** and **cholesterol** to low, make a sauce which is predominantly onion rather than an enriched white sauce. Soften 2 large onions in only 1 tablespoon oil. Thinly slice a potato, add this to the onions and cook for 2 or 3 more minutes before stirring in the stock. Omit the egg yolks and use smetana instead of cream; omit the lemon juice. (Calories lost: up to 970.)
This method omits the flour, so it is **gluten-free**.

TURKEY TOASTS

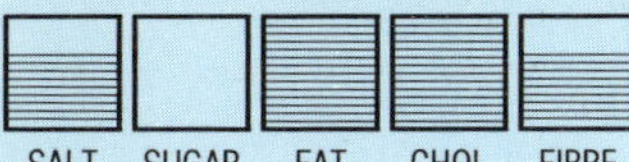

GLUTEN-FREE* WHOLEFOOD*
TOTAL CALORIES: ABOUT 3100

Reduce the **salt** to low by using bread made without salt and only 1 oz (25 g) Cheddar (or Parmesan) cheese, finely grated.

Reduce **fat** and **cholesterol** to low by using skim milk and only 2 teaspoons butter (or vegetable margarine) in the sauce. Do not butter the toast and use only half the cheese (as above). (Calories lost: up to 700.)

TURKEY ESCALOPES CORDON BLEU

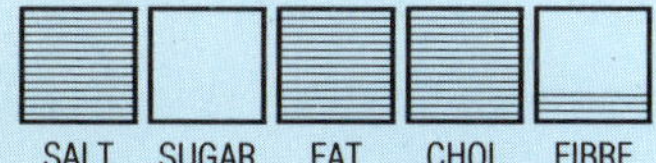

GLUTEN-FREE* WHOLEFOOD*
TOTAL CALORIES: ABOUT 2760

It is impossible to reduce the **salt** in this recipe unless you omit the ham and cheese, which give it its character. However, you can reduce the **fat** and **cholesterol**: check that the ham you use is very lean; soften the mushrooms in a pan lightly brushed with oil in place of butter; cook the escalopes also in a pan lightly brushed with oil and cover it tightly. Thin slices of cheese plus the small amount of oil for cooking will add up to a low-to-medium fat and cholesterol level. (Calories lost: up to 680.) Do not butter the noodles or add an oily salad dressing.

TURKEY ESCALOPES CORDON BLEU

Fresh turkey makes a good main course for a dinner party, especially as escalopes can now be bought ready-cut.

PREPARATION TIME: *20 min*
COOKING TIME: *25 min*
INGREDIENTS *(for 4)*:
4 turkey escalopes
4 slices lean cooked ham
4 thin slices Fontina, Bel Paese, or Gruyère cheese
4–6 oz (100–175 g) button mushrooms
3 oz (75 g) unsalted butter
Seasoned flour (page 100)
1 tablespoon olive oil
Black pepper
1–2 tablespoons chopped parsley
4–6 tablespoons stock (page 81)
GARNISH (OPTIONAL):
Watercress

Buy the turkey escalopes ready-cut, or cut them from a large uncooked bird which is intended for a casserole, risotto or for deep-freezing in portions. The white breast meat should give 5 slices from each side. Before slicing the breast, cut down slantwise behind the wishbone and remove this to give another escalope. Store the surplus escalopes in the home freezer.

Cut the ham and cheese slices to fit the escalopes. Trim the mushrooms and slice them thinly; cook until soft in ½ oz (10 g) of the butter and set them aside. Coat the turkey escalopes evenly, but not too thickly, with the seasoned flour.

Melt the remaining butter and the oil in a large frying pan over moderate heat. Fry the escalopes for about 5 minutes on each side. Place a slice of ham on each escalope, spoon over a thin layer of mushrooms and season lightly with freshly ground pepper. Sprinkle some of the parsley over the mushrooms and cover with a slice of cheese. Pour the hot stock over the escalopes. Cover the pan closely with a lid or foil and cook over low heat for about 10 minutes or until the cheese has melted.

Lift out the escalopes and arrange on a hot serving dish; sprinkle over the remaining parsley or garnish with sprigs of watercress. The richness of the escalopes is best offset by a dish of buttered ribbon noodles and a tossed green salad.

GUINEA FOWL WITH GRAPES

In this French recipe, guinea fowl is cooked with white grapes. This domesticated game bird has a flavour reminiscent of pheasant, which may be cooked in the same way. A guinea chick will provide two servings and a fully grown bird three. They are usually sold ready trussed and barded with pork fat.

PREPARATION TIME: *30 min*
COOKING TIME: *55 min*
INGREDIENTS *(for 3):*
1 guinea fowl
1 onion
1 bouquet garni (page 99)
Salt and black pepper*
½ lb (225 g) white grapes
Juice of a lemon
1 oz (25 g) butter
4 rashers fat bacon (optional)
4 fluid oz (100 ml) dry white wine
2 egg yolks
2½ fluid oz (65 ml) cream
GARNISH:
Lemon wedges and vine leaves or 6 oz (175 g) white grapes

Clean the giblets thoroughly and put them in a saucepan with 1 pint (570 ml) of cold water. Peel and quarter the onion, add it to the giblets with the bouquet garni and a good seasoning of salt and freshly ground pepper. Bring to the boil, remove any scum and simmer the stock, covered, for 20 minutes. Strain and set aside.

Meanwhile, peel the grapes (page 96) if they are thick-skinned, and remove the pips. Sprinkle them with a little lemon juice and salt before stuffing them into the guinea fowl. Sew up the vent. Melt the butter and brush it all over the bird. Remove the rind and gristle from the bacon and tie the rashers over the breast of the guinea fowl if not already barded.

Roast the guinea fowl in the centre of a pre-heated oven, at 400°F (200°C, mark 6), for 30 minutes. Remove the bacon or fat and continue cooking the guinea fowl for a further 15 minutes or until golden brown and tender. Place on a serving dish and keep it warm in the oven.

Pour the wine into the roasting tin and bring to the boil on top of the stove, scraping up all the residue. Pour it into a measuring jug, making it up to ¼ pint (150 ml) with the giblet stock. Beat the egg yolks with the cream in a bowl and gradually stir in the wine and stock mixture. Place the bowl over a saucepan containing ½ in (1 cm) of gently simmering water. Stir this sauce continuously until it has thickened enough to coat thinly the back of a wooden spoon. Do not let the sauce reach boiling point or it will curdle. Correct seasoning and sharpen to taste with lemon juice.

Garnish the guinea fowl with lemon wedges arranged on fresh vine leaves, or with small bunches of unpeeled white grapes. Pour the sauce into a warm sauce boat and serve with, for example, new potatoes and cauliflower or broccoli over which the crisp bacon has been crumbled as a garnish.

GUINEA FOWL IN RED WINE

The somewhat dry flesh of guinea fowl is made tender by cooking it in wine, using a method similar to that for the classic French *coq au vin*. Chicken may be cooked in the same way.

PREPARATION TIME: *20 min*
COOKING TIME: *1 hour*
INGREDIENTS *(for 4–6):*
1 or 2 guinea fowl (jointed)
3 oz (75 g) belly pork
2 oz (50 g) unsalted butter
Salt and black pepper*
16 button onions
3 fluid oz (75 ml) brandy
1 bottle Beaujolais
¼ pint (150 ml) chicken stock
1 bouquet garni (page 99)
2 cloves garlic
4 oz (100 g) mushrooms
SAUCE:
1 oz (25 g) plain flour
1 oz (25 g) unsalted butter
GARNISH:
Parsley sprigs

Cut the belly pork into small cubes and fry in half of the butter in a deep sauté pan. Wipe and season the poultry joints with salt and freshly ground pepper. Remove the pork from the pan and slowly brown the guinea fowl in the butter over gentle heat.

Peel the onions and add to the pan, together with the fried belly pork; turn the onions until they are glazed. Warm the brandy, pour over the guinea fowl and set alight. As soon as the flames have died down, pour over the wine and stock, add the bouquet garni and the crushed garlic. Increase the heat to bring the contents of the pan slowly to boiling point. Check the seasoning, cover the

GUINEA FOWL WITH GRAPES

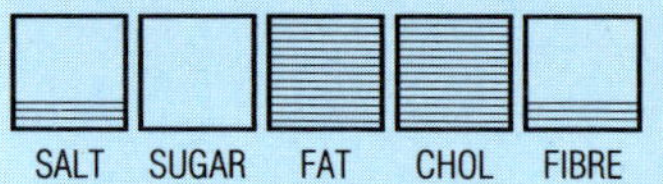

GLUTEN-FREE WHOLEFOOD
TOTAL CALORIES: ABOUT 2360

The low **salt** level assumes that the bacon is not used: if it is, the level of salt will be high. To reduce **fat** and **cholesterol** to low, omit the bacon; omit brushing the bird with butter; and replace the egg yolks and cream in the sauce with 4 tablespoons low-fat curd cheese (such as quark) or smetana. After blending this in do not let the sauce come back to the boil or the mixture will curdle. (Calories lost: up to 940.)

Pressure cooker: ✓ for the stock.

GUINEA FOWL IN RED WINE

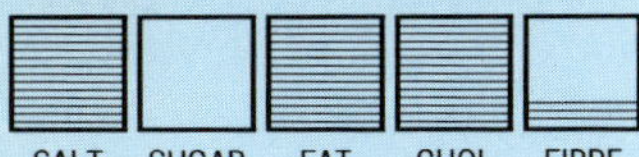

SALT SUGAR FAT CHOL FIBRE

GLUTEN-FREE WHOLEFOOD
TOTAL CALORIES: ABOUT 3740

The **salt** content is high because of the pork: if this is omitted the salt will be low.
To reduce **fat** and **cholesterol** to the low level natural in guinea fowl, brown the bird in a heavy pan lightly brushed with oil; omit the butter. Do the same with the mushrooms. To thicken the sauce, liquidise the mushrooms in the stock. If you would like the sauce to be still thicker, blend 1 tablespoon cornflour, rice flour (both **gluten-free**) or arrowroot with enough water to make a smooth paste. Work in a little hot stock, return to the pan and simmer for at least 4 minutes for it to thicken up. (Calories lost: up to 750.) Do not butter the side vegetables.

Freezing: √ up to 2 months.

pan with a lid and simmer for 30 minutes.

Meanwhile, trim and clean the mushrooms, sauté them in 1 oz (25 g) of butter, drain and add to the fowl after this has simmered for 30 minutes. Cover and cook for a further 10 minutes or until the guinea fowl is tender. Transfer the contents of the pan to a heated serving dish and keep it warm.

Turn up the heat and boil the liquid in the pan rapidly until it is reduced to about ¾ pint (425 ml). Work the flour and butter together to form a paste; remove the pan from the heat and beat in knobs of the paste until the sauce thickens. Return to the heat and bring slowly to the boil. Pour the sauce over the guinea fowl and garnish with parsley.

Boiled new potatoes and young blanched broccoli spears, cooked in butter, could be served as well.

PIGEONS WITH OLIVES

Small woodpigeons can be roasted or grilled like other game birds. But since the meat is rather dry, they are more suitable for braising or a casserole. Partridges may be cooked in the same way.

PREPARATION TIME: *1 hour*
COOKING TIME: *2 hours*
INGREDIENTS *(for 4)*:

4 pigeons
3 onions
1 carrot
4 oz (100 g) salted belly pork or green streaky bacon
2 cloves garlic
Seasoned flour (page 100)
2–3 tablespoons brandy
¼ pint (150 ml) dry white wine or vermouth
¼ pint (150 ml) pigeon stock
4 oz (100 g) green stuffed olives
1 bouquet garni (page 99)
4 large slices bread
1 tablespoon olive oil

Skin the pigeons carefully. Cut along and down each side of the breastbone on each pigeon so that each breast, leg and wing comes away in one piece.

Wash the pigeon halves thoroughly in cold water and dry them on a clean cloth. Clean the carcasses and giblets thoroughly.

Peel and finely slice one onion, scrape and roughly chop the carrot. Put the carcasses, giblets, onion and carrot in a saucepan and cover with cold water. Bring to the boil and simmer, covered with a lid, until all the meat has come off the bones. Strain the stock and set aside.

Meanwhile, remove the rind from the pork or bacon and cut the meat into ½ in (1 cm) wide strips, crossways. Put the strips in a large flameproof casserole over a moderate heat and cook until the fat runs. Peel and finely chop the remaining onions, and peel and crush the garlic. Add these to the pork and cook until soft.

Coat the pigeons thickly with the seasoned flour. Add them to the onion mixture and brown them well on both sides. Warm the brandy, set it alight and pour over the pigeons, shaking the casserole until the flames die down. Add the wine and ¼ pint (150 ml) of the stock. Put in the olives and bouquet garni and bring to the boil. Remove the casserole from the heat and cover closely with foil and a lid. Cook in the centre of a pre-heated oven at 300°F (150°C, mark 2), for 1½–2 hours or until tender.

Fry the bread golden in the oil and arrange two pigeon halves on each slice. Top with the pork and olives and pour over the strained gravy. Serve with mashed potatoes or boiled rice.

PIGEONS WITH FORCEMEAT BALLS

These inexpensive little game birds can be ordered cleaned and trussed, ready for cooking. Young, tender pigeons can be roasted or grilled, but when older they are best used for a casserole.

PREPARATION TIME: *1 hour*
COOKING TIME: *1¼ hours*
INGREDIENTS *(for 6)*:
3 pigeons
¼ lb (100 g) streaky bacon
1 oz (25 g) unsalted butter
2 level tablespoons plain flour
¾ pint (425 ml) hot chicken stock or water
*1 level teaspoon salt**
Black pepper
1 bouquet garni (page 99)
12 button onions
½ lb (225 g) button mushrooms
FORCEMEAT BALLS:
¼ lb (100 g) fresh breadcrumbs
2 oz (50 g) shredded beef suet
1 rounded tablespoon finely chopped parsley
Finely grated rind of half lemon
Salt and black pepper*
1–2 eggs
GARNISH:
Chopped parsley

Dice the bacon, having first removed the rind; heat the butter in a deep, heavy-based pan. Fry the bacon over moderate heat until the fat runs and the bacon pieces are crisp. Remove the bacon from the pan with a perforated spoon and leave to drain on crumpled absorbent paper. Put the pigeons in the pan to brown them, turning several times. Lift out the pigeons and put them in a casserole.

Pour away all but one tablespoon of the hot fat from the pan;

PIGEONS WITH OLIVES

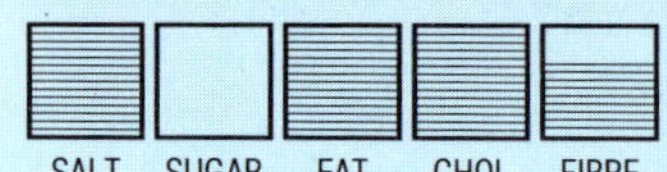

SALT SUGAR FAT CHOL FIBRE

GLUTEN-FREE* WHOLEFOOD*
TOTAL CALORIES: ABOUT 2280

Reduce the **salt** to low by omitting the pork (or bacon) and the olives, and using bread made without salt. The olives could be replaced with large chunks of dessert apple, very lightly poached (and the dish re-named).

For moderate **fat** and **cholesterol** brown the onions and pigeons in a heavy pan brushed with oil and serve on toast rather than fried bread. Although lower in fat than much red meat, pigeons contain about 13%, more than most game, so the overall fat content cannot be less than moderate. (Calories lost: up to 500.)

As a **gluten-free** alternative to the fried bread (and a way of compensating for the dryness of the pigeons), serve them on a bed of lightly cooked vegetables, such as braised celery, fennel or Chinese cabbage.

Pressure cooker: ✓ for the stock.

Freezing: ✓ up to 4 months (the casserole only, not the fried bread).

PIGEONS WITH FORCEMEAT BALLS

GLUTEN-FREE* WHOLEFOOD*
TOTAL CALORIES: ABOUT 3180

To reduce **salt** to low, omit the bacon and use breadcrumbs made without salt.
Limit **fat** and **cholesterol** to the moderate level naturally present in pigeons as follows: omit the bacon; brown the pigeons in a heavy pan brushed lightly with oil; do not add any extra fat before stirring in the flour. Make the forcemeat balls with ½ oz (15 g) butter or vegetable margarine instead of suet and use only one (small) egg to bind the mixture. (Calories lost: up to 1000.)
Cornflour or rice flour can be used for a **gluten-free** sauce, but the forcemeat balls are best made with crumbs from a gluten-free loaf.

Freezing: ✓ up to 4 months (the pigeons and the forcemeat balls should be frozen separately).
Microwave: ✓

stir in the flour and cook gently for a few minutes until browned. Gradually blend in the hot stock and bring the sauce slowly to the boil. Simmer for a few minutes, then strain the sauce over the pigeons in the casserole. Add the bacon pieces, the salt, a few twists of pepper and the bouquet garni. Peel the onions and add them whole to the pigeons. Cover the casserole with a lid and cook in the centre of a pre-heated oven for 1 hour at 350°F (180°C, mark 4).

Meanwhile, trim and finely slice the mushrooms. For the forcemeat balls, measure the breadcrumbs, shredded suet, chopped parsley and lemon rind into a mixing bowl; season with salt and freshly ground pepper. Beat the eggs lightly and stir them into the mixture with a fork until the forcemeat has a moist, but not too wet, consistency. Using the tips of the fingers, shape the forcemeat into 8–12 round balls and put these, together with the mushrooms, in the casserole. Replace the lid and continue cooking for 15–20 minutes.

Lift the pigeons from the casserole, cut them in half and arrange them on a hot serving dish. Surround them with the mushrooms, onions and forcemeat balls. Remove the bouquet garni from the sauce before pouring it over the pigeons.

Garnish with chopped parsley and serve the pigeons with new potatoes.

PARTRIDGE WITH CABBAGE

Partridge with cabbage is a classic French farmhouse method of cooking older game birds. Gourmets maintain that the casserole should be cooked with older partridge, which are replaced with young, oven-roasted partridge just before serving.

PREPARATION TIME: *30 min*
COOKING TIME: *2 hours*
INGREDIENTS *(for 4):*
2 plump partridge
4 rashers green streaky bacon
2 level tablespoons plain flour
1 oz (25 g) lard or bacon fat
4 pork chipolata sausages
4 oz (100 g) pickled belly pork
1 large onion
1 small white cabbage
Salt and black pepper*
5 fluid oz (150 ml) red wine

Truss the partridge neatly, bard (page 91) the breasts with the bacon rashers and secure with string. Peel and thinly slice the onion. Roll the birds in the flour and pat off the surplus.

Heat the lard or fat in a flameproof casserole or large pan and brown the birds and the sausages all over, then remove from the pan. Remove the rind and gristle and cut the pickled pork into ½ in (1 cm) chunks, then put into the casserole together with the sliced onion; fry until both are just turning colour. Pour off any remaining fat. Remove any coarse outer leaves from the cabbage, wash it and blanch for 5 minutes in boiling salted water. Cut into quarters, remove the tough centre stalk and shred the cabbage coarsely.

Put half the shredded cabbage in the pan and mix with the pork and onion. Add a few twists of pepper – the pork is already salty – put in the partridge and cover with the remaining cabbage.

Pour over the wine, cover the casserole tightly and cook over low heat on top of the stove, or in the centre of a pre-heated oven at 325°F (170°C, mark 3), for about 2 hours or until tender, depending on the age of the birds. If necessary add more wine or a little chicken stock.

To serve, lift out the partridge, remove the string and cut each bird in half. Arrange the partridge and sausages on the cabbage. Serve with jacket potatoes.

POACHED PARTRIDGE IN VINE LEAVES

Vine leaves impart an unusual flavour to these succulent game birds. Order the partridge ready for cooking and have the giblets included with the order.

PREPARATION TIME: *25 min*
COOKING TIME: *1½ hours*
INGREDIENTS *(for 4):*
2 young partridges
Salt and black pepper*
6 lemon slices
4 teaspoons quince, redcurrant or cranberry jelly
13–14 oz (375–400 g) tin of vine leaves
¾ lb (350 g) fat green bacon rashers
½ pint (300 ml) dry white wine
1½ pints (900 ml) chicken stock
GARNISH:
Watercress, lemon wedges

Wipe the partridges inside and out and season with salt and black pepper. Put 3 lemon slices and half the quince jelly inside each bird. Wrap the drained vine leaves round the birds, cover with the bacon rashers and tie firmly with fine string.

Bring the wine and stock to the boil in a large saucepan, together with the giblets. Add the partridges and simmer for 1¼ hours.

Chill the partridges quickly by immersing them in a bowl of iced water until quite cold. Remove from the water, unwrap the bacon and vine leaves; dry the partridges with absorbent paper.

Serve the partridges whole, on a bed of watercress, garnished with lemon wedges and Cumberland sauce. A lettuce and celery salad would be a good side dish.

CUMBERLAND SAUCE

PREPARATION TIME: *15 min*
COOKING TIME: *10 min*
STANDING TIME: *24 hours*
INGREDIENTS *(about 1 pint, 570 ml):*
2 oranges
2 lemons
1 lb (450 g) redcurrant jelly
8 fluid oz (225 ml) port or red wine
2 heaped teaspoons arrowroot

Thinly peel one orange and one lemon. Remove pith and shred the peel finely. Boil the shreds for 3 minutes. Drain and cover with cold water for 1 minute; drain again and set aside. Squeeze and strain all the fruit juices into a pan, add the jelly and bring slowly to the boil. Simmer for 5 minutes, then add the port and bring the sauce back to the boil. Remove from the heat and stir in the arrowroot, mixed to a paste with a little cold water. Cook for 1 minute more. Add the blanched peel and leave the sauce in a cool place for 24 hours.

PARTRIDGE WITH CABBAGE

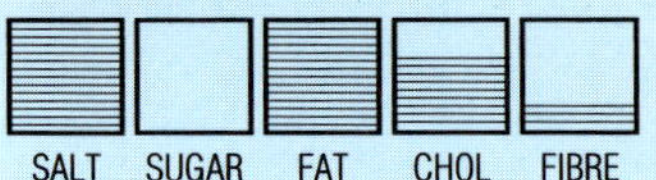

SALT SUGAR FAT CHOL FIBRE

TOTAL CALORIES: ABOUT 2900

The high **salt** level of this dish comes from the bacon, sausages and pork; if the quantities of these are halved, or if the bacon and pork are omitted, the level will be reduced to moderate. Omitting the pork and bacon and all (or all but one) of the chipolatas will also reduce the **fat** and **cholesterol** content to low. (Calories lost: up to 1120.)
Apart from the flour (for which cornflour, potato flour or rice flour all make good **gluten-free** substitutes), there is generally gluten in chipolatas (in the form of breadcrumbs), but local butchers can often make up gluten-free sausages on request.

Freezing: ☑ up to 2 months.
Microwave: ☑

POACHED PARTRIDGE IN VINE LEAVES WITH CUMBERLAND SAUCE

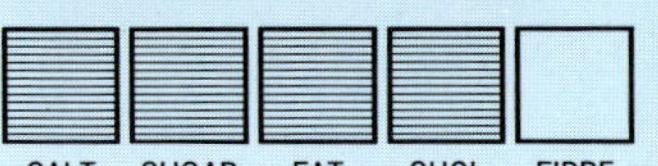

SALT SUGAR FAT CHOL FIBRE

GLUTEN-FREE* WHOLEFOOD*
TOTAL CALORIES: ABOUT 3690

To achieve a low **salt** level, use fresh vine leaves (or cabbage leaves), blanched in simmering water for 5 minutes, and omit the bacon.
The only way to reduce the **sugar** content of the sauce is to use fresh red currants or cranberries – about 1 lb (450 g) – and simmer them gently with

the fruit juices and arrowroot before sweetening to taste. Add honey a little at a time, tasting as you go, to avoid over-sweetening. Liquidise if you like. (Calories lost: up to 000.) Without the bacon this dish also becomes low in both **fat** and **cholesterol**, especially if the chicken stock has been carefully skimmed of all fat. (Calories lost: up to 2000.)

GROUSE À LA GRAND-MÈRE

GLUTEN-FREE* WHOLEFOOD*
TOTAL CALORIES: ABOUT 3280

The **salt** level can be reduced to very low by using bread made without salt, or by serving the grouse on a bed of plain rice, mashed potato or lightly cooked vegetables instead of bread. Replacing the bread also avoids the **fat** in fried bread. To reduce the fat further (to low), and the **cholesterol** also to low, brown the grouse and the onions in a heavy pan brushed lightly with oil, omitting the butter; add flour to the pan to make the sauce without adding any more fat. Replace the cream with smetana, low-fat curd cheese or thick plain yogurt into which you have stirred 1 teaspoon cornflour before heating (this will prevent it separating and curdling when heated). (Total calories lost: up to 1250.)
The alternatives to bread given above are all **gluten-free**.

Freezing: √ up to 2 months (as a casserole, not on the bread slices).
Microwave: √ for cooking the casserole.

GROUSE À LA GRAND-MÈRE

Mature grouse which have escaped the guns for some years are not tender enough for plain roasting. They can, however, be made into a tasty casserole, flavoured with herbs and brandy. Quail can be treated in the same way.

PREPARATION TIME: *30 min*
COOKING TIME: *1½ hours*
INGREDIENTS *(for 4):*
4 mature grouse
8–12 button onions
1 stick celery
8 oz (225 g) mushrooms
4 oz (100 g) butter
1–1½ tablespoons plain flour
1 pint (570 ml) stock or bouillon
Fresh thyme, marjoram and rosemary
Salt and black pepper*
3–4 tablespoons double cream
2 tablespoons brandy
Lemon juice
4 small slices crustless bread
GARNISH:
1 tablespoon chopped parsley

Peel the onions, leaving them whole. Scrub the celery, trim the mushrooms and chop both roughly. Melt half the butter in a flameproof casserole and, when hot, brown the neatly trussed grouse all over, together with the onions.

Lift out the grouse and onions, and fry the celery and mushrooms in the butter until soft. Remove the pan from the heat, stir in sufficient flour to absorb all the fat, and return the pan to the heat. Cook this roux until brown, then gradually blend in the stock or bouillon. Bring the mixture to simmering point and season to taste with the herbs, salt and some freshly ground pepper.

Return the grouse and onions to the casserole, cover with a lid and cook over low heat on top of the stove for about 1½ hours or until the grouse are tender. Mix the cream and brandy together, blend in 2 or 3 tablespoons of the sauce from the grouse, and stir it back into the casserole. Sharpen to taste with lemon juice and adjust seasoning.

In a clean pan, fry the bread in the remaining butter until crisp and golden. Drain the bread on crumpled absorbent paper, then arrange it on a hot serving dish. Place one grouse on each bread slice, pour over a little sauce and sprinkle with parsley. Pour the remaining sauce into a sauce boat. Serve the grouse with fluffy creamed potatoes and cauliflower or broccoli.

PHEASANT STEWED WITH APPLES

This is an excellent Normandy method of cooking older or slightly tough cock pheasants with apples. Frozen whole or jointed pheasants and guinea fowl are also suitable.

PREPARATION TIME: *40 min*
COOKING TIME: *45 min*
INGREDIENTS *(for 4)*:
1 pheasant
1 bay leaf
1 sprig parsley
Salt and black pepper*
1 onion
2 sticks celery
2 cooking apples
2–3 level tablespoons plain flour
1½ oz (40 g) butter
¼ pint (150 ml) cider
2 tablespoons calvados (optional)
2½ fluid oz (65 ml) double cream
GARNISH:
2 dessert apples
Celery leaves

Joint the pheasant by first removing the legs, then cut away the two breast sections down and along the backbone. Leave the flesh on the bone, so that it will not shrink during cooking, and cut off the lower part of the wings.

Put the pheasant carcass, the neck and the cleaned giblets into a pan, together with the bay leaf, parsley, and a seasoning of salt and freshly ground pepper. Cover the carcass with cold water, put the lid on the pan and simmer this stock over low heat for about 20 minutes.

Peel and thinly slice the onion. Cut the leafy tops off the celery and set aside for garnish. Scrub the celery sticks and chop them finely. Peel, core and roughly chop both the cooking apples.

Coat the pheasant joints lightly with a little flour, and heat the butter in a flameproof casserole or heavy-based pan. Fry the pheasant over high heat until golden brown all over, then remove from the casserole. Lower the heat and fry the onion and celery for 5 minutes. Add the apples and fry for a further 5 minutes. Draw the casserole from the heat and stir in sufficient of the remaining flour to absorb all the fat. Gradually blend in the cider (and calvados if used) and ½ pint (300 ml) of strained pheasant stock. Bring this sauce to simmering point over low heat.

Put the pheasant back into the casserole, and if necessary add more stock to the sauce until it almost covers the joints.

Season to taste with salt and freshly ground pepper, and cover the casserole with a lid.

Cook the casserole in the centre of a pre-heated oven, at 325°F (170°C, mark 3), for 45 minutes or until tender. Remove the pheasant and keep warm in the oven. Boil the sauce briskly on top of the stove, stir into the cream and pour this mixture back into the pan; adjust seasoning.

Return the pheasant joints to the sauce and serve straight from the casserole. Alternatively, arrange the joints on a warm deep serving dish and spoon the sauce over them. Surround with the cored, but unpeeled apples, cut into thick slices and fried in a little butter until golden. Push a small tuft of celery leaves through the centre of each apple slice.

Boiled or mashed potatoes could also be served.

PHEASANT STEWED WITH APPLES

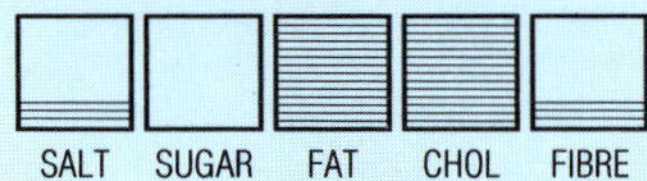

SALT SUGAR FAT CHOL FIBRE

GLUTEN-FREE* WHOLEFOOD*
TOTAL CALORIES: ABOUT 2025

Pheasant has a low to medium fat content of under 10%. To reduce both **fat** and **cholesterol** to this level, brown the bird in a casserole lightly brushed with oil, omitting the butter. To soften the vegetables, add them to the pan with 2 tablespoons stock and cover tightly. No extra fat will be needed. Replace the cream with 3 tablespoons smetana, low-fat curd cheese or thick plain yogurt; after blending in, do not let the dish boil again. Apple rings for the garnish can be cut from a baked dessert apple (dessert apples keep their shape when baked) instead of being fried. (Calories lost: up to 500.)

Pressure cooker: √ for the stock.
Freezing: √ up to 2 months.
Microwave: √ for cooking the casserole once it has been assembled.

PHEASANT WITH CABBAGE

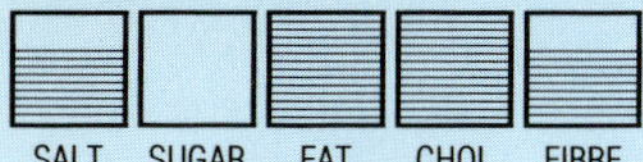

GLUTEN-FREE WHOLEFOOD
TOTAL CALORIES: ABOUT 3690

The **salt** comes mainly from the bacon and bacon fat. To reduce the level to low, halve the amount of bacon used (or omit it); omit the bacon fat and brown the pheasant in a casserole lightly brushed with oil.
These measures will also reduce the **fat** and **cholesterol** levels. To reduce them further (to low-medium), replace the cream with smetana, cultured buttermilk, low-fat curd cheese or low-fat plain yogurt. In each case, blend in $1\frac{1}{2}$ teaspoons of cornflour before heating, and heat over low heat for only just long enough to cook through. (Calories lost: up to 1750.)

PHEASANT WITH CABBAGE

This has long been a favourite of pheasant lovers and makes a satisfying meal on a cool autumn evening. However, if pheasant is unavailable or too expensive, the dish may be prepared with chicken.

PREPARATION TIME: *15 min*
COOKING TIME: *about 1 hour*
INGREDIENTS *(for 4):*
2 young pheasants
*Salt**
3 oz (75 g) bacon fat or butter
4 slices bacon
1 medium head green cabbage
$\frac{1}{2}$ pint (300 ml) double cream
12 juniper berries
Paprika
Pepper

Sprinkle the pheasants inside and out with salt and pepper. Brown the pheasants in hot bacon fat or butter on all sides in a large casserole. Top the breasts with bacon slices and secure the bacon with wooden cocktail sticks or toothpicks. Reduce the heat, cover, and cook gently for 1 hour until almost tender. Remove the pheasants and set aside.

While the pheasants are cooking, shred the cabbage and parboil it in salted water for 10 minutes. Drain.

Put the cabbage in a casserole, cover, and cook slowly for 10 minutes. Season with salt and freshly ground pepper. Add the pheasants to the cabbage, pour the cream over them, and add the juniper berries. Simmer, covered, for 5 minutes. Before serving, sprinkle the birds and cabbage with a little paprika.

Serve on a heated dish with boiled new potatoes.

MUSTARD RABBIT

Wild rabbit traditionally went into this French farmhouse stew, perfect for a chilly late summer day when autumn seems near. Today, most rabbits available are bred for the table.

PREPARATION TIME: *15 min*
COOKING TIME: *1½–2 hours*
INGREDIENTS *(for 4–6):*
2½–3 lb (1–1½ kg) rabbit or 6 rabbit joints
4 rounded tablespoons Dijon mustard
Seasoned flour (page 100)
2 oz (50 g) unsalted butter
2 oz (50 g) green streaky bacon
1 onion
1 clove garlic
½ pint (300 ml) double cream
GARNISH:
Chopped chervil or parsley
Bread croûtons (page 96)

Wash and dry the rabbit thoroughly. Cut it into six or eight neat joints and put them in a large bowl. Cover with cold salted water and leave to soak for 1–2 hours. Then drain and dry thoroughly. Coat the rabbit joints evenly with mustard and leave them in a cool place overnight, covered with muslin.

The following day dust the rabbit lightly with seasoned flour, shaking off any surplus. Melt the butter in a flameproof casserole and lightly brown the joints on both sides; lift them out and set aside. Remove the rind, and roughly chop the bacon. Peel and finely chop the onion and garlic. Fry the bacon for 2–3 minutes in the butter, then add the onion and garlic and continue cooking over low heat until the onion is soft.

Return the rabbit joints to the casserole, cover closely with a lid or foil and simmer over low heat for 30 minutes. Remove the casserole from the heat and stir in the cream. Cover again and cook over low heat on top of the stove, or in an oven pre-heated to 325°F (170°C, mark 3) for about 45 minutes, or until the rabbit is tender. Stir once or twice.

Serve the rabbit straight from the casserole, sprinkled with the fresh herbs and garnished with bread croûtons. Buttered rice or boiled potatoes can be served with the rabbit, together with a green vegetable.

RABBIT WITH PRUNES

Rabbit, which can be bought frozen in supermarkets the year round, makes a pleasant change from chicken. The delicate flesh is enhanced by a well-flavoured marinade and the fruity contrast of the prunes.

PREPARATION TIME: *45 min*
MARINATING TIME: *1 hour*
COOKING TIME: *1½ hours*
INGREDIENTS *(for 4–6):*
2 frozen, jointed rabbits, thawed
1 large onion
4 peppercorns, crushed
4 bay leaves
¼ pint (150 ml) wine vinegar
Seasoned flour (page 100)
2 oz (50 g) unsalted butter
2 onions
1 pint (570 ml) light beer
Juice of 1 lemon
1 sprig thyme
1 teaspoon Dijon mustard
1 tablespoon tarragon vinegar
2–3 tablespoons sugar
Salt and black pepper*
8 soaked prunes
2 teaspoons cornflour

Peel and slice the large onion and add it, with the crushed peppercorns and 2 of the bay leaves, to the rabbit. Mix the wine vinegar with 1 pint (570 ml) of water and

MUSTARD RABBIT

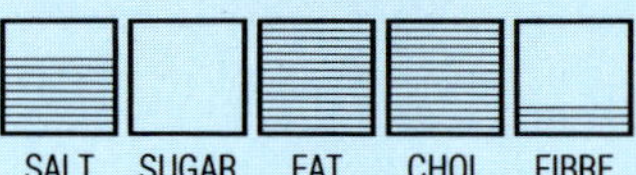

GLUTEN-FREE* WHOLEFOOD*
TOTAL CALORIES: ABOUT 4230

The **salt** content will be low if the bacon is omitted. This will also reduce the **fat** level; to limit both this and **cholesterol** to low, you should also brown the rabbit in a heavy pan lightly brushed with oil, omit the bacon, and replace the cream with the same amount of smetana, quark or thick low-fat plain yogurt, into which you have thoroughly blended 1½ teaspoons cornflour to help it keep stable when heated. With this method the cooking of the rabbit should be completed first, as once your chosen cream substitute is added the mixture should only be reheated gently for a few minutes, not brought back to the boil.
(Calories lost: up to 1200.)

Freezing: ✓ up to 2 months.

RABBIT WITH PRUNES

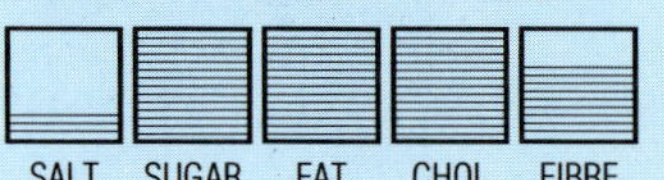

GLUTEN-FREE* WHOLEFOOD*
TOTAL CALORIES: ABOUT 3300

The **sugar** content can be reduced to medium simply by adding less: the recipe as it stands is very sweet, and ½ tablespoon would suit many people's palates, since sweet prunes and beer are also included.
Rabbit is one of the leanest meats with around 4% fat, despite its rich flavour. If it is browned in a heavy pan lightly

brushed with oil, omitting the butter, this dish will be very low in both **fat** and **cholesterol**. (Calories lost: up to 570.)

Pressure cooker: √ for the rabbit (not the prunes; they must be cooked separately).
Freezing: √ up to 2 months.
Microwave: √

CIVET DE LIÈVRE

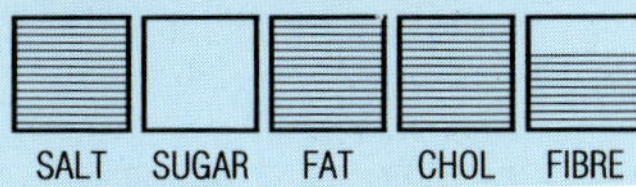

SALT SUGAR FAT CHOL FIBRE

GLUTEN-FREE* WHOLEFOOD*
TOTAL CALORIES: ABOUT 3780

The high **salt** level comes mainly from the piece of streaky bacon. Omitting this brings the level down to low, and also helps reduce the fat content.
To reduce the **fat** further, to the low 8% naturally present in hare plus a very little oil (and also reduce the **cholesterol** to low), brown the meat in a heavy pan lightly brushed with oil. Do the same with the mushrooms, and omit the butter and the 3 tablespoons of the oil from the marinade. Do not use beurre manié to thicken the sauce. (Calories lost: up to 1180.)

Pressure cooker: √

Freezing: √ up to 2 months.

Microwave: √

pour over the rabbit, covering the pieces completely. Leave the bowl in a cool place to marinate for about 1 hour, turning the meat occasionally.

Lift the rabbit from the marinade and dry the pieces thoroughly; coat them with seasoned flour. Melt the butter in a large frying pan, add the rabbit, and cook until evenly brown all over. Put the pieces of rabbit in a large flameproof casserole. Strain the marinade and pour ¼ pint (150 ml) of it over the meat. Peel and finely chop the onions and add to the rabbit, together with the beer, the lemon juice, the other 2 bay leaves, thyme, mustard, vinegar, and sugar. Season to taste with salt and freshly ground pepper. Bring the mixture to a boil; cover the pan with a lid and leave to simmer gently for 1½ hours, or until rabbit is tender. About 20 minutes before the end of cooking time add the soaked prunes.

When the rabbit is cooked, blend the cornflour with a little water to a smooth paste. Add some of the hot liquid from the pan and blend thoroughly before stirring it into the liquid. Bring the mixture back to the boil, stirring gently until the sauce has thickened.

Remove the pan from the heat and transfer the pieces of rabbit and the prunes to a hot serving dish. Correct seasoning, if necessary, and pour the sauce over the rabbit. Serve with creamed potatoes and a green vegetable.

CIVET DE LIÈVRE

Literally, hare stew, this is a classic recipe from French farmhouse cooking, reminiscent of traditional English jugged hare. The ingredients can be either a whole jointed hare or the legs and rib joints after the saddle has been roasted whole.

PREPARATION TIME: *45 min*
COOKING TIME: *about 3 hours*
INGREDIENTS *(for 6):*

2½–3 lb (1–1½ kg) hare pieces
2–3 carrots
2 onions
1 clove garlic
1 shallot
3 bay leaves
3 sprigs thyme
6 parsley stalks
Black pepper
3 tablespoons olive oil
1 bottle red wine
2 oz (50 g) butter
2 liqueur glasses brandy
1 oz (25 g) plain flour
⅓ pint (200 ml) chicken stock
¼ lb (100 g) green streaky bacon
¼ lb (100 g) button mushrooms
1 lb (450 g) small onions
GARNISH:
Freshly chopped parsley

Wipe the hare pieces and put them in a large basin. Peel and finely slice the carrots and the onions. Skin and finely chop the garlic and shallot. Add these vegetables, with the bay leaves, thyme, the parsley stalks and freshly ground pepper, to the hare. Pour over the oil and wine and marinate for 24 hours.

Remove the meat from the marinade and pat it dry on absorbent paper. Melt the butter in a large saucepan and fry the meat gently for about 15 minutes, until browned on all sides. Pour the brandy over the meat and, when hot, set it alight. As soon as the flames have died down, sprinkle in the flour, stirring to blend it well with the butter. Add the marinade ingredients and sufficient stock to just cover the meat. Bring to the boil, cover and simmer for 2–3 hours.

Cut the bacon into strips 1 in (2½ cm) long. Place in a saucepan, cover with cold water and bring to the boil. Simmer for 1 minute, then drain. Put the bacon strips in a dry frying pan and sauté gently until the fat runs. Wipe and trim the mushrooms, cut each in half and add to the pan. Sauté gently for a few minutes before seasoning, then remove from the pan and set aside. Peel the onions, leaving them whole; put them in a saucepan and cover with cold water. Bring to the boil and simmer gently for 10–15 minutes. Drain and set aside. Lift the hare pieces from the pan and keep them hot. Strain off the liquid and return it to the saucepan. Add more salt and pepper if necessary; if the sauce appears too thin, thicken with a little beurre manié (page 82). Put the hare into the pan, with the bacon, mushrooms and onions. Re-heat gently.

Arrange on a hot serving dish, pour over the sauce and sprinkle with parsley. Croquette potatoes and braised celery could also be served.

GAME SOUP WITH PORT WINE

This is a rich, sustaining soup for cold autumn days. It can be made from neck of venison or from any game bird, such as pheasant, partridge or grouse, that is too tough for roasting or grilling.

PREPARATION TIME: *55 min*
COOKING TIME: *2½–3 hours*
INGREDIENTS *(for 6):*
1 lb (450 g) venison or a 2 lb (900 g) game bird
1 large onion
1 parsnip or turnip
1 carrot
1 leek
3 sticks celery
½ lb (225 g) mushrooms
4 oz (100 g) butter
1 bay leaf
Thyme, marjoram and basil
Salt and black pepper*
1–2 cloves garlic
2 oz (50 g) plain flour
5 fluid oz (150 ml) port or burgundy
GARNISH:
Bread croûtons (page 96)

Cut the venison into 2–3 in (5–8 cm) chunks, trimming off any gristle. If a game bird is being used, chop it, through the bone, into small portions; clean thoroughly. Peel and roughly chop the onion, parsnip and carrot. Wash all dirt off the leek and celery under cold running water and chop them roughly as well. Trim and thinly slice the mushrooms.

Melt half the butter in a large pan over moderate heat and fry the meat, turning it frequently, until it begins to colour. Add the onion, leek and celery to the pan and brown it evenly. Put the parsnip, carrot and bay leaf, together with a pinch of thyme, marjoram and basil into the pan. Season with salt, freshly ground pepper and the crushed garlic. Pour in about 3 pints (1¾ litres) of water, or enough to cover the contents in the pan; bring to the boil over high heat.

Remove any scum which rises on the surface, then add the mushrooms. Cover the pan with a lid and simmer over low heat for about 2 hours or until the meat is perfectly tender.

Strain the stock through a fine sieve and leave to cool slightly. Remove the bay leaf and all bones, then put the meat and vegetables in the liquidiser with a little of the soup, to make a thick purée.

Melt the remaining butter in a large, clean pan over moderate heat; blend in the flour and cook, stirring continuously, until this roux is caramel coloured. Take the pan off the heat and gradually blend in the port and about ½ pint (300 ml) of stock. Return the pan to the heat, bring to simmering point, stirring all the time, then blend in the meat and vegetable purée and about 1½ pints (900 ml) of stock to make a thick soup. Heat the soup through over low heat for about 15 minutes and correct seasoning if necessary.

Serve the soup in individual bowls, garnished with small bread croûtons.

SADDLE OF VENISON

For a special dinner occasion, venison in port is an excellent choice. The saddle should have been hung for at least three weeks to ensure a truly succulent roast. A saddle will serve eight people handsomely, and the recipe is also suitable for a smaller joint.

PREPARATION TIME: *25 min*
COOKING TIME: *2¾ hours*
INGREDIENTS *(for 8–10):*
1 saddle of venison, 6–7 lb (about 3 kg)
2 carrots
1 Spanish onion
2 sticks celery
Salt and black pepper*
4 oz (100 g) unsalted butter
¼ pint (150 ml) olive oil
2 cloves garlic
2 bay leaves
1 sprig fresh or ½ level teaspoon dried thyme
½ pint (300 ml) chicken stock
½ bottle port
1 heaped tablespoon plain flour
2 oz (50 g) unsalted butter
1 heaped tablespoon red currant jelly

Peel and chop the carrots, onion and celery. Trim any gristle from the venison, wipe well with a cloth and season with salt and pepper. Melt the butter and combine with the olive oil in a large roasting or sauté pan; quickly brown the venison, then remove. Reduce the heat, peel and crush the garlic, and add to the pan together with the bay leaves, thyme and chopped vegetables; cook for 5 minutes without colouring. Return the venison to the pan and cover with foil, making sure it is tightly sealed. Cook for 45 minutes on the bottom shelf of an oven

GAME SOUP WITH PORT WINE

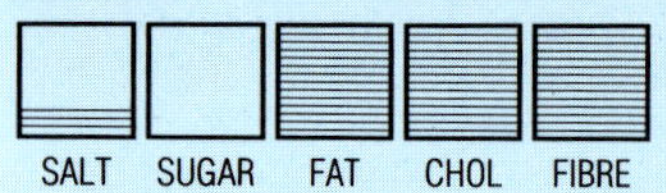

GLUTEN-FREE* WHOLEFOOD*
TOTAL CALORIES: ABOUT 2230

The high level of fat comes almost entirely from the butter, since venison is very lean at around 6.4% fat. To reduce both **fat** and **cholesterol** to low, brown the meat and soften the vegetables in 1 tablespoon of oil in a large casserole, adding a little stock if the mixture shows signs of sticking, and keeping it tightly covered over very low heat. (Calories lost: up to 770.) As **gluten-free** alternatives to flour and bread, thicken the soup by a technique that adds no fat instead of by the roux method: to do this, either add 3 oz (75 g) split red lentils to the mixture and simmer for 25 minutes before liquidising to a smooth texture, or increase the amount of vegetables used so that, when puréed, they produce a thick soup. Instead of croûtons, sprinkle with a little finely chopped carrot and parsley; or cut some firm tofu into dice and heat this up gently in the soup just before serving.

Pressure cooker: ✓
Freezing: ✓ up to 3 months.
Microwave: ✓

SADDLE OF VENISON

GLUTEN-FREE* WHOLEFOOD*
TOTAL CALORIES: ABOUT 8975

Although there is a certain amount of **sugar** in the port and red currant jelly, it should not cause too much worry among 8–10 people. If you do want to cut it down (perhaps because you are having something sweet to follow) you could replace the port with a sound red wine and use a purée of dried apricots instead of the jelly.

Venison itself is very lean and to avoid dryness in cooking it must be kept moist. This can be done however without adding the amount of butter and oil given, and the **fat** and **cholesterol** reduced to low. To achieve this, brown the meat in a heavy pan lightly brushed with oil and keep it moist by sealing it in with stock, as in the recipe. If wished, a cup of the port can be added at this stage, as it helps to tenderise the meat, thus shortening the cooking time and so reducing the risk of dryness.

To thicken the sauce without using the flour and butter paste, add some fresh red currants (or cranberries), say 4 oz (100 g), and when they burst after simmering, liquidise the mixture in a blender with 1 tablespoon arrowroot which has been slaked with water to a smooth paste. Re-boil the mixture for 2–3 minutes and allow to cool slightly before serving. (Calories lost: up to 2000.)

Instead of serving with fried mushrooms, simmer them in 2–3 tablespoons of stock for 5 minutes. Small boiled potatoes make a **gluten-free** alternative to croûtons.

pre-heated to 375°F (190°C, mark 5), then pour in the boiling stock, re-seal and cook for 1 hour.

Remove the pan to the top of the stove; pour the port over the venison and heat until the juices are simmering, then return to the oven. Do not re-seal, but cook for another hour, basting every 15 minutes. If the joint appears to be cooking too quickly, turn the heat down slightly for the last 30 minutes. Transfer the venison to a dish and keep it hot in the oven while making the sauce.

Strain the liquid from the roasting pan into a saucepan and keep at a fast boil until reduced by half. Meanwhile, combine the flour and butter to make a paste and use knobs of this to thicken the reduced sauce, stirring continuously. Finally mix in the red currant jelly, and as soon as this has dissolved, season the sauce with salt and pepper if necessary.

Carve the joint and arrange the slices on a serving dish. Pour some of the sauce over the meat and decorate it with glazed onions, mushroom caps fried in butter, and bread croûtons (page 96).

Serve the remainder of the sauce in a separate bowl.

White Fish

When buying fish make sure that they have a fresh, clean smell. Take a careful look at the eyes; they should be bright and bulging. If they have a sunken or cloudy look, the fish is not fresh. The gills should be bright red and free from slime. As the fish becomes stale, the colour of the gills gradually fades to light pink, then grey, then to a greenish or brownish colour. The skin of fresh fish has a shiny, iridescent look, and the scales will adhere firmly to the flesh. The flesh is elastic and springs back to its original shape when pressed.

To judge the freshness of steaks and fillets, look for a fresh-cut appearance–firm-textured flesh with no traces of browning around the edges or signs of drying out. The fish will have a fresh, mild smell. Wrapped steaks and fillets are packaged in moistureproof material, with little or no air between the fish and the wrapping. Frozen fish should be frozen solid, with no brownish tinge or other discoloration.

It is an advantage to have a local fishmonger. Even though supermarkets sell fish – usually a limited selection – a merchant whose business is fish will know much more and will help the customer to understand how to buy and cook fish.

Small white fish, whether flat or round, are sold whole or filleted. Large fish, such as turbot, halibut, haddock, hake and cod, may be purchased whole or as fillets, cutlets and steaks. These basic cuts of fish are shown below. The fillet from a large round fish, such as cod (top), is longer and thicker than a fillet from a flat fish such as plaice and sole (below). The steak, also cut from a round fish, is taken from between the middle part of the body and the tail. The cutlet comes from between the head and the middle part of the body.

THE FOUR BASIC CUTS OF FISH

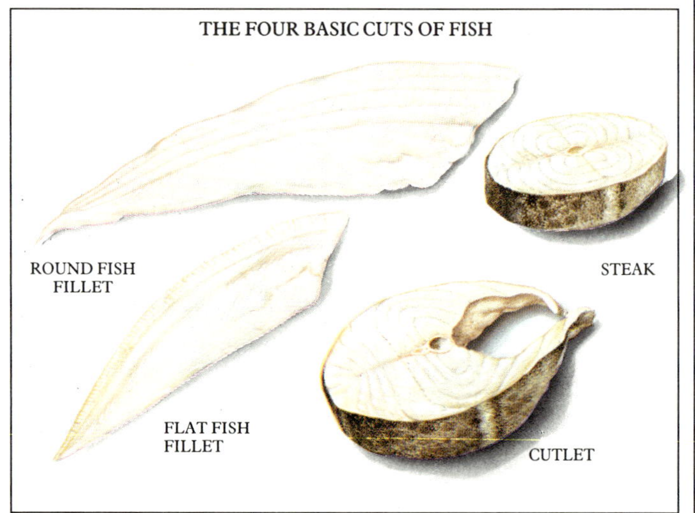

Bream, sea (bream, dorade, chad) A round, bony fish with a deep body, coarse scales and a black spot behind the head. The flesh is pink and delicate. Needs careful scaling. Bake, grill or fry.

Cod Large round fish which weighs up to 80 lb (36 kg). It has an olive-brown back with yellow and brown spots, small soft grey scales which should look bright, and white underside. The firm white flesh is sold whole, as fillets (fresh or wood-smoked) or steaks, often sold frozen. Avoid any fish with pink or grey discoloration. Can be poached, baked or grilled.

Cod roe The pinkish hard female roe and the soft male roe, known as chitterling, are sold boiled or uncooked. The hard roe is also smoked.

Haddock A round fish of the cod family, with grey skin. A dark line runs along both flanks and there is a dark smudge behind the gills. The white flesh, which should be very firm, is sold whole or as steaks and fillets. Suitable for poaching, baking, grilling and frying. Available all year round. **Smoked haddock** is smoked until pale yellow, on the bone (Finnan haddock) or as fillets. Very yellow haddock has probably been artificially coloured. It loses its flavour quickly.

Arbroath smokies Small whole haddock hot smoked to a brown colour.

Hake A round, long and slender fish with scaly silver-grey skin and tender, white, flaky flesh. Practically boneless. Sold as cutlets and fillets and suitable for baking.

Halibut This flat fish weighs from 9 lb (4 kg) up to 300–400 lb (140–180 kg). It has dark olive skin, marbled with lighter olive. The white dry flesh should be quite firm. Chicken halibut is smaller, 1–8 lb ($\frac{1}{2}$–$3\frac{1}{2}$ kg) in weight.
Greenland or mock halibut, weight 2–5 lb (1–$2\frac{1}{2}$ kg), has dark skin on both sides and oily, less expensive flesh. Considered inferior to proper halibut.

Plaice Flat fish, creamy-white on the underside, grey-brown with orange spots on the upper side. On fresh fish, the spots should be quite bright and the soft white flesh should be bright with no signs of discoloration. Sold whole or as fillets. Grill, poach, bake or fry.

Skate This flat, ray-shaped fish has slightly moist, slimy and smelly skin, with pink flesh. Only the wings, with prominent bones, are sold. Poach, grill or fry.

Sole (common, Dover or black) The elongated to oval body is almost completely surrounded by fins and is covered with tiny hard scales, firmly attached to the skin. The colour is usually olive-brown with irregular black markings on the upper side. The underside is white. The flesh is finely textured and delicate in flavour. Fresh sole is covered with slime and the skin is difficult to peel off. Sold whole or in fillets, for poaching, grilling and frying.
Lemon sole This is wider and more pointed than Dover sole and has light brown skin with darker brown spots on the upper side. The flesh is more stringy and has less flavour.

Witch (Aberdeen sole, megrim) Similar to lemon sole, but thinner. The pure white flesh lacks the flavour of real sole.

Turbot A flat fish with black skin and raised growths on its back. Creamy-white on the underside and with white, firm flesh. Similar to halibut, but with less dry, more delicately flavoured flesh. Poach, bake or grill.

Whiting A round fish belonging to the cod family. Grey-olive-green on the back, with pale yellow shading to silvery on the underside. When fresh the soft flesh is flaky, but deteriorates rapidly. Poach, bake or fry.

Oily Fish

Oily fish are so called because the oil content is found throughout the flesh, while in white fish the oil is present only in the liver. Oily fish come from the sea and some are also caught in freshwater lakes, rivers and streams or produced in fish farms.

When buying oily fish, look for fresh fish with firm, even-textured flesh, clear, full and shiny eyes, bright red gills and a clean smell.

The herring is the most common oily fish; it is delicious when cooked fresh, but is perhaps more popular salted and smoked. It is probable that more people eat kippers – the most famous smoked variety – than fresh herring, or any other kind of fish.

Generally speaking, there are two methods of smoking fish: hot-smoking in which the temperature in the smoking kiln is raised sufficiently to cook the fish which then requires no cooking prior to eating; and cold-smoking in which the finished product is normally cooked in the kitchen before consumption. Hot-smoked fish must be eaten soon after curing; cold-smoked fish will keep longer if lightly wrapped in plastic film and stored in the refrigerator.

Eel, common A richly flavoured freshwater fish up to 3 ft (1 metre) in length. It has shiny grey-black skin and firm, white flesh. It is always sold alive and should be cooked as soon as possible after killing. The fishmonger will kill and skin an eel whole. Steam, braise or deep fry.

Herring A small, delicately flavoured and bony saltwater fish, usually weighing about 6 oz (175 g). It has silvery-blue scales on the back, silvery flanks and underside, and firm brownish flesh. The skin should have a shiny, bright look, and the flesh should be firm to the touch. Sold whole; suitable for frying and grilling.
Buckling Hot-smoked herring, requiring no cooking.
Herring roes Both hard and soft roes are in short supply.
Kipper The most common smoked herring. It is split and put in brine before being smoked. Some kippers look dark because artificial colouring is added. These should be eaten as soon as possible after buying. Some kippers are not dyed at all and keep well. All kippers should have a sheen and the flesh should be soft to the touch. Kippers are sold whole, usually in pairs or as fillets.

Mackerel A long, slender, saltwater fish with striped blue and green back, silvery underside and firm flesh. It deteriorates quickly and must be used on the day of purchase. Sold whole, for grilling, frying and baking. On fresh mackerel, the skin should be shiny and the flesh quite stiff.
Smoked mackerel Hot-smoked and ready for eating.

Salmon The king of fish is caught in cool, fast-running rivers. It is a saltwater fish which travels up rivers to spawn. A fresh salmon has bright silvery scales, red gills and pink-red, close-textured flesh. Sold whole, weighing 8–20 lb ($3\frac{1}{2}$–9 kg), or as steaks. Avoid steaks with watery, grey-looking flesh. Canadian, Irish, Norwegian and Alaskan salmon is available frozen.
Smoked salmon Scotch smoked salmon has strips of fat between the meat and is considered the finest. Smoked Canadian, Norwegian and Pacific salmon is less expensive but drier.

Sardine A small and immature pilchard. It is usually sold tinned, in oil or tomatoes. Fresh sardines, imported from France and Portugal, are becoming increasingly popular.

Smelt or sparling Tiny saltwater fish which, like salmon, spawns and is caught in rivers. It has bright silvery scales and pure white flesh when quite fresh. It has a strong aroma which has been compared to that of violets and cucumbers, and a delicate flavour. Clean by pressing the entrails out through a cut just below the gills, and serve smelts shallow or deep-fried.

Sprat Small, silvery-skinned salt-water fish of the herring family. Prepare and cook like smelts. Young sprats, known as brislings, are tinned in oil or a sauce. Whole smoked sprats are also available.

Trout, rainbow The most common trout, reared on fish farms. It is green-gold in colour with whitish flesh. Grill or bake in foil.

Trout, river or brown This has darker skin than rainbow trout and is spotted. The flesh is superior to that of rainbow trout. Grill or fry.

Trout, sea or salmon A freshwater fish, similar to salmon, with silvery scales when fresh. The firm flesh has a delicate salmon flavour and is pale pink. Always sold whole, at an average weight of 2–6 lb (1–3 kg). Cooked as salmon.

Trout, smoked Rainbow trout smoked to a rich brown colour. Requires no cooking.

Shellfish

Shellfish are divided into two groups: crustaceans, such as crabs, lobsters and shrimps, which have jointed shells; and molluscs, such as mussels, oysters and scallops. Outside Britain, the division of small and not so small crustaceans into shrimps and prawns is unknown. When these types of fish are imported elsewhere, some confusion can therefore arise concerning the names of these crustaceans. In particular, the various large prawns imported from the Pacific have no precise equivalent in other waters although they may be used in substitution for the Dublin Bay prawn. This itself is now officially labelled scampi.

The crawfish, also known as spiny lobster or rock lobster (*langouste* in French), should not be confused with the freshwater crayfish (*écrevisse*). This is a common shellfish in France, but not to be found elsewhere.

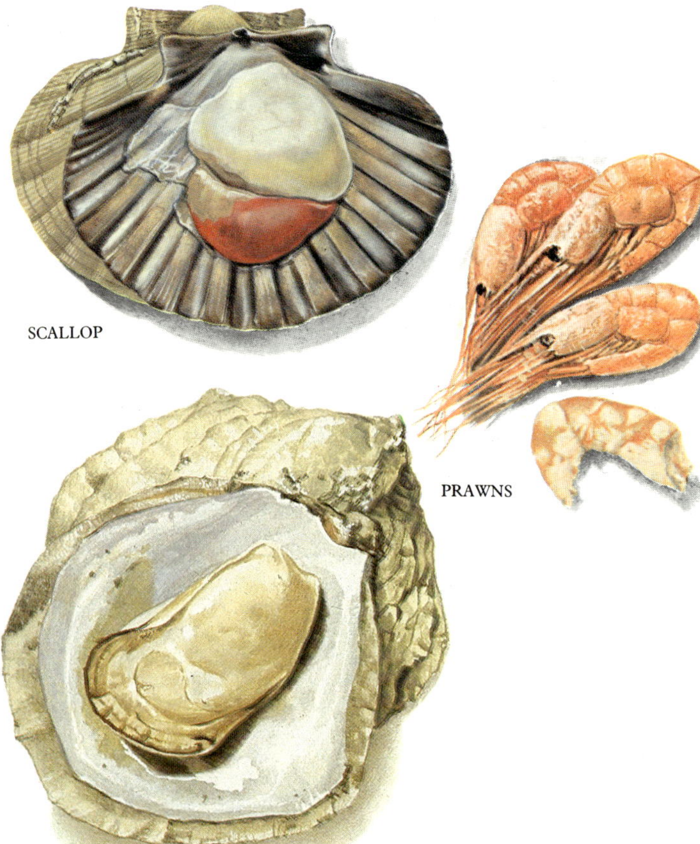

Crab This crustacean is grey-brown when alive, brownish-red when cooked. It is sometimes sold alive, but usually freshly boiled by the fishmonger. Also sold 'dressed', that is prepared ready for eating. The weight of a crab varies from $1\frac{1}{2}$–8 lb ($\frac{3}{4}$–$3\frac{1}{2}$-kg). The claws provide white meat and the shell brown meat. Male crabs (cocks) have larger claws, and the female crabs (hens) often contain edible roes or red coral. Crabs are best when medium-sized, about 3 lb ($1\frac{1}{2}$ kg), and should have both claws attached. When buying crab, shake it lightly; it should feel heavy but with no sound of water inside. Also sold as fresh, frozen or tinned crabmeat.

Crawfish (spiny lobster, rock lobster) A crustacean similar to lobster, but heavier, weighing 5–6 lb (about $2\frac{1}{2}$ kg). It lacks the large claws, and all the meat is in the tail. The flesh is coarser in texture than lobster meat, but is prepared in the same way. Most crawfish tails are sold frozen.

Lobster Crustacean, dark blue when alive and scarlet when boiled. The male lobster is brighter in colour, smaller than the female, but with larger claws. Best at a weight of 1–2 lb ($\frac{1}{2}$–1 kg). The female has a broader tail and more tender flesh. The female also contains the coral, or eggs, used for lobster butter. Sold live or cooked. When buying lobster, choose a medium-sized one which feels heavy for its size. The tail should spring back when straightened out. Avoid lobsters with white shells on their backs as this is a sign of age.

Mussels These molluscs with blue-black shells are boiled and served in a sauce. Before cooking, discard any with broken shells and any which do not close when tapped. Mussels are sold by the pint; allow $1\frac{1}{2}$ pints (about 1 litre or $\frac{3}{4}$ kg) per person.

Oysters These highly priced molluscs are usually eaten raw, but may also be cooked. Shells should be closed, or shut when tapped. Oysters must be absolutely fresh and should be opened just before serving. Allow six for each person.

Prawns Small, soft-shelled grey crustaceans, the shells of which turn bright red and the flesh pink when boiled. They are usually sold already boiled, with or without their shells. Unshelled they are sold by the pint (570 ml), and shelled by weight. Available all year round, fresh or frozen.
Dublin Bay prawn, scampi, Norway lobster The largest prawn, about 4 in (10 cm) long. Pale pink with a hard shell when alive, pink when boiled. Sold alive or cooked, with or without shells. Also sold frozen.

Scallops Native molluscs with white flesh and orange roe. They are enclosed in pinkish-brown shells. They are usually sold opened. Ask the fishmonger to include the deep shells with the order. Look for firm white flesh and bright roe. Suitable for poaching, baking, grilling and for stews.

Shrimps, common or brown Small crustaceans with almost translucent shells which turn brown when boiled. British shrimps are caught mainly in Morecambe Bay and the Solway Firth and are usually sold cooked in their shells. Available all year round. Frozen, shelled shrimps are imported from Greenland. Also available tinned and potted.

Pink shrimps These have grey shells which turn rosy-pink when boiled. They are less tasty than brown shrimps and usually sold cooked, but unpeeled.

Poultry

Poultry, which are domestic birds specially bred for the table, include chicken, duck, goose, guinea fowl and turkey. Nowadays free-range chickens are available only from specialist shops, and most chickens are battery-reared. These, although less tasty, are cheaper.

The flavour of a chicken depends on its age. In a young bird the tip of the breastbone is soft and flexible, and the feet smooth with small scales. When cooked, the flesh is tender and mild in flavour. As the bird ages, the breastbone becomes harder and more rigid, and the scales on the feet coarser. The cooked flesh is also coarser and drier, but the flavour is better developed. The length of time a bird is left after killing and before drawing also influences the flavour – the longer it is left, the stronger the taste.

Duck is one of the more expensive breeds of poultry, all the more so because it yields little meat in comparison to its weight and size. Geese are also expensive because, like ducks, they cannot be reared successfully under factory-farming conditions. It was traditional to serve goose for Christmas dinner, but it was ousted from the festive table by the turkey.

Like all poultry, turkey is now available throughout the year, fresh or frozen, in all sizes. It is also sold in individual portions, many supermarkets offering turkey breast and leg portions.

Poultry giblets are sold either with the bird or separately. They can be used for stocks, stuffings and pâtés.

Chicken Available throughout the year, fresh or frozen, and usually sold oven-ready – that is plucked, drawn and trussed. Fresh chickens are sometimes sold plucked but not drawn or trussed. A fresh chicken should have a plump, white breast, smooth and pliable legs and a pliable beak and breastbone. Young birds have short, sharp claws. Chickens are usually sold under different names, according to their age and weight, and can be cooked in numerous ways. Whole chickens may be roasted, spit-roasted, pot-roasted and braised. They can be boiled or cooked in a casserole. They can be boned and made into galantines; and jointed they are grilled, fried or stewed.

Poussin A baby chicken, four to six weeks old and weighing up to 1 lb (450 g). Allow one poussin per person. Suitable for roasting, spit-roasting and grilling.

Spring chicken About six weeks old, with an average weight of $2\frac{1}{2}$ lb (1·1 kg). Best roasted to give three portions.

Roasting chicken (or broiler) The most popular size for a family. It is eight weeks old and weighs 3–4 lb (1·4–1·8 kg), enough for four people. The larger roasting chicken, weighing 4–6 lb (1·8–2·7 kg), serves about six. It is also sold divided into individual joints for frying, grilling or baking.

Boiling fowl An older bird, usually a hen after the laying season and about eight months

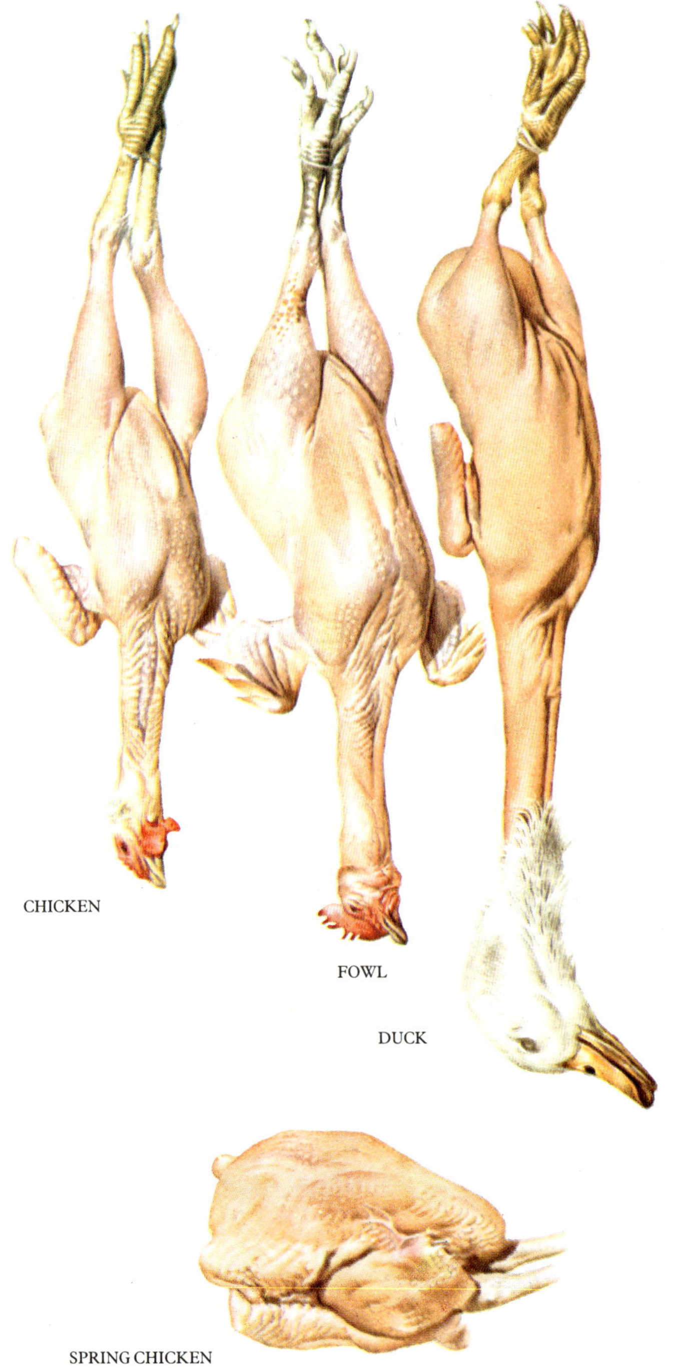

CHICKEN

FOWL

DUCK

SPRING CHICKEN

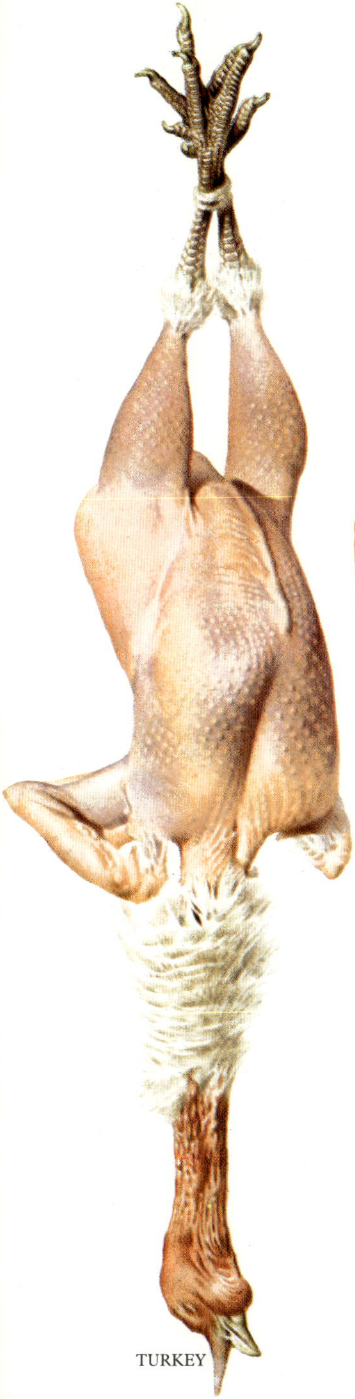

old, average weight 6 lb (2·7 kg). It is meaty but also fatty, and is suitable for stews or casseroles. Boiling fowl, being in less demand than roasting chicken but less expensive, generally has to be ordered in advance.

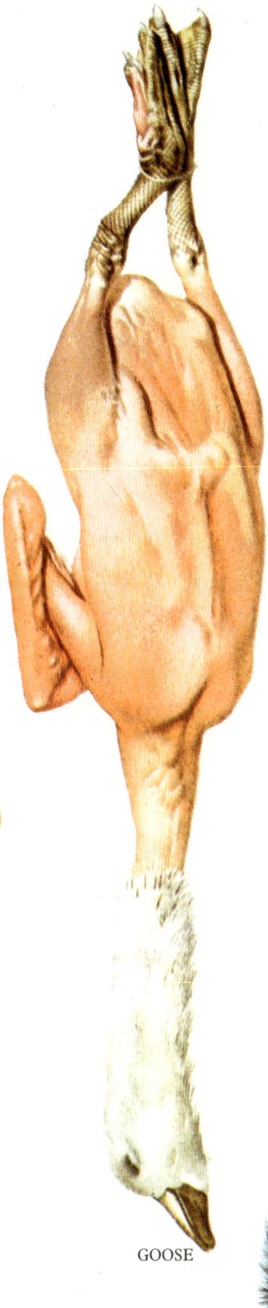

Frozen chickens These are drawn and trussed, ready for roasting, and are sold whole or in joints. They must be completely thawed in the wrapping before being cooked. Never put a frozen chicken in hot water to thaw – the only effect this has is to toughen the flesh. A bird which has to be thawed quickly can be put under cold, slow-running water. The giblets are sometimes wrapped separately and put inside the chicken.

Duck The most famous breed is the Aylesbury duck. It is usually sold weighing 4–6 lb (1·8–2·7 kg), but a duck does not serve as many as a chicken of similar weight. A 6 lb (2·7 kg) duck is only enough for four people. Duck is a fatty bird that is best roasted. The breast should be plump, the bird's underbill soft enough to bend and the feet pliable.

Duckling A young duck weighing 3½–4 lb (1·6–1·8 kg). It is always roasted and will serve no more than two persons.

Goose This is considered by many gourmets to be the best of all poultry. It is a fatty bird with creamy-white flesh which cooks to a light brown, and has a slightly gamey flavour. Average weight is 6–12 lb (2·7–5·4 kg), but again it serves less per pound than chicken. Allow 12–14 oz (350–400 g) per person. Choose a young bird with soft yellow feet and legs which still have a little down on them. Older birds have stiff, dry webs.

Guinea fowl Originally a game bird, but now bred for the table, guinea fowl should be hung for several days. It has grey plumage, tinged with purple and spotted with white. The flesh is firm and creamy-white with a flavour slightly reminiscent of pheasant. Suitable for roasting, braising and casseroles. Available all the year round.

Turkey The weight of a turkey ranges from about 6 lb (2·7 kg) to 30–40 lb (14–18 kg), the average weight being 10–14 lb (4½–6½ kg). Allow 10–12 oz (about 300 g) per serving. Hen birds are the best buy at seven to nine months old. The legs should be black, the neck short, the breast plump and the flesh pale white, with a faint blue tinge.

TURKEY

GOOSE

DRESSED GUINEA FOWL

GUINEA FOWL

Game

The term game is applied to wild animals and birds which are hunted and eaten. For roasting and grilling, all game should be young – a condition that is easiest recognised in unplucked game. The beak and feet should be pliable, the plumage or fur soft, and the breast plump.

If not bought already prepared for cooking, game must be hung in order to tenderise the flesh and develop the gamey flavour. Hanging time depends on the weather – game matures more quickly in warm humid weather – and on individual taste. Game birds are hung, unplucked and undrawn, by their beaks in a cool airy place and are ready for cooking when the tail feathers can be pulled out easily. Furred game is hung by the feet for one or two weeks.

Although many types of game are commercially frozen and therefore available throughout the year, the flavour is at its best in freshly killed and well-hung game.

VENISON

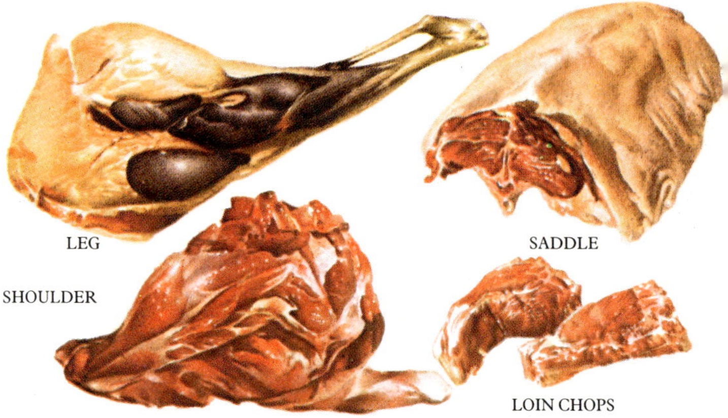

LEG

SADDLE

SHOULDER

LOIN CHOPS

RABBIT AND HARE

FORE AND HIND LEGS OF RABBIT

SADDLE OF RABBIT

SADDLE OF HARE

GAME BIRDS

Grouse Young birds, with soft downy breast feathers and pointed flight wings, are roasted and served one per person. Older birds, with rounded tips to the wings, are better casseroled. Hang young and old birds for about three days.

Partridge There are two varieties, the English or grey partridge, which has the better flavour, and the slightly larger, red-legged French partridge. Young birds have pointed tips to the feathers, yellow-brown pliable feet and light-coloured plump flesh. Hang for three or four days before roasting or grilling; serve one per person.

Pheasant The cock and hen may be sold singly or as a brace. Young birds of both sexes have pliable beaks and feet, soft and pointed feathers; on cocks the short spurs are rounded. A hen pheasant, which is considered the tastiest, will serve three people, and a cock four people.

Pigeon Wood pigeons are inexpensive game birds, often tough and best casseroled. Very young birds, with pink legs, downy feathers and plump breast, may be roasted or grilled. Hang for one day, and serve one per person.

Quail Quail has a less gamey flavour than other birds and should not be hung. On young birds, the feathers are pointed and the feet soft with rounded spurs. Roast or grill, serving one bird per person.

Wild duck The most common is teal, with short pointed feathers and thin soft feet in young birds. It generally requires no hanging. Roast or grill, serving one bird per person. Mallard is larger, with lean, dry flesh. Hang for one day only. Serve roasted. One bird serves two to three.

Wild goose Canada goose is occasionally seen, although it is illegal to offer it for sale. On young birds, with lean dark flesh, the flight feathers are pointed and the long dark feet pliable.

Hang a wild goose for four or five days. One goose, average weight 7 lb (3·2 kg, will serve six persons.

FURRED GAME

Hare There are two types, the English or brown hare and the Scottish or blue hare. A young hare (weight 6–7 lb, about 3 kg), known as a leveret, can be recognised by its small, sharp, white teeth, smooth fur and hidden claws; the soft ears tear easily. Hang for about one week. Young hares may be roasted whole, to serve four to six persons; older animals are better casseroled although the saddle can be roasted.

Rabbit The flesh of the wild rabbit often has a gamey flavour. Smaller than the hare (it serves three persons), a young rabbit can be recognised by the same signs. It is prepared and cooked in the same way, but is skinned at once after killing and should not be hung. Rabbits on sale in the shops are domesticated, with a flavour like chicken.

Venison The best meat comes from the young male deer (buck), at an age of $1\frac{1}{2}$–2 years. The lean meat is dark red and close-grained, with firm white fat. Hang for at least one week. Venison is sold in joints, the leg and saddle being the choicest cuts. Loin chops, neck cutlets and shoulder may be braised.

Stocks

A good stock is made from the bones and flesh of fish, meat and poultry, often with added vegetables, herbs and spices. It is the basis for most soups and also adds flavour to casseroles and sauces.

Fresh bones and meat are essential: the carcass of a previously roasted chicken, for example, will give the stock a stale taste. Vegetables give additional flavour, but avoid potatoes, which make the stock cloudy. Strong-flavoured vegetables, such as turnips, swedes and parsnips, should be used sparingly.

Chicken Stock

The main ingredient for this is the carcass of a chicken. A turkey or game bird can also be used, together with the scalded feet of the bird and the cleaned giblets. Alternatively, a whole chicken, poached, produces very good stock: if the chicken itself is carved and served straight away, the bones may in this case be added back and simmered for another hour to give more flavour.

PREPARATION TIME: *5 min*
COOKING TIME: *2–3 hours*
INGREDIENTS *(for 4–6 pints, about 2½–3½ litres):*
1 chicken carcass, together with feet and giblets
1–2 leeks
1 large onion
1–2 celery sticks, including the green tops
½ lb (225 g) carrots
2 bouquets garnis (page 99)
Salt and black peppercorns*

Clean the vegetables and slice them or chop them roughly. Put all the ingredients in a large pan, cover with cold water and bring gently to simmering point. Remove any scum from the surface and cover the pan with a tight-fitting lid. Simmer the stock over the lowest possible heat for about 2 hours. Top up with hot water if the level of the liquid falls below the other ingredients.

Strain the stock through a fine sieve or muslin into a large bowl. Leave it to settle for a few minutes, then remove the fat from the surface by drawing absorbent paper over it. If the stock is not required immediately, leave the fat to settle in a surface layer which can then be easily lifted off.

Once the fat has been removed, correct the seasoning if necessary.

Fish Stock

The basis for this stock is bones and trimmings, such as the head and the skin. White fish such as cod, haddock, halibut, whiting and plaice can all be used. Sole is particularly good.

PREPARATION TIME: *5–10 min*
COOKING TIME: *30 min*
INGREDIENTS *(for 1 pint, 570 ml):*
1 lb (450 g) fish trimmings
*Salt**
1 onion
Bouquet garni (page 99) or 1 large leek and 1 celery stick

Wash the trimmings thoroughly in cold water and put them in a large pan, with 1 pint (570 ml) lightly salted water. Bring to the boil over low heat and remove any surface scum. Meanwhile, peel and finely chop the onion and add to the stock with the bouquet garni or the cleaned and chopped leek and celery. Cover the pan with a lid and simmer over low heat for 30 minutes. Strain the stock through a sieve or muslin.

Cooking stock in a pressure cooker

Place the stock ingredients, with lightly salted water, in the pressure cooker – it must not be more than two-thirds full. Bring to the boil and remove the scum from the surface before fixing the lid. Lower the heat and bring to 15 pounds (6·8 kg) pressure. Reduce the heat quickly and cook steadily for 1 hour. Strain the stock and remove the fat.

Storing stock

After the fat has been removed, pour the cooled stock into a container and cover with a lid. It will keep for three or four days in the refrigerator, but to ensure absolute freshness, boil up the stock every two days. Fish and vegetable stocks spoil quickly and should be made and used on the same day. If refrigerated they will keep for two days.

Freezing stocks

Stocks can be satisfactorily stored in a home freezer, where they will keep for up to two months. Boil the prepared stock over high heat to reduce it by half. Pour the concentrated cooled stock into ice-cube trays, freeze quickly and transfer the cubes to polythene bags. Alternatively, pour the stock into freezing containers, leaving a 1 in (2½ cm) space at the top.

To use frozen stock, leave it to thaw at room temperature, or simply turn it into a saucepan and heat over low heat, stirring occasionally. Add 2 tablespoons water to every cube of stock.

Ready-made stocks

Many ready-made stock preparations are available, usually in the form of cubes or extracts. In an emergency, these preparations are acceptable replacements for home-made stocks, but they lack body and jellying qualities. As they are highly seasoned, be careful about extra flavourings until the soup has been tasted.

SKIMMING STOCK

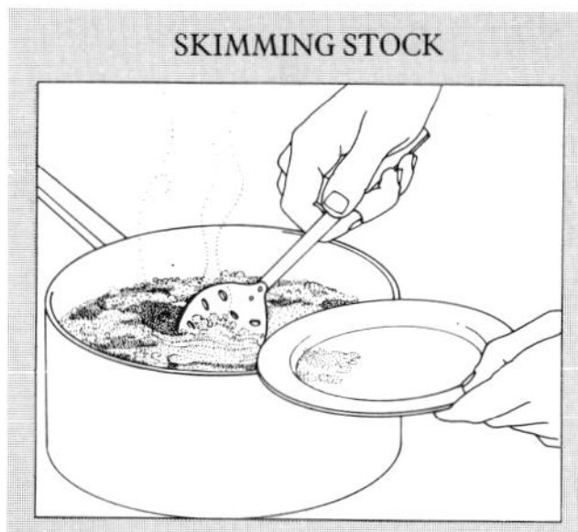
Lifting scum from boiling stock

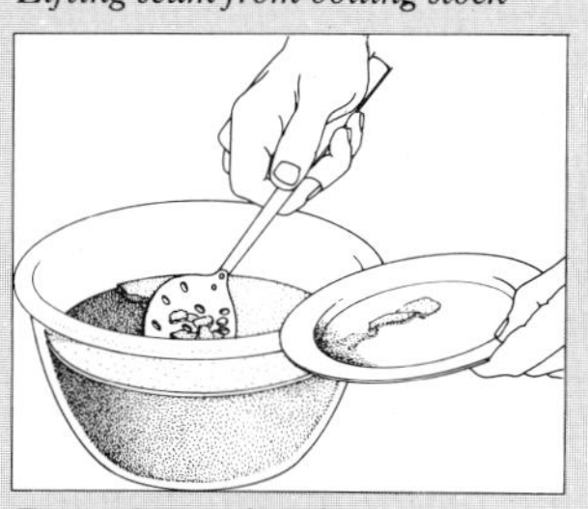
Removing surface fat

Sauces and Dressings

Sauces first came into widespread use in the Middle Ages, to disguise the flavour of long-stored meat that had been inadequately cured. Today, they are used to add flavour to bland food, colour to simple meals and moisture to otherwise dry foods.

BASIC WHITE SAUCE

This is prepared either by the roux or the blending method:

Roux method
A roux is usually composed of equal amounts of butter and flour which are then combined with liquid (usually milk) to the required consistency. Melt the butter in a heavy-based pan, blend in the flour, and cook over low heat for 2–3 minutes, stirring constantly with a wooden spoon.

Gradually add the warm or cold liquid to the roux, which will at first thicken to a near solid mass. Beat vigorously until the mixture leaves the sides of the pan clean, then add a little more milk. Allow the mixture to thicken and boil between each addition of milk. Continuous beating is essential to obtain a smooth sauce. When all the milk has been added, bring the sauce to the boil; let it simmer for about 5 minutes and add the seasoning.

A basic white sauce can also be made by the one-stage method. This consists of putting the basic ingredients (fat, flour and liquid) into a pan at the same time. Cook over low heat, beating until the sauce has thickened. Boil for 3 minutes and season.

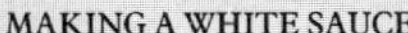
MAKING A WHITE SAUCE

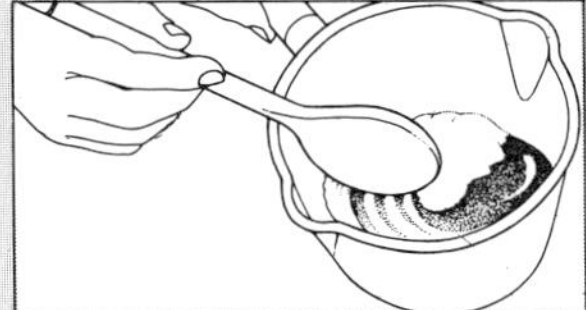
Blending butter with flour

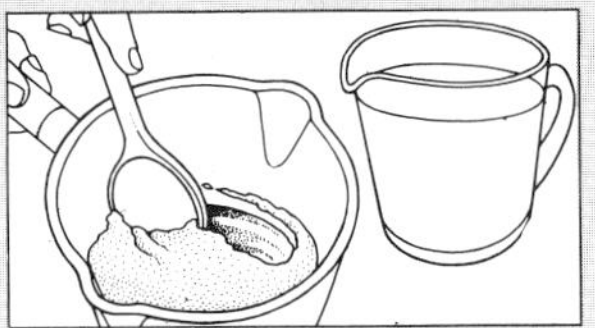
Thickening the roux

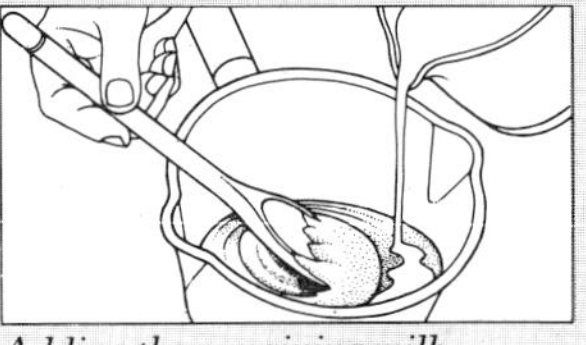
Adding the remaining milk

Blending method
For this method the thickening agent is mixed to a paste with a little cold milk. Mix 1 oz (25 g) plain flour with a few tablespoons taken from ½ pint (300 ml) of cold milk. Blend to a smooth paste in a bowl, and bring the remaining milk to the boil.

Pour the hot milk over the paste and return the mixture to the pan. Bring to the boil over low heat, stirring continuously with a wooden spoon. Simmer the sauce for 2–3 minutes, until thick. Add a knob of butter and seasoning and cook for 5 minutes.

A basic white sauce can be made into other savoury sauces, such as béchamel and velouté.

Béchamel Sauce

PREPARATION TIME: *20 min*
COOKING TIME: *5–10 min*
INGREDIENTS (*½ pint, 300 ml*):
½ pint (300 ml) milk
½ small bay leaf
Sprig of thyme
½ small onion
¼ level teaspoon grated nutmeg
1 oz (25 g) butter
1 oz (25 g) plain flour
Salt and black pepper*

Put the milk with the bay leaf, thyme, onion and nutmeg in a pan, and bring slowly to the boil. Remove from the heat, cover with a lid and leave the milk to infuse for 15 minutes.

In a clean heavy-based pan, melt the butter, stir in the flour and cook the roux for 3 minutes.

Strain the milk through a fine sieve and gradually blend it into the roux. Bring to the boil, stirring continuously, then simmer for 2–3 minutes. Adjust the seasoning.

Velouté Sauce

PREPARATION TIME: *5–10 min*
COOKING TIME: *1 hour*
INGREDIENTS (*½ pint, 300 ml*):
1 oz (25 g) butter
1 oz (25 g) plain flour
1 pint (570 ml) white stock
Salt and black pepper*

Make the roux with the butter and flour. Gradually stir in the hot stock until the sauce is quite smooth. Bring to boiling point, lower the heat, and let the sauce simmer for about 1 hour until reduced by half. Stir occasionally. Strain through a sieve.

Thickening agents for sauces

Basic white and brown sauces can be thickened or enriched with various other liaisons: cornflour or arrowroot with water; beurre manié (kneaded butter and flour); egg yolks and cream.

Cornflour and arrowroot
To thicken ½ pint (300 ml) of liquid to a sauce of coating consistency, stir 1 level tablespoon cornflour with 1½ tablespoons cold water, and mix into a smooth paste. Blend a little of the hot liquid into the liaison, then return this to the sauce. Bring the sauce to the boil, stirring constantly for 2–3 minutes to allow the starch to cook through.

Arrowroot is best used to thicken clear sauces that are to be served at once. To thicken ½ pint (300 ml) sauce use 2¼ level teaspoons arrowroot mixed to a paste with water.

The sauce cannot be reheated and quickly loses its thickening qualities.

Beurre manié
This liaison is ideal for thickening sauces, casseroles and stews at the end of cooking. Knead an equal amount of butter and flour, about 1 oz (25 g) each, into a paste with a fork or the fingers. Add small pieces of the beurre manié to the hot liquid. Stir or whisk continuously to dissolve the butter and disperse the flour. Simmer the sauce until it is thick and smooth and has lost the starchy taste of raw flour. Do not let the sauce boil or the beurre manié will separate out.

EGG-BASED SAUCES

These rich sauces require care and practice to prevent them curdling. They are made from egg yolks and a high proportion of butter. Through continuous whisking, these two main ingredients are emulsified to the stage where they form a thick and creamy consistency.

Hollandaise Sauce

PREPARATION AND COOKING TIME: *20 min*
INGREDIENTS (*½ pint, 300 ml*):
3 tablespoons white wine vinegar
1 tablespoon water
6 black peppercorns
1 bay leaf
3 egg yolks
6 oz (175 g) soft butter, preferably unsalted
Salt and black pepper*

Boil the vinegar and water with the peppercorns and the bay leaf in a small pan, until reduced to 1 tablespoon. Leave to cool. Cream the egg yolks with ½ oz (10 g) butter and a pinch of salt. Strain the vinegar into the eggs, and set the bowl over a pan of boiling water. Turn off the heat. Whisk in the remaining butter, ¼ oz (5–10 g) at a time, until the sauce is shiny and has the consistency of thick cream. Season with salt and freshly ground pepper.

Until the technique of egg-based sauces has been mastered, a Hollandaise sauce may sometimes curdle during preparation. This is generally because the heat is too sudden or too high, or because the butter has been added too quickly.

If the finished sauce separates, it can often be saved by taking it off the heat immediately and beating in 1 tablespoon of cold water.

Whisking in pieces of butter to thicken Hollandaise sauce

Béarnaise Sauce

This sauce is similar to Hollandaise sauce, but has a sharper flavour. It is served with grilled meat and fish.

PREPARATION AND COOKING TIME: *20 min*
INGREDIENTS (*½ pint, 300 ml*):
2 tablespoons tarragon vinegar
2 tablespoons white wine vinegar
½ small onion
2 egg yolks
3–4 oz (75–100 g) butter, preferably unsalted
Salt and black pepper*

Put the vinegars and finely chopped onion in a small saucepan; boil steadily until reduced to 1 tablespoon. Strain and set aside to cool. Follow the method used for making Hollandaise sauce.

Mayonnaise

Mayonnaise and its variations are the most widely used of savoury cold sauces. They are served with hors d'oeuvre, salads, cold meat, poultry and vegetable dishes. Mayonnaise, like Hollandaise and Béarnaise sauce, is based on eggs and fat, but oil is used instead of butter.

It is essential that all the ingredients and equipment are at room temperature. Assemble the bowl, egg and oil at least 1 hour before making a mayonnaise.

PREPARATION TIME: *20 min*
INGREDIENTS (*¼ pint, 150 ml*):
1 egg yolk
¼ level teaspoon salt
½ level teaspoon dry mustard
Pinch caster sugar
Black pepper
¼ pint (150 ml) olive oil
1 tablespoon white wine vinegar or lemon juice

Beat the egg yolk in a bowl until thick. Beat in the salt, mustard, sugar and a few twists of freshly ground pepper. Add the oil, drop by drop, whisking vigorously between each addition of oil so that it is absorbed completely before the next drop. As the mayonnaise thickens and becomes shiny, the oil may be added in a thin stream. Finally, blend in the vinegar.

A mayonnaise may curdle if the oil was cold or was added too quickly, or if the egg yolk was stale. To save a curdled mayonnaise, whisk a fresh yolk in a clean bowl, and gradually whisk in the curdled mayonnaise. Alternatively, whisk in a teaspoon of tepid water until the mayonnaise is thick and shiny.

SALAD DRESSINGS

A good dressing is essential to a salad, but it must be varied to accord with the salad ingredients. A sharp vinaigrette sauce is probably best for a green salad, but more substantial salads might need additional flavours.

Sauce Vinaigrette

PREPARATION TIME: *3 min*
INGREDIENTS (*¼ pint, 150 ml*):
6 tablespoons oil
2 tablespoons vinegar
2 teaspoons finely chopped herbs
Salt and black pepper*

Put the oil and vinegar in a bowl or in a screw-top jar. Whisk with a fork or shake vigorously before seasoning to taste with herbs, salt and freshly ground pepper.

French Dressing

PREPARATION TIME: *3 min*
INGREDIENTS (*⅓ pint, 200 ml*):
8 tablespoons oil
4 tablespoons vinegar
2 level teaspoons French mustard
½ level teaspoon each salt and black pepper*
Caster sugar (optional)

Whisk or shake all the dressing ingredients together, seasoning with sugar (optional). Either of the following ingredients can be added to a basic French dressing: 1–2 crushed garlic cloves; 2 tablespoons chopped tarragon or chives; 1 tablespoon tomato paste and a pinch of paprika; 2 tablespoons each finely chopped parsley and onion; 1 teaspoon anchovy essence (for cold fish).

Fish

Fish are sold fresh, frozen, salted from the barrel, smoked, pickled or tinned. Flat fish, such as plaice, sole, turbot and whiting, are sold whole or filleted. Whole round fish, such as cod, haddock and hake, are also sold as steaks and cutlets.

Many shellfish are sold already boiled and even prepared. The exceptions are mussels and oysters which must always be bought live.

Cook fish on the day it is bought; for a main course allow 7–8 oz (200–225 g) of fish per person, or one good-sized fillet, steak or cutlet.

PREPARATION OF FISH

Fishmongers will usually clean and fillet fish ready for cooking. But if this has not been done, a few simple preparations are necessary. Unwrap the fish as soon as possible and if it has to be stored in the refrigerator, wrap it in plastic or foil to prevent its smell spreading to other food.

Scaling

Cover the wooden board with several sheets of newspaper. Lay the fish on the paper and, holding it by the tail, scrape away the scales from the tail towards the head, using the blunt edge of a knife. Rinse the scales off under cold water. Alternatively, cook the fish without removing the scales, and skin it before serving.

Cleaning

Once scaled, the fish must be cleaned, or gutted. This process is determined by the shape of the fish – in round fish the entrails lie in the belly, in flat fish in a cavity behind the head.

Round fish

(cod, herring, mackerel, trout, for example). Slit the fish, with a sharp knife, along the belly from behind the gills to just above the tail. Scrape out and discard the entrails. Rinse the fish under cold running water and, with a little salt, gently rub away any black skin inside the cavity.

The head and tail may be left on the fish if it is to be cooked whole, but the eyes should be taken out. Use a sharp knife or scissors to cut off the lower fins on either side of the body and the gills below the head. Or cut the head off below the gills and slice off the tail.

Small round fish (smelts, sardines and sprats) need less preparation. Wipe the fish with a damp cloth, cut off the heads just below the gills, leaving the tails intact. Squeeze out the entrails. Fresh eels are sold live; the fishmonger will cut off the heads and may also skin the fish. Otherwise, loosen the skin at the head with the tip of a knife. Grip the skin in a rough cloth and peel it down and over the tail. Cut the skinned eel into pieces and rinse in cold water to remove blood.

Flat fish

(plaice, sole, for example). Make a semi-circular slit just behind the head, on the dark skin side. This opens up the cavity which contains the entrails. Scrape these out and wash the fish. Cut off the fins, and cook the fish whole.

CLEANING FLAT FISH

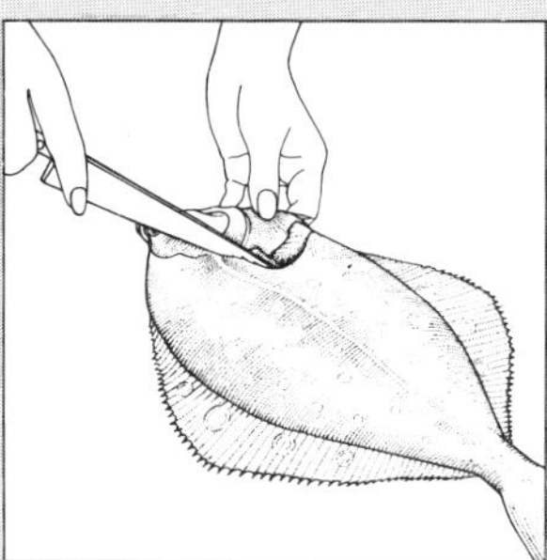

1. *Slitting behind the head*

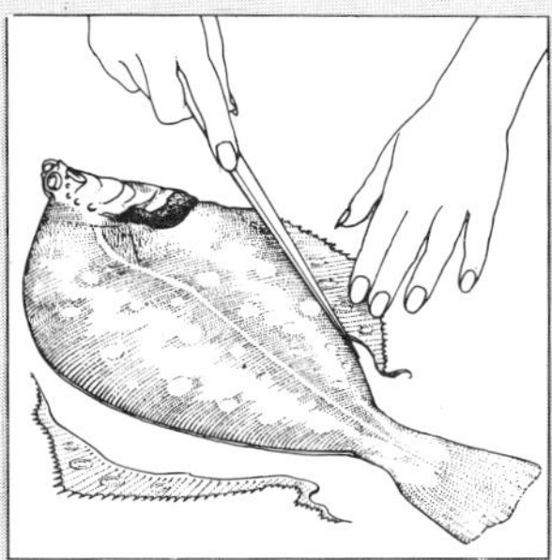

2. *Cutting off the fins*

CLEANING ROUND FISH

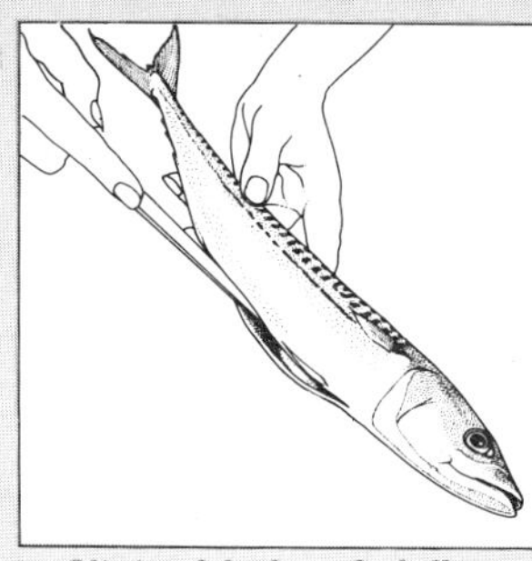

1. *Slitting fish along the belly*

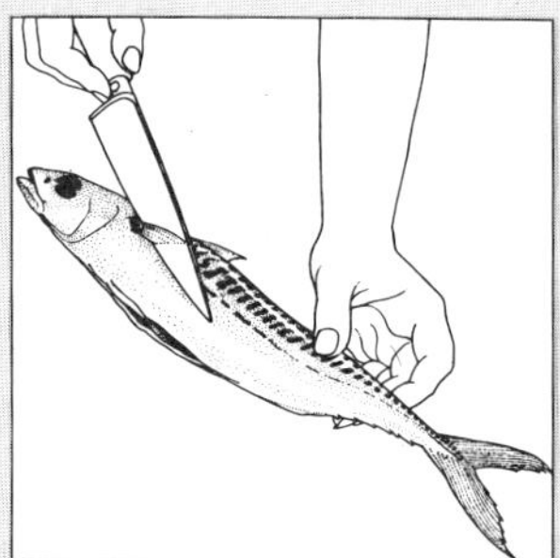

2. *Cutting off the gills*

SKINNING A FLAT FISH

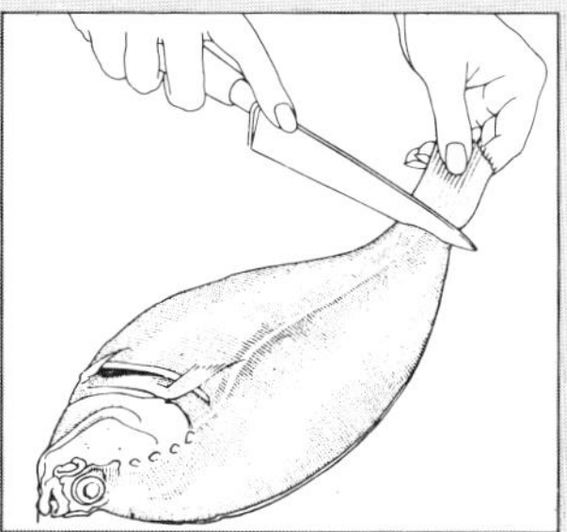

1. *Slitting skin above the tail*

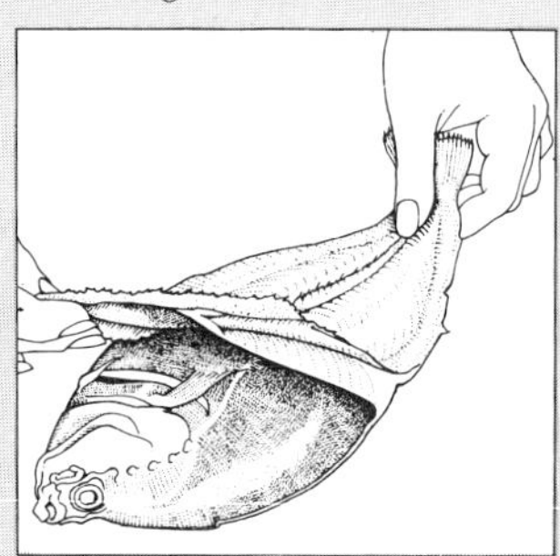

2. *Drawing skin towards the head*

SKINNING A ROUND FISH

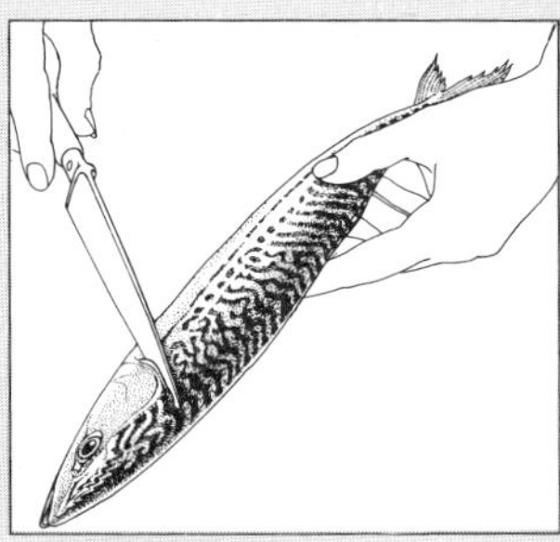

1. *Loosening skin below head*

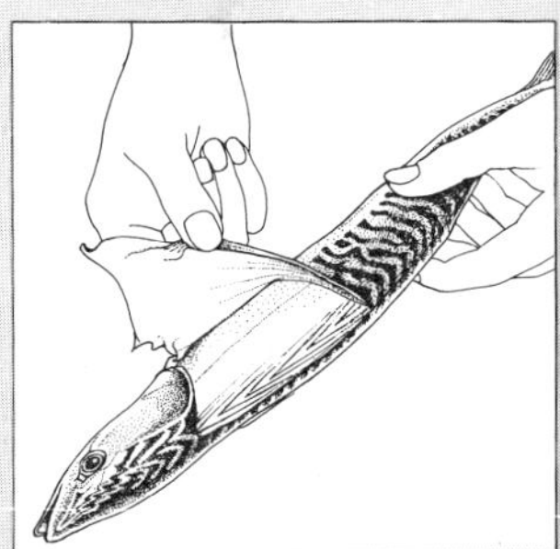

2. *Drawing skin towards the tail*

CUTTING A ROUND FISH INTO TWO FILLETS

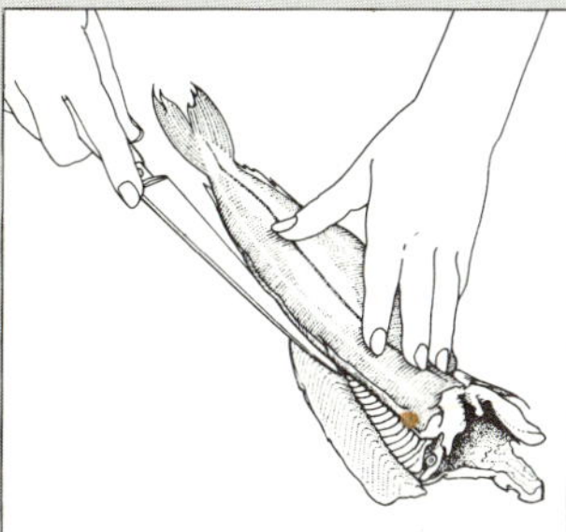
1. *Cutting along the backbone*

2. *Freeing the first fillet*

3. *Removing the backbone*

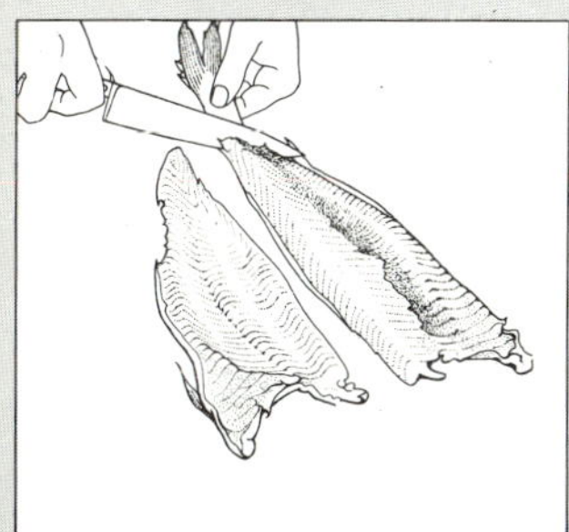
4. *Cutting off the tail*

Skinning
Again, the method varies according to the type of fish.

Round fish
These are usually cooked with the skin on, but it is also possible to remove the skin before cooking. Using a sharp knife, loosen the skin round the head and then gently draw it down towards the tail. Cut it off. Repeat the process on the other side.

Flat fish
Lay the fish, dark skin uppermost, on the board. Make a slit across the skin just above the tail. Slip the thumb into the slit, and gently loosen the skin. Holding the fish firmly by the tail, pull the skin quickly towards the head (dip the fingers in a little salt to get a better grip), and cut it off. The white skin on the other side may be removed in the same way, but it is usually left on.

Filleting and boning
The fish can now be cut into serving portions. Fillets of both round and flat fish are popular as they provide a solid piece of fish without any bones.

Round fish
To fillet a large fish, such as haddock, cut the head off the cleaned fish, and then cut along the backbone, working towards the tail. Insert the knife blade at a slight angle to the bone and, keeping the sharp edge towards the tail, gently ease the flesh from the bone with slicing movements.

Continue cutting in line with the backbone, until the whole fillet is freed. Open out the fish and cut off the fillet at the tail. With the tip of the knife, ease off the backbone to reveal the other fillet, and cut off the tail. If the fish is large, the fillets can be cut into smaller portions of a size suitable for serving.

Boning large round fish
(salmon and salmon trout)
Using a sharp knife or scissors, cut the fins and gills off the cleaned fish, and cut an inverted V into the tail. Wash the fish under cold water to remove all traces of blood, then place it in a fish kettle or large flameproof dish and poach it in court bouillon (see page 87).

Lift the poached fish on to a board, and with a sharp knife or scissors snip the skin just below the head and above the tail. Carefully peel off the skin, leaving head and tail intact. Snip the backbone below the head and above the tail, then with the blade of a sharp knife split the fish along the backbone. Ease the bone out from the back without breaking the fish.

Boning small round fish
Smaller round fish such as herrings and mackerel may be filleted as already described, but are more often boned and cooked whole or with a stuffing.

To bone a cleaned herring, cut off the head, tail and fins. Open out the split fish and spread it flat, skin side up. Press firmly along the centre back of the fish to loosen the backbone, then turn the fish over. Starting at the head, ease away the backbone with the tip of the knife, removing at the same time as many of the small bones as possible. The herring can now be folded back into its original shape or cut into two long fillets.

Steaks and cutlets
Large round fish are often sold in thick cutlets, from the middle of the fish, or as steaks, from the tail end. These should be cleaned, but not skinned before cooking. The small central bone is best removed after cooking. If it is removed before cooking, the centre should be stuffed.

Filleting flat fish
A large sole or plaice will yield four small fillets, two from each side. Lay the fish, dark skin up, on the board and with a sharp knife cut off the fins. Make the first cut along the backbone, working from the head towards the tail. Then make a semi-circular cut, just below the head, through half the thickness of the fish. Slant the knife against the backbone, and with short sharp strokes of the knife separate the left fillet from the bone. Make a thick cut just above the tail and remove the fillet. Turn the fish round and remove the right fillet in the same way. Turn the fish over and remove the fillets on the other side.

COOKING METHODS

A number of basic cooking methods are suitable for all fish whether they are whole, filleted or cut into steaks. But whatever cooking method is chosen, fish should be cooked for a short time only and at low heat. Prolonged cooking time and high heat toughens the flesh and destroys the flavour.

Baking
This method is suitable for small whole fish and for individual cuts, such as fillets and steaks.

Brush the prepared fish with melted butter and season with lemon juice, salt and freshly ground pepper. Make three or four diagonal score marks on each side of whole round fish so that they will keep their shape. Lay the fish in a well-buttered, ovenproof dish. Bake in the centre of a pre-heated oven at 350°F (180°C, mark 4), allowing 25–30 minutes for whole fish and 10–20 minutes for fillets and steaks.

During baking, baste the fish frequently – this is particularly important with white fish.

Alternatively, lay streaky bacon rashers over the fish to provide basting during cooking.

Before baking, fish may be stuffed with a filling of fine breadcrumbs seasoned with salt, pepper, herbs or parsley and bound with a little melted butter. Spoon the filling loosely into the cavity, as it tends to swell during cooking. Close the opening on round fish with cocktail sticks.

Whole flat fish have only small cavities which must be opened up to allow room for stuffing. To do this make an incision down the centre of the back. Ease the flesh from the backbone on either side, as far as the fins, with the knife blade to form a cavity and loosely stuff this. Leave the pocket open.

For individual stuffed fillets, spread the mixture over the fish, roll it up and secure with wooden skewers.

Baking can also be done in foil, which is excellent for sealing-in both flavour and aroma. It also cuts down on oven cleaning. Place the prepared fish on buttered foil and sprinkle with lemon juice, salt and pepper. Wrap the foil loosely over the fish, place in a baking tin, and cook in the centre of a pre-heated oven at 350°F (180°C, mark 4). Allow 20 minutes for steaks, and about 8 minutes per pound for large fish plus 10 minutes extra in all.

Braising

Large flat fish, such as brill and turbot, can be cooked by this method which adds flavour to their somewhat dry flesh. Peel and finely chop 2 carrots, 1 onion, 1 leek or parsnip. Sauté these vegetables in a little butter and spread them over the base of an ovenproof dish. Lay the prepared fish on top and sprinkle with salt and freshly ground pepper. Add a few sprigs of fresh herbs, such as parsley and thyme, or a bay leaf. Pour over enough fish stock or white wine to come just level with the fish.

Cover the dish and cook in the centre of a pre-heated oven at 350°F (180°C, mark 4) until the fish flakes when tested with a fork. Lift out the fish carefully and strain the cooking liquid. This may be used as a sauce and can be thickened with egg yolks or cream, or by fast boiling until the sauce has reduced to the desired consistency.

Frying

This is one of the most popular cooking methods, and is suitable for steaks and fillets of cod, haddock, hake and eel and for small whole fish such as herrings, mackerel, mullet, plaice, sole, sprats, whitebait and trout. Coat the prepared fish in seasoned flour (page 100) or dip them first in lightly beaten egg, then in dry breadcrumbs, shaking off any surplus. Heat an equal amount of butter and cooking oil in a frying

BONING A COOKED SALMON

1. *Peeling skin towards the tail*

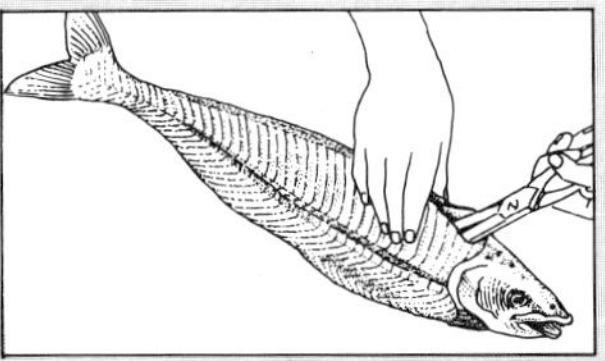
2. *Snipping the backbone*

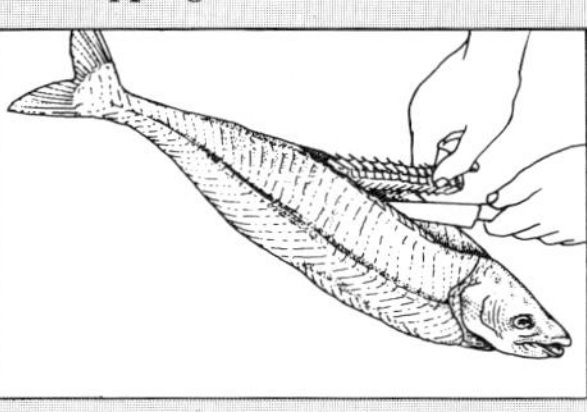
3. *Easing backbone from the fish*

BONING A HERRING

1. *Slitting fish along the belly*

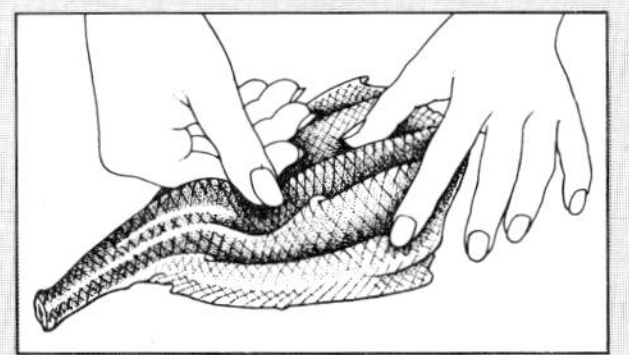
2. *Pressing along the backbone*

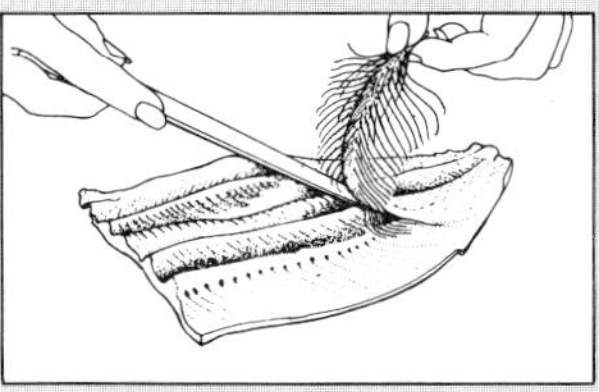
3. *Easing away the backbone*

REMOVING THE FOUR FILLETS FROM A FLAT FISH

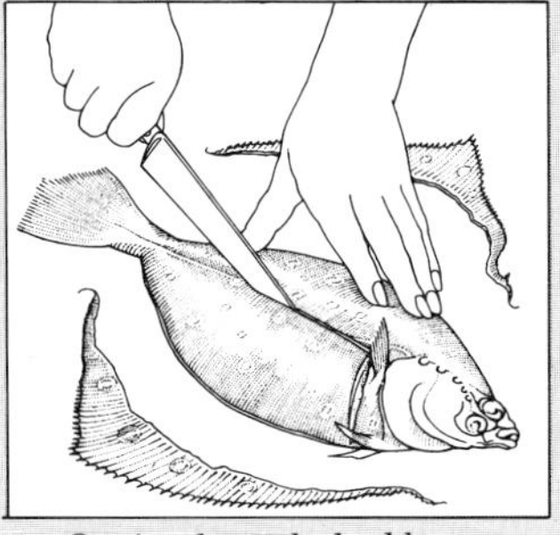
1. *Cutting down the backbone*

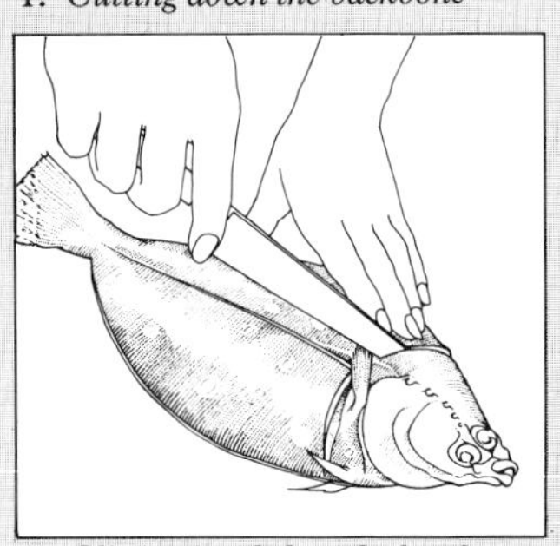
2. *Slitting just below the head*

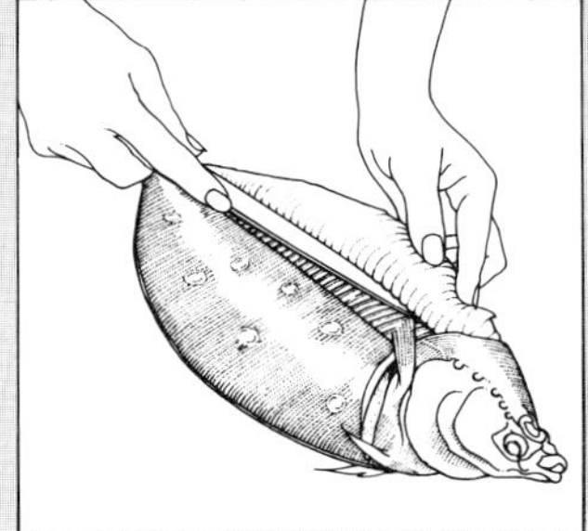
3. *Separating fillet from the bone*

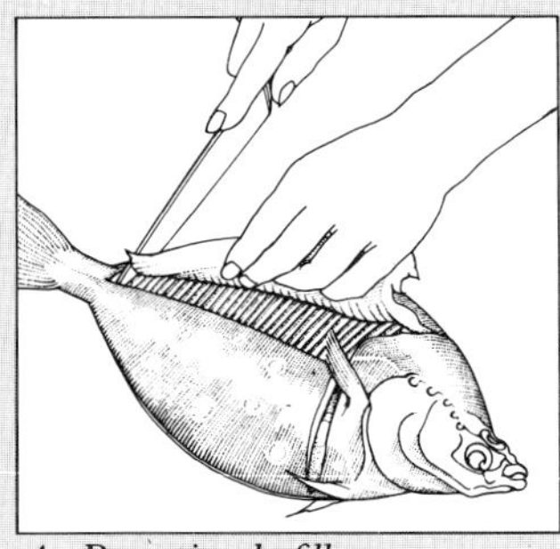
4. *Removing the fillet*

pan over moderate heat. Put in the fish and fry until brown on one side; turn it over with a fish slice. Allow approximately 10 minutes frying depending on the thickness of the fish. Remove from the pan and drain on absorbent paper.

Grilling
This quick cooking method is suitable for small whole fish, round or flat, and fillets, cutlets and steaks. Whole fish should be scored with three or four diagonal cuts on each side of the body. This allows the heat to penetrate more evenly and prevents the fish splitting.

Brush white fish, such as plaice or sole, with melted butter or oil, and sprinkle them with lemon juice or a little finely chopped onion. Baste two or three times during grilling to prevent the flesh from drying out. Oily fish need no brushing or basting.

Grill all fish under a pre-heated grill at moderate heat. Allow 4–5 minutes for fillets, and 10–15 minutes for thick steaks, cutlets and whole fish. The fish is cooked when the flesh separates into flakes when tested with a knife.

During grilling, whole fish and thick steaks should be turned over once to ensure that both sides are evenly cooked. Thin steaks and fillets need to be cooked on one side only.

Poaching
This is ideal for all types of fish, whether whole, filleted or cut into steaks. Poaching – slow simmering in liquid – can be done in a large saucepan or fish kettle on top of the stove, or in a shallow covered dish in the oven at 350°F (180°C, mark 4). For easy removal, tie the fish loosely in a muslin cloth.

Cover the fish completely with lightly salted water (1½ level teaspoons salt to 2 pints (1·2 litres) of water). Add to the pan a few parsley or mushroom stalks, a good squeeze of lemon juice, a slice of onion and carrot, together with a bay leaf and 6 peppercorns.

Bring the liquid to the boil over moderate heat, then cover the pan and lower the heat. Simmer the fish until it flakes when tested with a fork, allowing 8–10 minutes per pound (450 g). Lift out the cooked fish with a perforated spoon, and use the poaching liquid as the base for a sauce.

Whole fish, such as salmon, trout and salmon trout, are usually poached in a classic preparation or fish stock known as court bouillon.

Court Bouillon
PREPARATION TIME: *10 min*
COOKING TIME: *20 min*
INGREDIENTS:
2 carrots
1 onion
2 sticks celery
2 shallots
1 bay leaf
3 parsley stalks
2 sprigs thyme
2 tablespoons lemon juice
½ pint (300 ml) dry white wine
Salt and black pepper*

Peel and finely chop the vegetables. Put them in a large saucepan with all the other ingredients and 1½ pints (900 ml) of water. Bring to the boil, cover with a lid and simmer over low heat for 15 minutes. Leave the court bouillon to cool slightly, then strain it and pour over the fish to be poached.

Steaming
Fillets and thin cuts of fish cooked in this manner are ideal for invalids and young children.

Roll the fillets or lay them flat in the perforated steamer compartment and sprinkle lightly with salt and freshly ground pepper. Set the steamer over a pan of boiling water and cook the fish for about 10–15 minutes.

SHELLFISH

Small shellfish are served as hors d'oeuvre, and in soups and sauces. Large shellfish, such as crabs, lobsters and crawfish, can be served either as a first or a main course. If they are bought ready-prepared, they must be used on the day of purchase.

All fresh shellfish must be boiled before being dressed or used in a recipe. Oysters, which are usually eaten raw, are the one exception. Shellfish require little cooking time, and over-boiling causes the flesh to become tough and fibrous.

Most shellfish have indigestible or unwholesome parts, such as the beard of the mussel, and the 'dead men's fingers', or gills, in crabs and lobsters. These parts, together with the stomach sac and the intestinal tubes, must be removed during preparation.

Crab
This is usually bought cooked, and has often been dressed by the fishmonger. When buying a fresh crab, make certain that it has two claws and that it is heavy for its size. The edible parts of a crab are the white meat in the claws and the creamy-brown meat in the body shell. Allow 8–10 oz (225–275 g) dressed crab per person.

Wash the crab and put it in a large saucepan with plenty of cold water seasoned with 1 tablespoon lemon juice, a few parsley stalks, 1 bay leaf, a little salt and a few peppercorns. Cover the pan with a lid and bring the water slowly to boiling point. Cooking time is short: a 2½–3 lb (1–1½ kg) crab, measuring about 8 in (20 cm) across the body shell, should be boiled for only 15–20 minutes. Leave the crab to cool in the cooking liquid.

Dressed crab
Place the cooked crab on a board and twist off the legs and two large claws. Twist off the pincers and crack each claw open with a claw cracker, a hammer or the handle of a heavy knife.

Empty the white meat into a bowl and use a skewer or the handle of a teaspoon to scrape all the white meat from the crevices in the claws. Set the small legs aside for decoration or, if they are large, crack them open with a hammer and extract the white meat with a skewer.

Place the crab on its back and firmly pull the body (to which the legs were attached) away from the shell. Remove and discard the greyish-white stomach sac which lies behind the head in the shell, and the grey feathered gills known as 'dead men's fingers'.

Using a spoon, gently scrape the soft brown meat from the shell and put it in another bowl until required.

Cut the body part in two and pick out the white meat left in the leg sockets. Using the handle of a knife, tap and trim away the shell edge along the natural dark line round the rim. Scrub the inside of the shell thoroughly under cold

DRESSING A COOKED CRAB

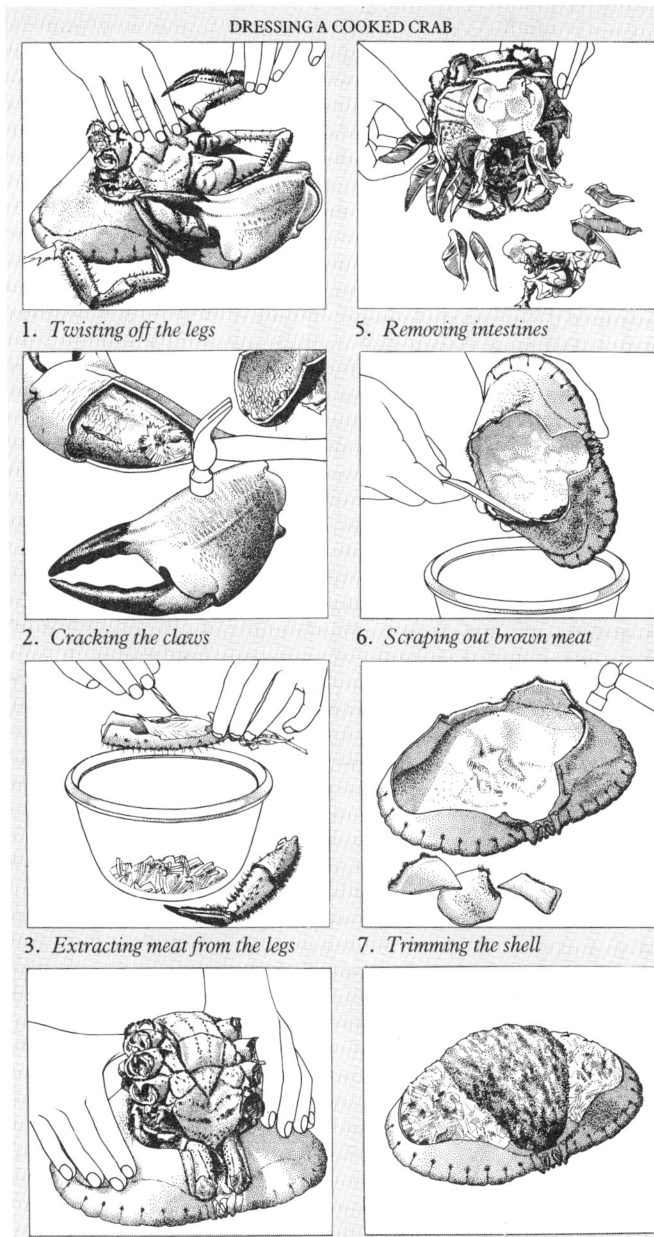

1. *Twisting off the legs*
2. *Cracking the claws*
3. *Extracting meat from the legs*
4. *Pulling the body from the shell*
5. *Removing intestines*
6. *Scraping out brown meat*
7. *Trimming the shell*
8. *Dressed crab ready for serving*

water, dry, brush with oil and set aside.

Finely chop the white meat and season it to taste with salt, black pepper, cayenne and a few drops of white wine vinegar. Mix the brown meat with 1–2 tablespoons fresh breadcrumbs and

DRESSING A COOKED LOBSTER

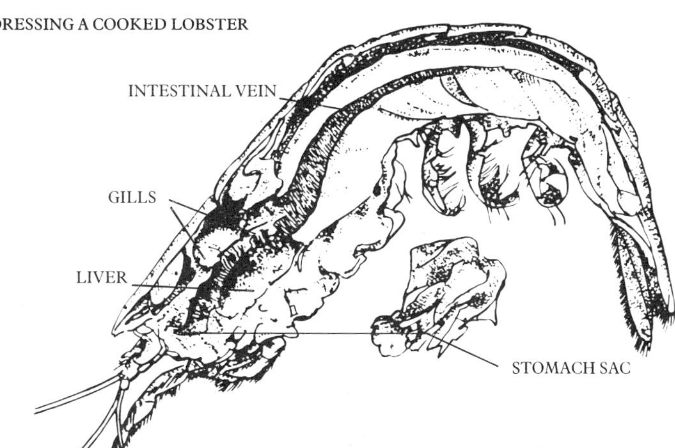

season with salt, pepper, lemon juice and finely chopped parsley. Place the brown meat in the centre of the shell and set the white meat on either side.

Lobsters

These are usually sold ready-cooked. The average lobster will serve two people.

If bought alive, rinse the lobster under cold running water. Grip it firmly round the body part and drop it into a large pan of boiling salted water. Cover with a lid and bring back to the boil. Simmer over low heat, allowing 20 minutes for a 1 lb (450 g) lobster and 30 minutes for a $1\frac{1}{2}$ lb (700 g) lobster. Leave to cool.

Dressed lobster

Twist the claws and pincers off the boiled lobster. Using a hammer, or a special lobster cracker, crack open the large claws and carefully extract the meat. Remove the thin membrane from the centre of each claw. The head may be cut off or left on.

Place the lobster on a board, back upwards, and split in half along its entire length with a sharp knife. Open out the two halves and remove the gills, the dark intestinal vein which runs down the tail, and the small stomach sac which lies in the head. The green creamy liver in the head is a delicacy and should not be discarded. The spawn – or roe – in a female lobster should also be kept; it is bright coral red and contained in the tail. It is usually added to the accompanying sauce.

Extract the meat from the tail, and with a small skewer pick out the meat from the feeler claws or set them aside for decoration. Wash and polish the empty half shells and put all the meat back in them. Garnish with the claws and serve cold with mayonnaise or a sauce vinaigrette (page 83), or grilled.

Mussels

These must always be bought alive and absolutely fresh. As soon as possible put them into a pail of cold salted water and throw away any mussels with open or broken shells. If time allows, sprinkle a little oatmeal or flour into the water. The live mussels will feed on the oatmeal and excrete their dirt. Throw away any mussels that float to the surface.

Scrub the shells with a stiff brush to remove all grit. With a sharp knife, scrape away the beard or seaweed-like strands protruding from each shell, and also scrape off the barnacles growing on the shells. Rinse the mussels in several changes of cold water to remove remaining grit.

Put the cleaned mussels in a large, heavy-based pan containing ½ in (1 cm) of water or white wine, chopped parsley and shallots or onions. Cover the pan with a lid and steam the mussels over low heat. As soon as the shells open, take the pan off the heat and remove a half shell from each. Keep the mussels warm under a dry cloth, and strain the cooking liquid through muslin. Serve with the liquid poured over them.

Oysters

Oysters are usually served raw as an hors d'oeuvre; six oysters per person should be allowed.

Scrub the tightly closed shells with a stiff brush to remove all sand. Open the shells over a fine strainer, set in a bowl to catch the oyster juice. Hold the oyster in one hand, rounded shell up, and insert the tip of an oyster knife, or a knife with a short strong blade, into the hinge. Twist the knife to prise the hinge open and cut the two muscles which lie above and below the oyster. Run the knife blade between the shells to open them and discard the rounded shell. After opening the shell, cut away the oyster with a knife.

Serve the oysters lightly seasoned with salt and pepper in their flat shells, and on a bed of cracked ice. They are traditionally served with lemon wedges and with thin slices of brown bread and butter.

Prawns and shrimps

These small shellfish are available all year round and are usually sold ready-cooked and often shelled. Live prawns and shrimps are grey-brown in colour, but turn bright red during cooking. Drop the live prawns or shrimps into a pan of boiling water, cover with a lid and boil for 5 minutes. Leave to cool in the cooking liquid.

To shell cooked prawns and shrimps, hold the fish between two fingers, then pull off the tail shell and twist off the head. Peel away the soft body shell, with the small crawler claws.

These shellfish are served hot or cold, as hors d'oeuvre, in seafood cocktails, salads, curries, soups and sauces. The large prawns may be coated in batter or in beaten egg and breadcrumbs and then deep fried.

Scallops

Fresh scallops are often sold already opened and cleaned, with the beards and intestines removed.

Wash and scrub the tightly closed shells of live scallops in cold water. Place the scallops, rounded shells uppermost, on a baking tray set on the top shelf of an oven, pre-heated to 300°F (150°C, mark 2), until the shells open, after about 5 minutes.

Once the shells have opened, cut through and remove the hinge muscles, and detach the rounded shells. Clean these thoroughly and set them aside – they make excellent small hors d'oeuvre containers. The scallop, attached to the flat shell, is surrounded by a beard-like fringe which must be scraped off. Also remove the black intestinal thread. Slide a sharp knife blade under the scallop and carefully ease off the white flesh with the coral attached.

Put the white and orange scallop flesh in a pan of cold water. Bring to the boil, remove any scum and simmer the scallops for 5–10 minutes. Do not overcook.

Scallops may also be baked, deep fried or grilled.

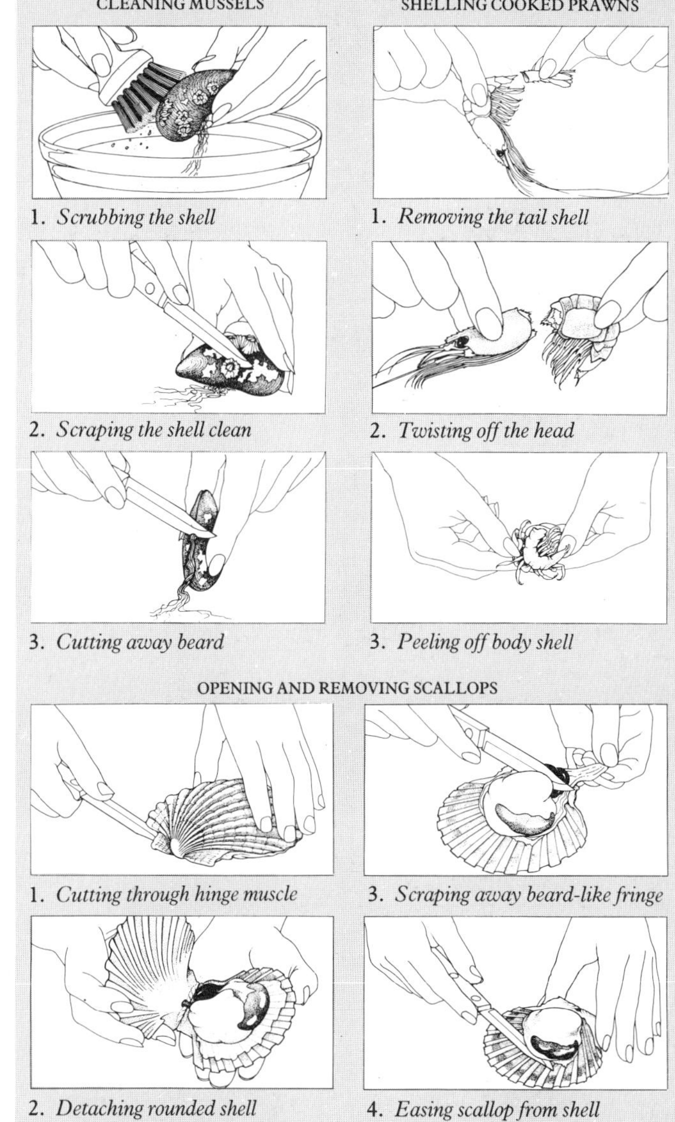

CLEANING MUSSELS: 1. *Scrubbing the shell* 2. *Scraping the shell clean* 3. *Cutting away beard*

SHELLING COOKED PRAWNS: 1. *Removing the tail shell* 2. *Twisting off the head* 3. *Peeling off body shell*

OPENING AND REMOVING SCALLOPS: 1. *Cutting through hinge muscle* 2. *Detaching rounded shell* 3. *Scraping away beard-like fringe* 4. *Easing scallop from shell*

Poultry and Game

As with many foods which were once seasonal, poultry and game are now available all the year round, because of the advent of freezing. Even so, freshly killed poultry is superior in taste to frozen birds, and game is at its best when it is in season, which lasts from late summer until early spring.

PREPARATION OF POULTRY

Most poultry is sold ready for cooking – that is hung, plucked, drawn and trussed. Oven-ready frozen poultry must be thawed slowly before cooking. It should be left in its film wrapping and placed in a refrigerator or cool larder for 24–48 hours, according to size, to thaw. It must never be thawed in hot water.

Stuffing

Before being trussed ready for cooking, poultry is usually stuffed. A stuffing improves the flavour of poultry, and makes the meat go further.

Stuffings are based on breadcrumbs – made from day-old bread – meat and rice to which butter or chopped suet is added together with herbs and seasonings. As a stuffing expands during cooking, stuff the bird loosely; a basic 4 oz (100 g) stuffing or forcemeat mixture is sufficient for a $3\frac{1}{2}$ lb ($1\frac{1}{2}$ kg) chicken.

Basic Forcemeat Stuffing

PREPARATION TIME: *15 min*

INGREDIENTS:

4 oz (100 g) breadcrumbs
1 oz (25 g) butter (melted)
1 small onion
Salt and black pepper*
1 egg
Stock or water

Put the breadcrumbs in a bowl and stir in the melted butter. Peel and finely chop the onion and blend into the breadcrumbs. Season with salt and pepper; beat the egg lightly and mix into the breadcrumbs. Add enough stock or water to give a moist but firm consistency.

Using a small spoon, fill the cavity of the bird with the stuffing. Chicken is stuffed from the neck end, duck and goose from either neck or vent end. Turkey is usually stuffed from both neck and vent ends.

The basic stuffing can be mixed with 2 tablespoons finely chopped parsley or 1 teaspoon sage.

Celery stuffing

Chop 3 sticks of celery finely and sauté them in a little butter for a few minutes. Add to the basic stuffing. This mixture may be flavoured further by adding 4 oz (100 g) dried, finely chopped apricots.

Apple stuffing

Chop 2 medium-sized cooking apples finely. Replace the butter in the basic stuffing with 1 oz (25 g) bacon fat or finely chopped streaky bacon and blend in the apples.

Mushroom stuffing

Trim and chop 4 oz (100 g) of mushrooms and sauté them in the melted butter for the basic stuffing. Mix with the breadcrumbs, onion, egg and seasonings.

Sausage stuffing

For a large bird, a meaty stuffing helps to keep the flesh moist. Make up the basic stuffing and mix it with 8 oz (225 g) sausage meat. Alternatively, melt 1–2 oz (25–50 g) of butter and lightly fry 1 finely chopped onion and 1 lb (450 g) of sausage meat for 2–3 minutes. Turn the mixture into a bowl and add 1 oz (25 g) breadcrumbs, salt and pepper to taste, 1 beaten egg and water to bind. Leave the mixture to cool before stuffing the bird.

Jointing

A chicken – or duck – can be cooked whole or cut into joints. A small bird can be halved by placing it, back down, on a board and cutting lengthways down and through the breastbone and then through the backbone.

Each half can be further divided into two. Tuck the blade of the knife underneath the leg joint and slice this away from the wing portion, holding the knife at an angle of 45 degrees.

To joint a chicken, pull the chicken leg away from the body, and slice down to where the thigh joins the carcass. Break the bone and cut the whole leg away with a knife. A large leg joint can be cut into the drumstick and thigh. Next, cut down from the breast towards the wing joint, severing the wing from the body, and fold the breast meat over the wing joints. Cut along the natural break in the rib cage to separate the top of the breast from the lower carcass. Divide the top. Divide this breast meat into two or three pieces. The remaining carcass can be used for making stock.

Trussing

Once stuffed, the bird should be trussed so as to keep it in shape during cooking, and to make it look attractive when it reaches the table. To tie up a bird, use a trussing needle, which has an eye large enough to take a piece of fine string. If a trussing needle is not available, use poultry skewers and string to secure the bird.

Using a trussing needle

Place the chicken, breast down, on a board. Fold the loose neck skin over the back, closing the neck opening. Fold the wing tips over the body so as to hold the neck skin in position. Turn the chicken, breast side up.

Make a slit in the skin above the opening at the vent of the body, and put the tail (parson's nose) through this.

Thread the trussing needle with string. Insert the needle through the second joint of the right wing, push it through the body, and out through the corresponding joint on the left side. Insert the needle through the first joint, where the wing is attached to the body, on the left side. Pass the needle through the body again and out through the corresponding joint on the right side. Tie the ends of the string securely.

To truss the legs, press them close to the body; thread the needle again and pass it through the right side of the parson's nose. Loop the string first around the right leg and then around the left leg. Pass the needle through the left side of the parson's nose, pull the string tightly to draw the legs together and tie the ends.

Trussing with a skewer
Fold the neck skin and wing tips over the back of the bird and pull the parson's nose through the slit above the vent.

Lay the bird on its back and, pushing the legs up towards the neck, insert a poultry skewer just below the thigh bone. Push the skewer through the body so that it comes out below the thigh bone on the other side.

Turn the bird on its breast. Pass a piece of string over the wing tips and beneath and up over the ends of the skewer. Cross the string over the back of the bird.

Turn the bird on to its back again, loop the string round the drumsticks and parson's nose, then tie the string securely.

Barding
After trussing, the bird is ready for cooking. If it is to be roasted, the lean breast flesh should be protected to prevent it from drying out. This is known as barding and consists of covering the breast with bacon rashers.

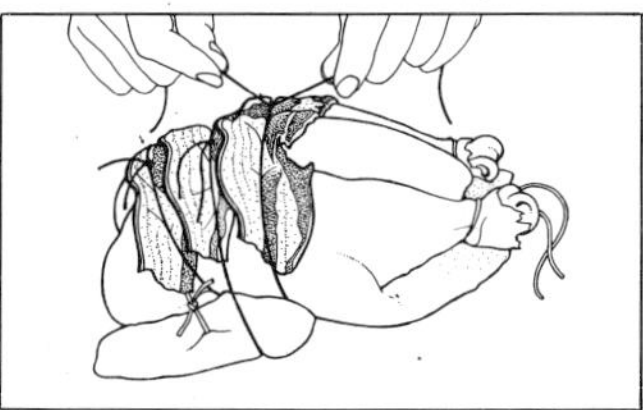

During cooking, the fat from the bacon melts and bastes the flesh. About 20 minutes before the end of cooking time, remove the bacon rashers and return the bird to the oven.

COOKING METHODS

Roasting is the most popular method of cooking whole chicken, duck, goose, guinea fowl and turkey. With the exception of duck and goose, which are fatty birds, all poultry should be barded or generously brushed with butter before roasting.

Boiling and steaming is suitable for older birds and joints. The cooked flesh is mainly used in other dishes, such as fricassées and curries. Braising and casseroling are ideal, but slow, methods of cooking older birds or joints.

Grilling or frying is reserved for whole small and young birds, and for chicken joints.

CHICKEN

Boiling
Rub the surface of a whole chicken with lemon juice to preserve the colour, and put it in a large pan. Add a bouquet garni (page 99), a peeled carrot and onion, and just enough water to cover the bird. Bring the water to the boil, and remove any scum from the surface. Reduce the heat to a gentle simmer, then cover with a lid and cook until the bird is tender, after 2–3 hours; chicken joints need only 15–20 minutes. Lift the chicken from the pan and serve hot or cold with a white sauce (page 82).

JOINTING A CHICKEN OR DUCK

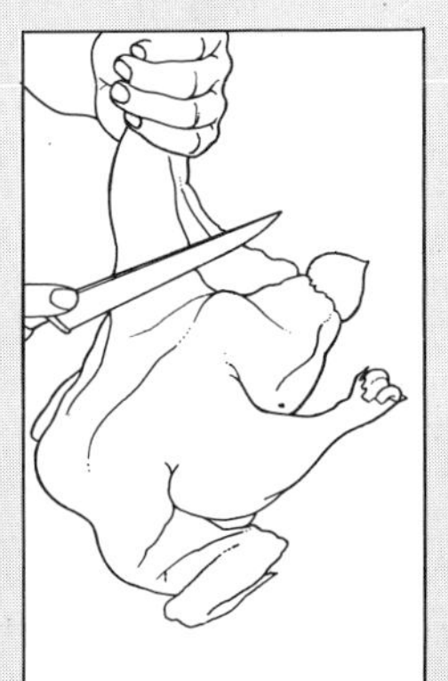
1. *Cut off legs*

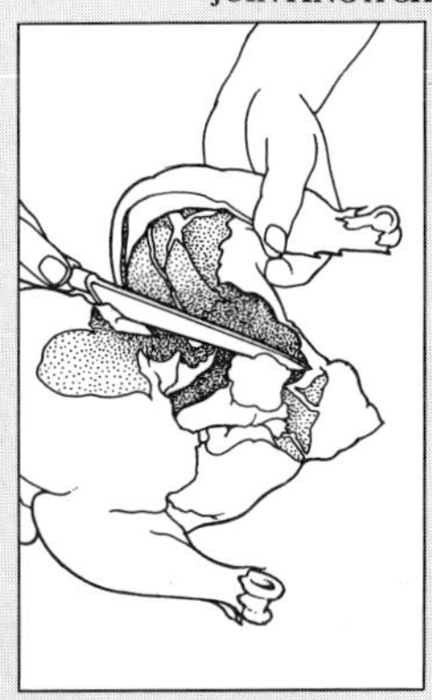
2. *Break the leg joints*

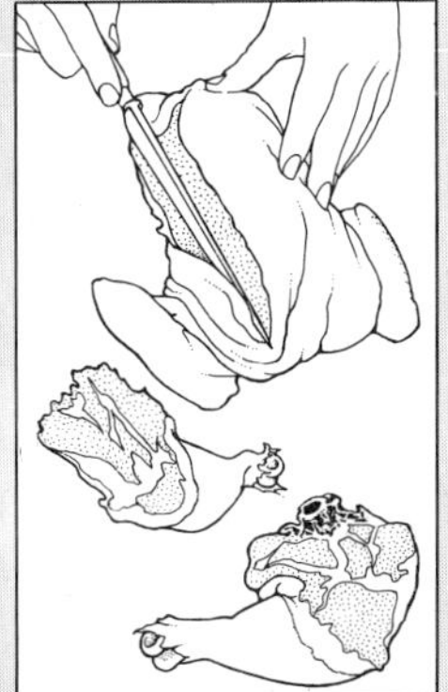
3. *Slice towards wing joint*

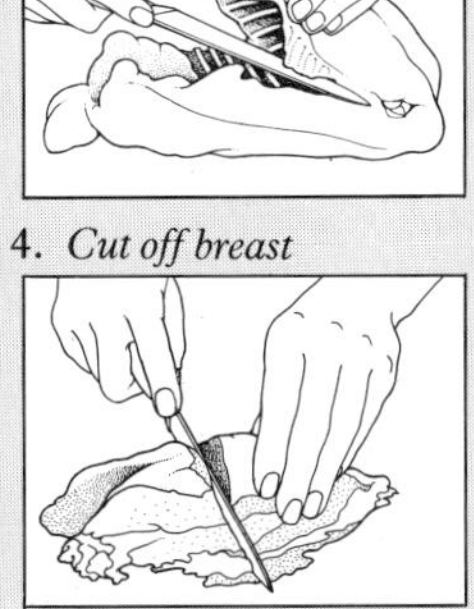
4. *Cut off breast*

5. *Cut breast in half*

Braising and casseroling
Lightly fry a whole bird or joints in a little butter until golden. Remove the bird from the pan and fry about 1 lb (450 g) of cleaned, roughly chopped vegetables, such as carrots, onions, celery and turnips, in the butter. Replace the poultry on the bed of vegetables, and cover the pan tightly with a lid. Cook over low heat on top of the stove or in the centre of an oven, at 325°F (170°C, mark 3), until tender. Braising is a slow process, up to 3 hours, but cooking time depends on the size and age of the bird.

For a chicken casserole, fry the joints in butter until golden, then put them in a flameproof casserole dish. Pour stock, wine or a mixture of both over the base of the dish to a depth of 1 in ($2\frac{1}{2}$ cm). Add seasoning, chopped herbs or a bouquet garni, and cover the dish with a lid. Cook as for braising, on top of the stove or in the oven, for $1–1\frac{1}{2}$ hours or until tender. A selection of lightly fried vegetables, such as button onions and mushrooms, baby carrots and small new potatoes, may be added halfway through cooking.

Grilling and frying
Spring chicken, poussins and small guinea fowl are excellent for grilling. One average bird (weight about $1\frac{1}{2}$ lb, 700 g) will serve two persons. To prepare a whole bird for grilling, place it on its breast, cut through the backbone and open the bird out. Flatten the bird with a meat mallet, breaking the joints where necessary.

Brush the bird all over with melted butter, and season lightly with salt and pepper. Cook the bird on the grill pan under moderate heat for 20–30 minutes, turning it over frequently.

Before frying chicken joints, coat them with seasoned flour (page 100), or with beaten egg and breadcrumbs. Brown the joints quickly in hot fat, then lower the heat and fry gently until the meat is tender, after 15–20 minutes.

Roasting
A roasting chicken weighing up to 3½ lb (1½ kg) will serve 3–4 persons. Place the barded chicken in a roasting tin in the centre of a pre-heated oven at 375°F (190°C, mark 5). Allow 20 minutes per pound (450 g), plus 20 minutes over. A chicken weighing 4–6 lb (1·8–2·7 kg) will give 4–6 servings. It should be roasted at 325°F (170°C, mark 3), allowing 25 minutes per pound (450 g), plus 25 minutes over. A capon, with an average weight of 6–8 lb (2·7–3·6 kg), provides 8–10 portions; it should be roasted at 325°F (170°C, mark 3).

Alternatively, loosely wrap the chicken in foil and roast at 400–425°F (200–220°C, mark 6–7), allowing 20 minutes per pound (450 g), plus an extra 20 minutes. Open the foil 20 minutes before cooking is completed to allow the bird to brown. Use a skewer to test that the bird is cooked. Insert the skewer through the thickest part of the thigh; if clear juices run out, the bird is cooked.

Steaming
Place the trussed but unstuffed chicken on a wire rack or trivet over a deep pan of boiling water. Cover the chicken with foil and steam for 3–4 hours. Remove the skin from the cooked chicken and use the flesh in invalid diets or in made-up dishes.

DUCK

Duck is prepared for roasting in the same way as chicken. Because duck is a fatty bird, it does not need barding or brushing with butter before cooking, but the skin should be pricked all over with a needle to allow the fat to run out of the bird during cooking. Season the duck with salt and pepper, and cook in a moderately hot oven, 400°F (200°C, mark 6), allowing some 20 minutes per pound (450 g).

Duck can also be jointed and braised for about 1 hour in the oven, at 350°F (180°C, mark 4).

Because the meat is very rich, duck is best served with sharply flavoured sauces and fruit, such as oranges, peaches and cherries. When buying, allow 1 lb (450 g) of duck per person.

GOOSE

Goose is more fatty than chicken, and therefore does not need to be brushed with melted butter before cooking. Before roasting a young bird, stuff it from the neck end, sprinkle with salt, and bard the bird with any fat taken from its inside. Loosely cover the bird with a piece of foil and roast at 400°F (200°C, mark 6), allowing 15 minutes per pound (450 g), plus an extra 15 minutes. Or, slow-roast the goose, near the bottom of the oven, at 350°F (180°C, mark 4), allowing 25 minutes per pound (450 g). Serve with apple sauce. When shopping, always allow ¾ lb (350 g) of goose for each person.

GUINEA FOWL

All the methods of cooking chicken can be applied to guinea fowl, particularly braising. When roasting the bird, bard the lean breast meat well.

TURKEY

A drawn turkey is usually filled with two different stuffings. The neck end can be stuffed with chestnut or veal forcemeat, and the body cavity filled with a sausage stuffing (page 90). An average (10–12 lb (4½–5½ kg)) turkey will require a sausage stuffing made from at least 2 lb (900 g) of sausage meat.

Chestnut stuffing
PREPARATION TIME: *20 min*
INGREDIENTS:
1 portion veal forcemeat stuffing
2 level tablespoons chopped parsley
2 oz (50 g) streaky bacon
8 oz (225 g) chestnut purée
Grated rind of a lemon

Make up the basic veal forcemeat stuffing and blend in the finely chopped parsley. Remove rind and gristle and chop the bacon finely; fry it without any extra fat for 2–3 minutes or until crisp. Mix the drained bacon thoroughly into the stuffing, together with the chestnut purée and finely grated lemon rind.

Veal Forcemeat
PREPARATION TIME: *20 min*
INGREDIENTS:
3 oz (75 g) breadcrumbs
1 oz (25 g) butter (melted)
1 small onion
4 oz (100 g) lean veal
2 oz (50 g) lean bacon
Salt and black pepper*
1 egg
Stock or water

Mix the breadcrumbs with the butter and the finely chopped onion. Finely mince the veal and bacon and add to the breadcrumbs. Season with salt and pepper, then add the lightly beaten egg and enough stock or water to bind the stuffing.

Roasting
The stuffed and trussed turkey should be coated with softened butter and barded with fat bacon strips. Roasting methods depend on the size of the bird and the time available. At low oven temperature, the turkey must be frequently basted. At the higher temperature, wrap the bird loosely in foil to prevent the flesh from drying out. About ½ hour before cooking is complete, open the foil to allow the bird to brown.

When buying turkey, allow ¾ lb (350 g) oven-ready weight per person, and 1 lb (450 g) if the bird is not drawn and trussed.

ROASTING TIMES FOR TURKEY

Weight of bird	**Method 1** (325°F, 170°C –mark 3)	**Method 2** (450°F, 230°C –mark 8)
6–8 lb (2·7–3·6 kg)	3–3½ hours	2¼–2½ hours
8–10 lb (3·6–4.5 kg)	3½–3¾ hours	2½–2¾ hours
10–14 lb (4·5–6·4 kg)	3¾–4¼ hours	2¾–3 hours
14–18 lb (6·4–8·2 kg)	4¼–4¾ hours	3–3½ hours
18–20 lb (8·2–9 kg)	4¾–5¼ hours	3½–3¾ hours
20–24 lb (9–10·8 kg)	5¼–6 hours	3¾–4¼ hours

GAME BIRDS

All game birds should be hung before plucking and drawing to allow the flavour to develop and the flesh to become tender. Most game birds are bought already hung, plucked and trussed (and sometimes barded). Freshly killed birds should be hung by their heads in a cool, airy place. The period of hanging depends on the age of the bird, the weather and individual taste. Young game is hung for a shorter time than old, and warm, damp weather causes the flesh to decompose quicker than cold, dry weather. On average, hang game birds for 7–10 days or until the breast feathers can be easily plucked out.

After hanging, game birds are plucked, drawn and trussed in the same way as poultry, but the feet are left on. They are best cooked quite simply, and young birds are excellent for roasting; they do not require stuffing. Older and tougher birds are better braised or casseroled.

Braising
Older birds and those of uncertain age are best cooked by this method. Before cooking, cut the bird into joints, coat with seasoned flour (page 100) and brown in hot fat in a pan. Remove the browned game from the pan and place in a casserole dish. Rinse the pan with ¼ pint (150 ml) dry red wine or game stock. Add the liquid to the casserole, cover tightly with a lid and cook in the centre of a pre-heated oven, at 325°F (170°C, mark 3), for 1 hour, or until the meat is tender.

Grilling
Small, tender birds, such as grouse, partridge and quail, can be grilled. Split them through lengthways along the breastbone and flatten the bird; brush generously with melted butter. Place under a hot grill and cook for 25–30 minutes, basting continuously and turning frequently.

ROASTING TIMES FOR GAME BIRDS

Bird	Temperature	Time
Grouse and Capercaillie	400°F (200°C, mark 6)	30–45 minutes
Partridge and Ptarmigan	400°F (200°C, mark 6)	30–45 minutes
Pheasant and Pigeon	425°F (220°C, mark 7)	20 minutes per pound (450 g)
Plover	425°F (220°C, mark 7)	30–45 minutes
Quail and Ortolan	425°F (220°C, mark 7)	20 minutes
Snipe and Woodcock	425°C (220°C, mark 7)	20 minutes

Roasting
Before roasting, game birds must be barded with strips of fat pork or bacon. Sprinkle the inside with salt and pepper and put a large knob of butter inside the bird to keep it moist. Place the prepared game bird on a piece of toast in the roasting tin. Baste frequently during cooking and remove the fat strips for the last 10–15 minutes. Sprinkle the breast lightly with flour and continue cooking until brown.

Serving roast game
Small birds, such as grouse, partridge, quail, snipe and woodcock, are served whole on their toast, and garnished with watercress. One bird should be allowed per person. Larger birds are split through lengthways to give two portions. Chips or matchstick potatoes are traditional with roast game and so too are fried breadcrumbs or bread sauce. A well-flavoured brown gravy, a tossed green salad, buttered sprouts or braised celery are served separately.

WILD DUCK

These game birds, which include mallard, teal and widgeon, should be hung for only 2–3 days. After hanging, the birds are plucked, drawn and trussed as other game.

Wild duck should not be overcooked. Coat the bird with softened butter, and roast at 425°F (220°C, mark 7), allowing 20 minutes for teal, and 30 minutes for mallard and widgeon. For extra flavour, baste with a little orange juice or port.

Serve with game chips, fried breadcrumbs and orange salad.

WILD GOOSE

This can be prepared and roasted in the same way as the domestic kind but, as the flesh is dry, it should be barded thoroughly.

FURRED GAME

This includes hare, which is a true game animal, and rabbit which is now specially bred for the table. A wild rabbit is cooked in the same way as one bred for the table. Hare is prepared for cooking by hanging, skinning and paunching (removing the entrails).

Rabbit is eaten when 3–3½ months old. Fresh or frozen prepared rabbits are sold paunched and skinned. If necessary, rabbit can be prepared at home in the same way as hare. However, it should never be hung, but skinned and paunched as soon as killed.

Preparing hare and rabbit
Hare is usually sold already hung, otherwise it should be hung by the feet for a week to 10 days. Place a bowl under the head of the hare to collect its blood, which may be used to thicken the gravy. One or two drops of vinegar added to the collected blood prevents it coagulating.

Jointing
A hare or rabbit is more often stewed or braised rather than roasted whole. Cut the skinned and paunched animal into eight joints. First cut off, with a sharp knife, the skin flaps below the rib cage and discard them. Divide the carcass in half lengthways along the backbone, then cut off the hind legs at the top of the thigh, breaking the bone. Cut off the forelegs round the shoulder bones, then cut each half into two.

If the saddle – the section between the hind legs and forelegs – is to be roasted whole, cut off the belly flaps, hind and forelegs as already described, but do not slit the hare through the backbone.

COOKING HARE AND RABBIT

Braising
This is a suitable cooking method for a jointed hare or rabbit. Coat the joints in seasoned flour and brown them in hot fat in a pan. Remove and place in a casserole. Rinse the pan with ½ pint (300 ml) red wine or game stock, scraping up the pan residues. Pour this

liquid over the joints, cover tightly and cook at 325°F (170°C, mark 3) for about 2 hours, or until the meat is tender. Add a little more stock or wine, if necessary, and thicken the juices with a little of the reserved blood, or beurre manié (page 82).

Roasting
Fill the body cavity of the animal with forcemeat (page 92) and sew the flesh together. Lay slices of fat bacon over the back and add 2 oz (50 g) dripping to the pan. Roast the hare at 350°F (180°C, mark 4) for 1½–2 hours. Baste frequently. Remove the bacon 15 minutes before cooking is completed to allow the hare to brown.

VENISON

This must be hung in a cool airy place for 2–3 weeks. Wipe away any moisture as it accumulates on the flesh during hanging.

Meat from a young deer is delicate and can be cooked without marinating, but the flesh of an older animal is tougher and is usually steeped in a marinade for 12–48 hours before cooking.

CARVING POULTRY AND GAME

The technique for carving poultry follows certain basic steps which consist of first removing the legs and wings and then carving the breast meat downwards in thick or thin slices. When carving turkey, serve each person with both white meat – from the breast – and brown meat – from the body or legs.

Chicken and large game birds are carved in the same way as turkey. Small game birds are either served whole, one per person, or they may be cut in half.

To carve whole saddle of hare and venison, cut across the base of the chump and at a right angle down the centre of the saddle, forming a T shape. The French method is to cut fairly thick even slices down the length of the saddle. The English way is to remove the meat completely before it is carved. Carve the chump end from each side in turn, slanting the knife towards the middle. Turn the joint over and slice the fillet lengthways.

DUCKLING

Small duckling – and some larger game birds – are often jointed after cooking and half a bird is served to each person. Remove the trussing string or skewers from the roast duckling, then split the bird in half with a carving knife or with a pair of poultry shears or strong kitchen scissors. Insert the scissors in the neck end and cut along the centre of the breastbone to the vent; split the bird in half by cutting through the backbone.

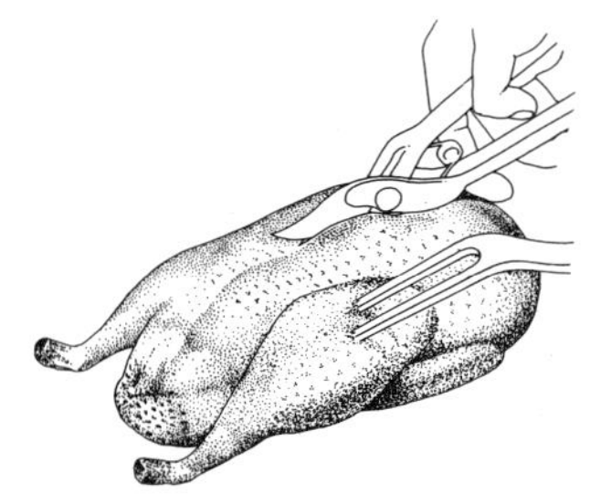

GOOSE

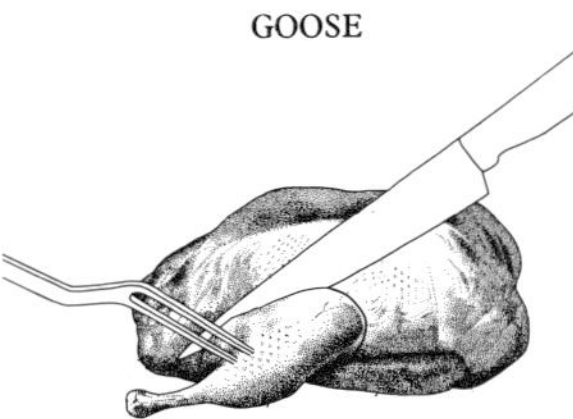

First cut off the leg joints from either side of body.

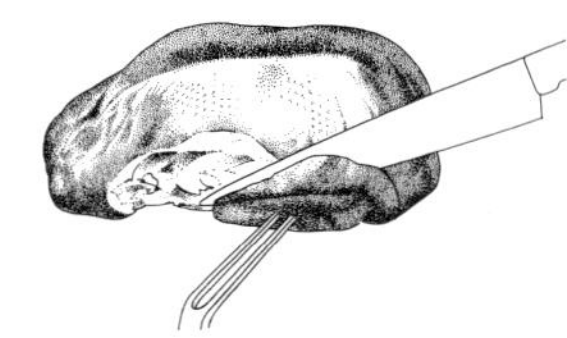

Remove the wings on either side of the breast, and detach the wishbone and meat from the neck end.

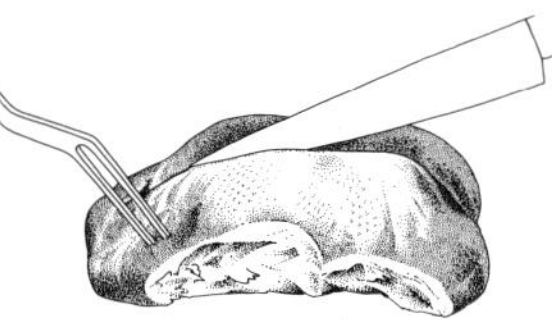

Slice down through the centre of the breast meat.

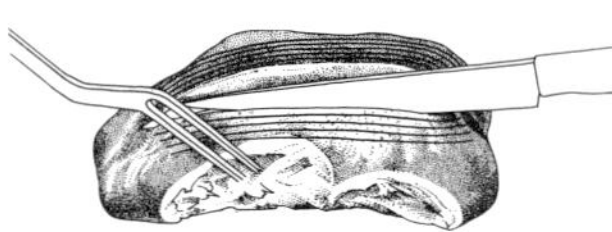

Holding the knife blade at an angle of 45 degrees to the breast, carve the meat in fairly thick, slightly wedge-shaped slices. Make them parallel to the first cut along the breast bone.

TURKEY

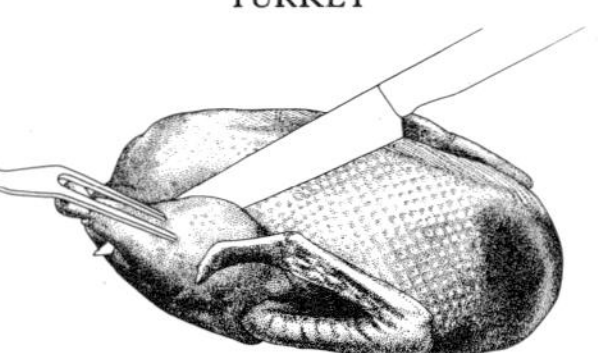

Begin by carving the legs from the bird at the point where the thigh bones meet the body.

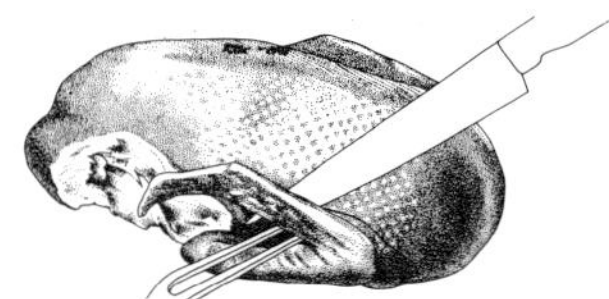

Remove the wing joints from either side of the breast.

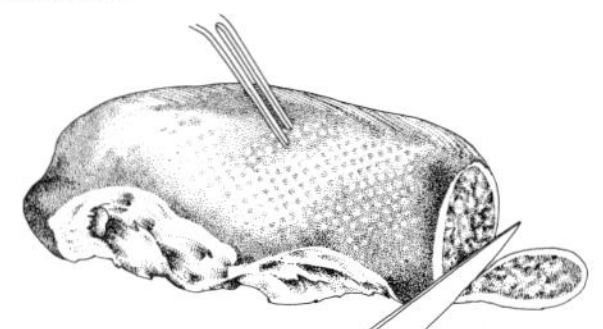

If the goose has been stuffed from the neck end, first cut thick slices across the stuffing.

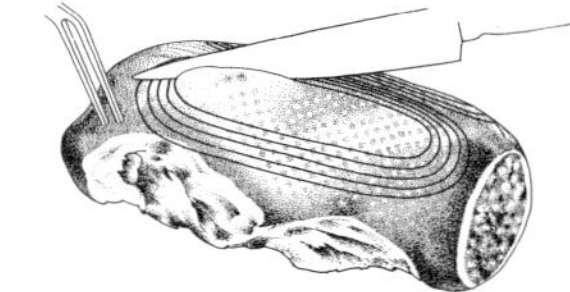

Fairly thick slices are then taken from both sides of the breast bone along the whole length of the bird. Carve downwards with the knife blade held almost flat against the body of the bird.

DUCK

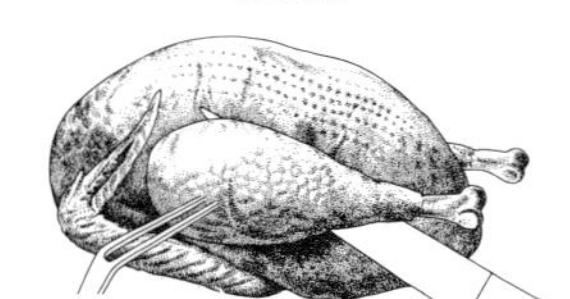

Cut the large drumsticks from either side of the body.

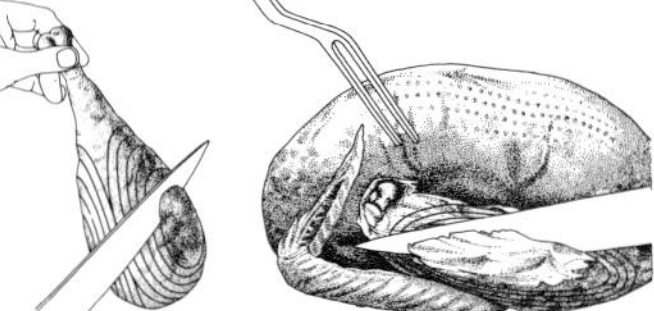

Hold the knuckle end of the drumstick in one hand and slice the meat downwards following the direction of the bone. Rotate the drumstick and carve off all the meat. Next, carve thin slices from the thigh bones.

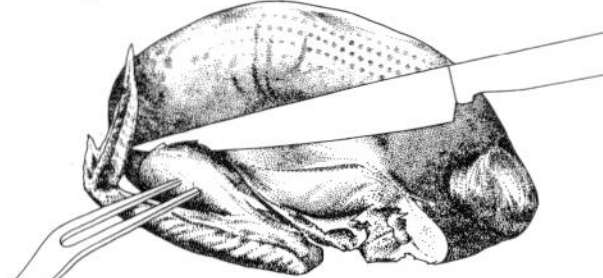

Cut off both wing joints and set them aside.

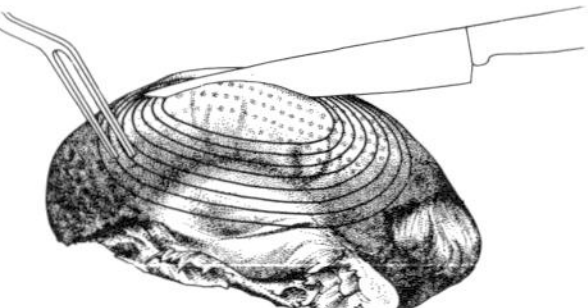

Carve the breast meat in long thin downward slices, from either side of the breast bone.

Fats and Oils

Fats and oils play an important part in cooking, as they contribute to or sometimes alter the flavour of food, especially when frying. The term "fat" can be taken generally to include all fatty substances, but it can also mean those which are solid at room temperature, those which are liquid being called "oils". Conveniently, this division more or less coincides with the division into saturated and unsaturated fats.

FATS

These are mainly derived from animal foods, such as meat and dairy products, but can also be produced from oily fish, nuts and vegetables.

Butter
Butter is made from the fatty substances skimmed from full cream milk. It is churned and then pressed to squeeze out water, and sometimes salt is added. It is used as the cooking medium for egg dishes and for sautéing and shallow frying over moderate heat. It is not suitable for frying at high temperatures as it burns easily, but a mixture of oil and butter will withstand quite a high heat without turning black.

Clarified butter, or ghee
This can be heated to a much higher temperature than ordinary butter without burning, and is therefore more suitable for frying and also for brushing food, for example fish, that is to be grilled. It is an expensive cooking medium, as 1 lb (450 g) of butter produces only about 10 oz (275 g) of clarified butter. To make it, melt the butter in a small pan over gentle heat and cook without stirring until the butter begins to foam. Continue to cook without letting it brown until the foaming stops. Remove the pan from the heat and let it stand until the milky deposits have sunk to the bottom, leaving a clear yellow liquid. Pour this carefully through muslin into a bowl. Clarified butter can be used in liquid or solid form and will keep well in the refrigerator.

Maître d'hôtel butter
A popular garnish for grilled meat or fish. Blend a tablespoon of finely chopped parsley with 4 oz (100 g) of softened butter and season to taste with salt, freshly ground pepper and a few drops of lemon juice. Other herbs, such as tarragon, chervil or chives, can also be used.

Dripping
This is the rendered fat from beef, mutton or poultry. A roast joint or bird will usually yield quite a lot, or it can be bought already rendered down. As it has a fairly high water content, it tends to splatter and is better used for roasting and shallow-frying than for deep-frying.

Lard
This is processed from pure pork fat and is excellent for frying. It is also used in baking some pastries and cakes.

Margarine
Made from vegetable oils blended with milk and vitamins, and sometimes with butter, margarine is interchangeable with butter for baking purposes and for sautéing. Most margarines are highly processed and therefore not acceptable to wholefood devotees. The fat content is the same as that of butter. From the point of view of low cholesterol content, soft margarines made from polyunsaturated vegetable oils are the best. Harder margarines are likely to have been processed in a way which in effect turns unsaturated fats into saturated ones.

Suet
Suet is the fat deposit from the loins and round the kidneys of beef or sheep. It is sold fresh for grating or already shredded and packed; it can be used in pastries, puddings and stuffings.

OILS

Edible oils are derived from fish, vegetables, cereals, fruit, nuts and seeds. They vary in colour and flavour, and choice is a matter of individual taste. Cold-pressed oil is the most natural (and most expensive) form, smelling and tasting strongly of its origin. Refined oil (often misleadingly called "pure") has had most of the vitamins and virtue bleached out or otherwise chemically removed, although some vitamins may be added back.

Corn oil
Fairly inexpensive and a good all-purpose oil with a mild taste.

Olive oil
Valued for its distinctive fruity taste and its affinity with certain foods. Suitable for frying and also for salad dressings: for these the best, but alas expensive, is the first pressing, also known as virgin oil.

Peanut oil
Also known as groundnut or arachide oil, this is a pleasant-tasting oil which will withstand quite high heat without burning.

Safflower oil
Expensive, but often recommended for a cholesterol-lowering diet as it is extremely high in polyunsaturated fats and in particular linoleic acid, the one essential fatty acid which cannot be manufactured by the body.

Sesame oil
Made from sesame seeds, this has a distinctive taste. It is much used in the Middle East for baking and also makes a good salad dressing.

Soya oil
A neutral-tasting oil, this is high in polyunsaturates and not too expensive.

Sunflower oil
An excellent all-round oil: can be used for frying and for salad dressings, high in polyunsaturates but cheaper than safflower oil.

Walnut oil
Very expensive; its strong nutty taste is much appreciated in salad dressings.

Garnishes

A well-chosen garnish adds texture, colour and flavour to a dish. It should be fresh and simple rather than cluttered, and if the dish is hidden by a sauce, the garnish should give a clue to what is in the sauce. For instance, a dish served *à la véronique* – that is, with a sauce containing white grapes – is always garnished with small bunches of grapes. Many garnishes are classic – lemon and parsley, for example, are traditional with fried fish.

Bread croûtons
Bread croûtons are a classic garnish with thick soups. Remove the crusts from ½ in (1 cm) thick slices of bread; cut into cubes and toast or fry in a little butter until crisp and golden. Serve in a separate dish or sprinkled over the soup.

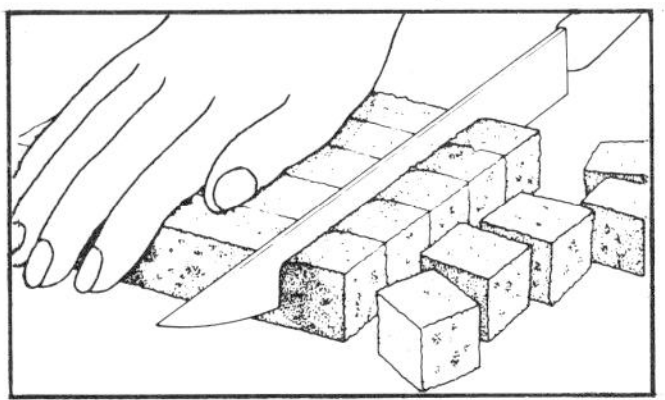

Cutting bread croûtons

Breadcrumbs
Fried crumbs are a traditional garnish for game and *au gratin* dishes. Melt 1 oz (25 g) butter or margarine in a frying pan, stir in 4 oz (100 g) fresh breadcrumbs and fry over moderate heat until the crumbs are evenly browned and golden. Turn frequently.

Celery tassels

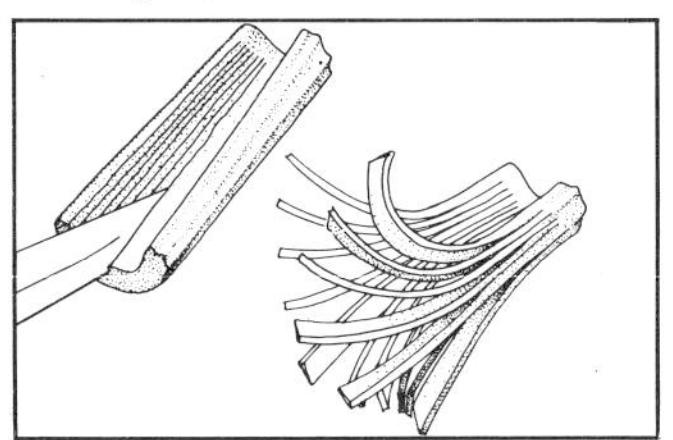

Edible garnish used with dips. Scrub the celery stalks, cut them in 2 in (5 cm) lengths, then cut down the lengths at narrow intervals almost to the base. Leave the stalks in a bowl of water to curl.

Cucumber

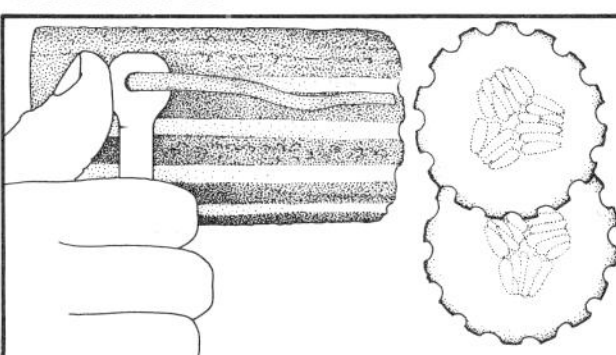

Sliced cucumber is a traditional garnish to a cold mousse or terrine. Deckled or ridged cucumber makes a more unusual decoration: wipe but do not peel a piece of cucumber; score it along the length with a fork or canelling knife, so that it has a serrated edge when cut into slices.

Gherkin fans

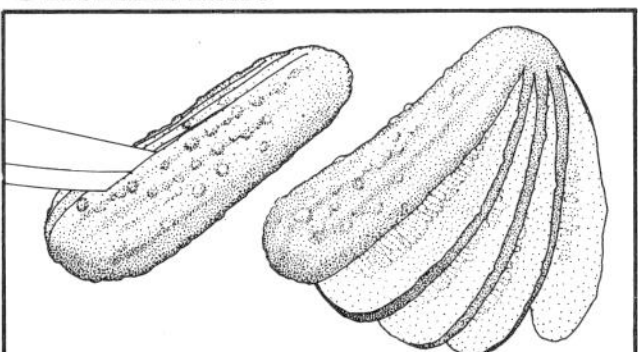

Drain cocktail gherkins thoroughly, then slice each three or four times lengthways almost to the stalk end. Ease the slices apart to open out like a fan.

Grapes
Most grapes are easily peeled, away from the stem end using the fingernails. If the skins are difficult to remove dip a few grapes at a time in boiling water for 30 seconds, then plunge them immediately into cold water.

Remove the pips from whole grapes by digging the rounded end of a clean new hair grip into the stem end of the grape; scoop out the pips. Alternatively, make a small cut down the length of the grape, being careful not to cut right through, and ease out the pips with the tip of the knife.

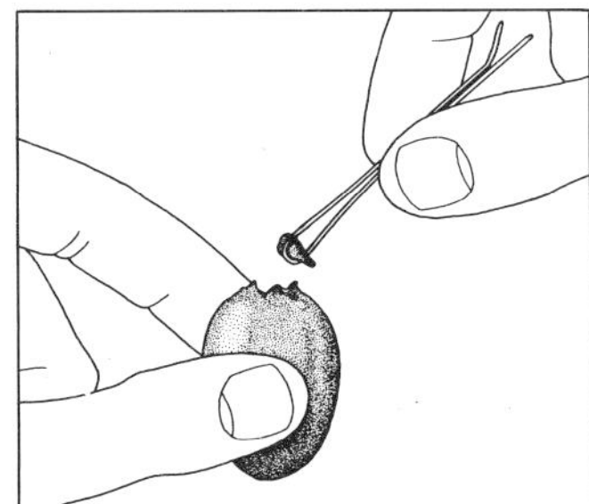

Mushrooms

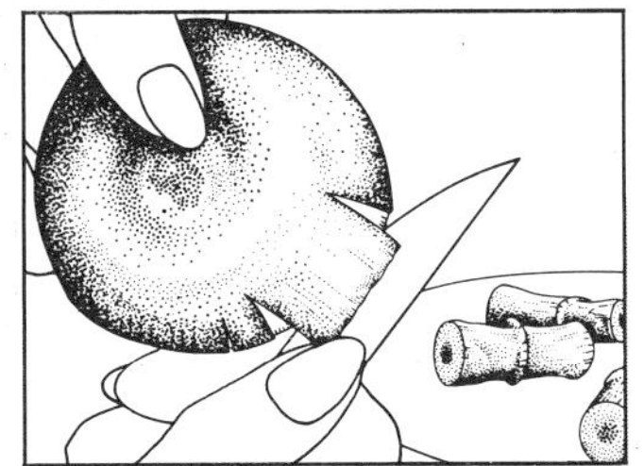

Trim by removing stalks, and peeling ragged skin

'Turned', these are a traditional garnish with grilled meat. Choose large button mushrooms, wipe with a damp cloth and trim the stem level with the cap. Peel off any ragged skin. With a sharp knife make a series of curving cuts, ¼ in (½ cm) apart, following the natural shape of the cap and from the top of the cap to the base. Take out a narrow strip along each indentation.

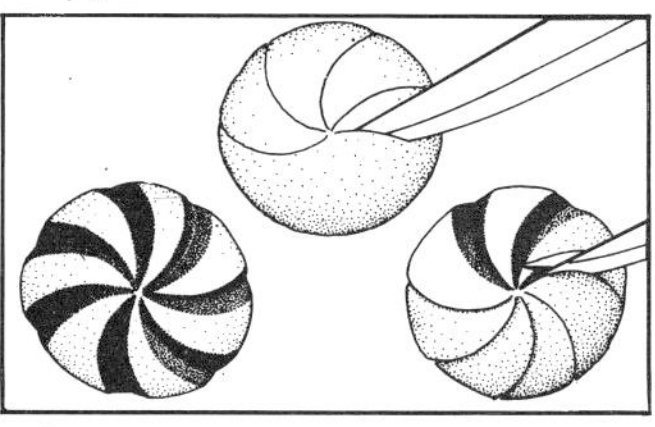

Nuts
Almonds are bought whole, halved or finely chopped (nibbed almonds), or flaked. Whole almonds, bought with or without their skins, can be used whole, split in two along their natural seam, cut into slivers or chopped. For slivered almonds blanch whole unskinned almonds in boiling water for 2–3 minutes; rub off the skins and, while still soft, cut the almonds into strips. For toasted almonds, spread the nuts in a shallow pan and brown under a grill.

Hazel nuts need to be toasted before the skins can be removed. Place the shelled nuts in a single layer on a shallow pan and toast under a medium grill until the skins are dry and the nuts begin to colour. Cool slightly, then rub the nuts against each other in a bag to loosen the skins.

Onions
Diced onions can be scattered over salads and other dishes. Peel

off the skin and trim the root. Cut the onion in half through the root, then cut downwards in slices. To chop, turn the onion and slice across the first cuts. To dice, chop again across these cuts.

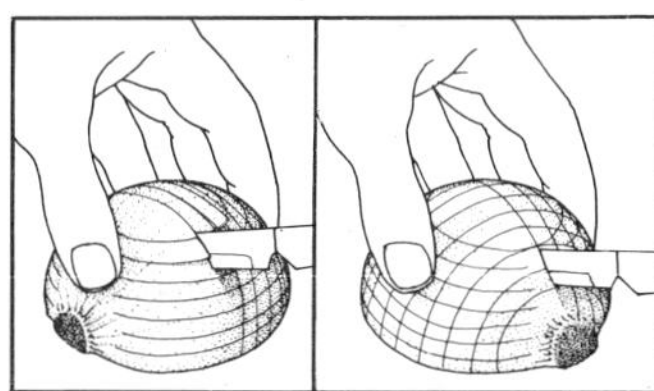

Parsley
Wash freshly picked parsley as soon as possible, shake well and remove long stems. Place in a jar of water reaching to the base of the leaves, or put in a polythene bag, tied at the neck. Parsley will then stay crisp and green for several days. Change the water in the container daily.

Scissors can be used for chopping parsley, but the result is coarser than when chopped with a knife. Gather the parsley into a tight bunch and with scissors snip off as much as is required straight on to the dish to be garnished.

To chop parsley, put the leaves on a chopping board. Hold the handle of a sharp straight-bladed knife firmly with one hand and the tip of the knife blade with the other; lift the handle in a see-saw action, gradually chopping the parsley finely or coarsely as required. Alternatively, bunch the parsley leaves in one hand on the chopping board and, using the knife, gradually shred the parsley, moving the fingers back to reveal more parsley.

Radish roses

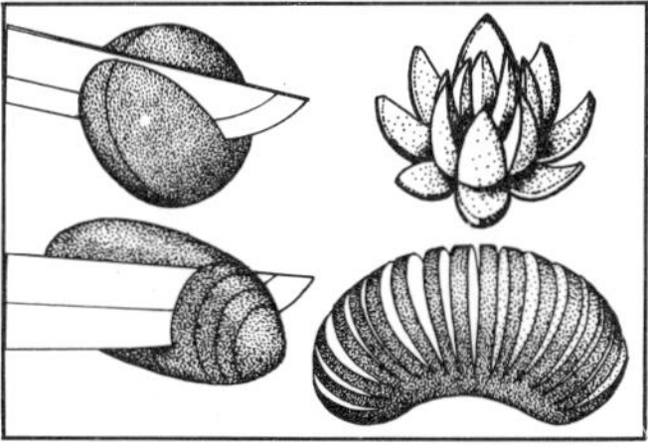

Used to garnish cold entrées, open sandwiches, hors d'oeuvre and salads. Make 6–8 cuts lengthways through a radish from the base towards the stalk; put the radishes in a bowl of iced water until they open like flowers. Long radishes look attractive when cut at intervals along the length to open out concertina-fashion.

Tomatoes

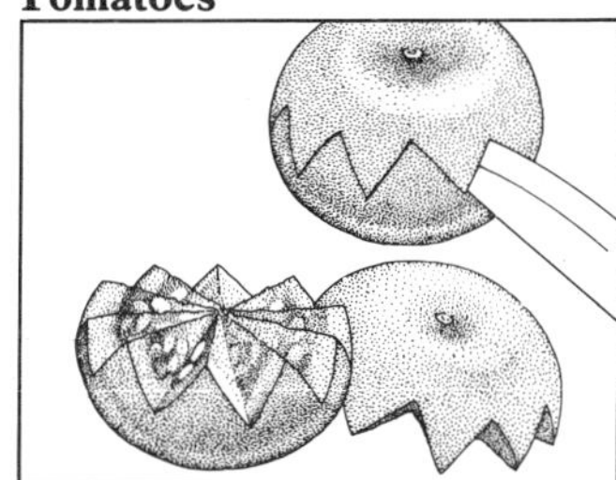

Serrated or vandyked tomatoes can be stuffed or used as tomato halves as a garnish for salads, flans, fried or grilled fish and meat. Choose firm tomatoes of even size. Using a small sharp knife, make a series of small V-shaped incisions around the circumference of the tomato. Carefully pull the two tomato halves apart. Oranges, grapefruit and melons may also be separated in this way.

Twists and butterflies

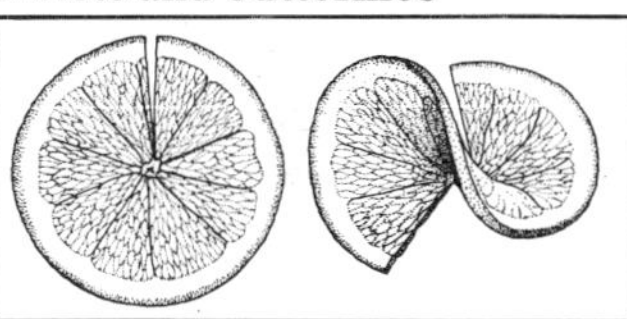

Tomatoes, cucumbers, beetroot, lemons and oranges make attractive garnishes to any number of dishes, both savoury and sweet. Slice the vegetable or fruit thinly, though not wafer-thin. For twists, cut each slice through to the centre, then twist the two halves in opposite directions and place in position. For butterflies, cut two deep V-shaped incisions to meet near the centre of each round lemon slice. Remove the two wedges in order to leave a butterfly shape.

Watercress
Another favourite garnish for meat, poultry and fish dishes. Trim off the stems, and wash the watercress leaves in plenty of salted water. Lift out, rinse and shake well. Discard any ragged and yellow leaves; arrange the watercress in small bunches to be added as garnish just before the dish is served. Washed watercress, with part of the stem left on, will keep for 1 day in the refrigerator if stored in a polythene bag.

TWO WAYS OF SKINNING FRESH TOMATOES

1. *Put in hot water for 1 min*

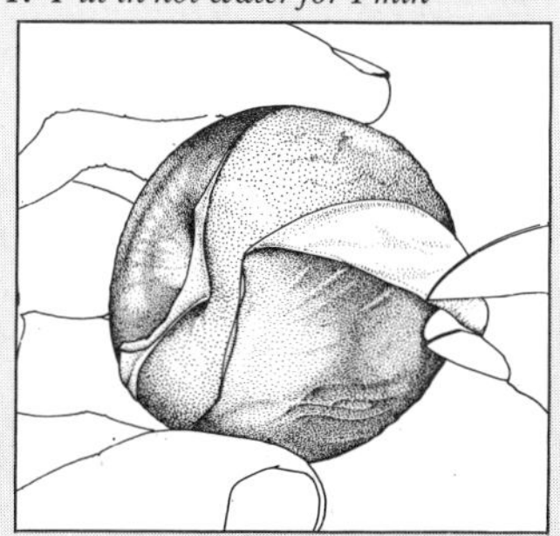

2. *Peel soft skin from wet tomato*

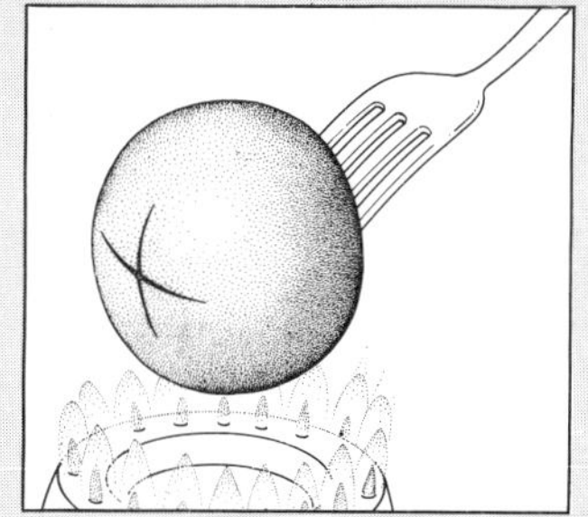

1. *Hold tomato over open gas flame*

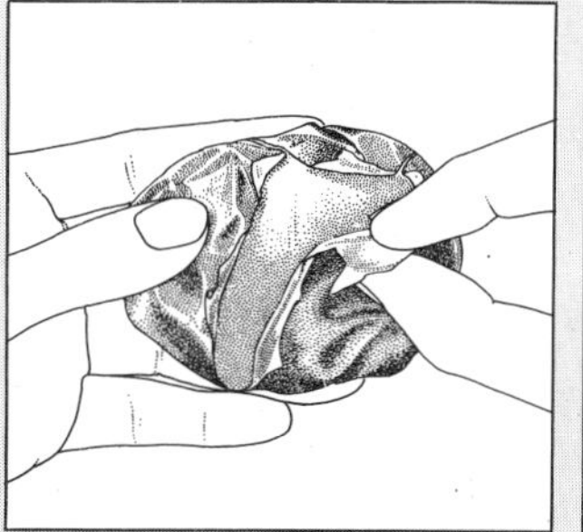

2. *Peel away charred tomato skin*

Home Freezing

A freezer is a time and money saver for anyone cooking for a family. It enables a cook to plan well ahead, both in bulk-buying and in cooking. And, if the rules for the preparation, packaging and thawing of the raw materials are carefully followed, frozen food loses nothing in freshness and quality.

FREEZING PRE-COOKED FOOD

For successful freezing follow these pointers.

1. Working surroundings must be scrupulously clean, as freezing does not destroy germs in food.

2. Use top-quality ingredients and season lightly; more seasoning can always be added later.

3. Always slightly undercook dishes which are to be frozen, allowing for the time the food will be in the oven to heat up.

4. When recipes for soups, sauces and casseroles call for the addition of cream or egg yolks, omit these before freezing and add them when the dishes are being reheated. Do not freeze dishes with custard or mayonnaise.

5. Omit garlic before freezing (it can be added later) unless the food is going to remain in the freezer for only a short time.

6. Be generous with sauces, so that the chicken, fish and game will not dehydrate when frozen.

7. Cool all dishes thoroughly before packing and freezing.

8. Garnish re-heated food before serving, not before freezing.

9. Pack and label all pre-cooked foods carefully and note the number of portions.

10. Do not freeze whole roast joints or poultry, or cold meat without a sauce, as the results are disappointing.

FREEZING FRESH FOOD

Fish

Fish should be frozen fresh and within 12 hours of being caught. It is not advisable to freeze even fresh shellfish at home, but some bulk suppliers offer frozen crab and lobster meat, as well as containers of prawns and shrimps. These may be stored in the home freezer for about one month.

Small round fish may be frozen whole after scaling and gutting. Larger round fish should have heads and tails removed. Flat fish is best frozen in fillets, interleaved with waxed paper. To preserve moisture in the prepared fish rub with a little olive oil. Wrap in heavy-duty polythene, or pack in rigid containers; label as usual.

The delicate flavour of whole salmon and trout can be maintained by freezing these fish in a sheet of ice. Dip the fish in cold salted water several times (placing it on a tray in the freezer between immersions) so that a layer of ice forms round the fish and seals it from the air. Then pack carefully in heavy-duty polythene.

Thaw whole fish slowly, preferably in the refrigerator, and cook immediately it is thawed. Cutlets, steaks and fillets may be cooked from the frozen state, if you are short of time.

Poultry and game

Only young plump birds should be frozen fresh, whole or jointed. Older birds, whether poultry or game, are best cooked as casseroles before freezing.

Remove giblets, clean and freeze separately as they have a shorter storage life. Clean the birds thoroughly, do not stuff them, but truss ready for cooking. Pad the legs with foil, before wrapping the whole bird in heavy-duty polythene. Label with weight, description and date. Pack jointed birds interspersed with waxed paper, in portions.

Stuffings should be frozen separately, as they store only for one month. Pack livers in polythene bags and freeze for use in pâtés and risottos.

Poultry and game birds should ideally be thawed slowly, in their wrappings in the refrigerator. In an emergency a frozen bird can be thawed, wrapped, in cold water.

Young game birds, well-hung, are frozen as poultry. Hare must be hung, skinned and cleaned; it is best frozen in joints ready for cooking. Rabbit is frozen like hare, but is not hung first. Venison should be hung before jointing and freezing.

Fish (storage time in brackets)	**Packaging**	**Thawing**
Whole fish (6 months)	Pack tightly in heavy-duty polythene	Thaw large fish in wrapping in a refrigerator for about 6 hours. Small whole fish may be cooked frozen over low heat
Fillets, steaks (6 months)	Wrap each piece in waxed paper, then pack in suitable portions in heavy-duty polythene	Thaw in wrapping in a refrigerator for about 3 hours
Poultry	**Preparation and Packaging**	**Thawing**
(Chicken 12 months; duck 4–6 months; goose 4–6 months, turkey 6 months; giblets 3 months; livers 3 months)	Wrap whole birds in heavy-duty polythene. Trim bones from joints and wrap individually before packing in heavy-duty polythene. Pieces for pies and casseroles may be packed in rigid containers. Pack giblets and livers separately in polythene bags	Thaw in wrapping in the refrigerator, a whole bird for 8 hours, joints and pieces for 2–3 hours. Thaw livers and giblets in wrapping in the refrigerator for 2 hours
Game	**Preparation and Packaging**	**Thawing**
Birds (6–8 months)	as poultry	as poultry
Hare, rabbit (6 months)	Wrap each joint in plastic film and pack several portions in heavy-duty polythene	Thaw in wrapping in the refrigerator for 2–3 hours
Venison (up to 12 months)	Freeze well-hung meat in joints or cutlets. Wrap joints in plastic film and polythene bags; overwrap with stockinet. Pack cutlets individually	Thaw in wrapping in the refrigerator for 5 hours

A to Z of Cookery Terms

A

arrowroot Starch made by grinding the root of an American plant of the same name. Used for thickening sauces

aspic Clear jelly made from the cooked juices of meat, chicken or fish

au bleu Blue; fish cooked immediately after being caught will turn blue

au gratin Cooked food, covered with a sauce, sprinkled with crumbs or grated cheese, dotted with butter and browned under the grill

B

barding Covering lean meat, game and poultry with thin slices of pork fat or bacon to prevent the flesh drying out during roasting

basting Moistening meat or poultry with pan juices during roasting by using a spoon or bulb baster

beating Mixing food to introduce air, to make it lighter and fluffier, using a wooden spoon, hand whisk or electric mixer

binding Adding eggs, cream or fat to a dry mixture to hold it together

blanching Boiling briefly 1. To loosen the skin from nuts, fruit and vegetables. 2. To set the colour of food and to kill enzymes prior to freezing. 3. To remove strong or bitter flavours

blanquette Veal, poultry or rabbit stew in a creamy sauce

blending Combining ingredients with a spoon, beater or liquidiser to achieve a uniform mixture

boiling Cooking in liquid at a temperature of 100°C (212°F)

bouquet garni A bunch of herbs, including parsley, thyme, marjoram, bay, etc., tied with string; or a ready-made mixture of herbs in a muslin bag. Used for flavouring soups and stews

braising Browning in hot fat and then cooking slowly, in a covered pot, with vegetables and a little liquid

brine Salt and water solution used for pickling and preserving

C

casserole 1. Cooking pot, complete with lid, made of ovenproof or flameproof earthenware, glass or metal. 2. A slow-cooked stew of meat, fish or vegetables

chaud-froid Elaborate dish of meat, poultry, game or fish, masked with a creamy sauce, decorated and glazed with aspic. Served cold

chilling Cooling food, without freezing it, in the refrigerator

chowder Fish dish, half-way between a soup and stew

civet Brown game stew

clarified butter Butter cleared of water and impurities by slow melting and filtering

colander Perforated metal or plastic basket used for draining away liquids

crêpe Thin pancake

cure To preserve fish or meat by drying, salting or smoking

D

darne Thick slice cut from round fish

déglacer To dilute pan juices by adding wine, stock or cream

devilling Preparing meat, poultry or fish with highly seasoned ingredients, for grilling or roasting

dice Cut into small cubes

dough Mixture of flour, water, milk and/or egg, sometimes enriched with fat, which is firm enough to knead, roll and shape

dress 1. To pluck, draw and truss poultry or game. 2. To arrange or garnish a cooked dish. 3. To prepare cooked shellfish in their shells, e.g. crab and lobster

dressing 1. Sauce for a salad. 2. Stuffing for meat or poultry

dripping Fat which drips from meat, poultry or game during roasting

E

en croûte Encased in pastry

F

fines herbes Mixture of finely chopped fresh parsley, chervil, tarragon and chives

flake 1. Separating cooked fish into individual flaky slivers. 2. Grating chocolate or cheese into small slivers

flambé Flamed; e.g. food tossed in a pan to which burning brandy or other alcohol has been added

florentine Of fish and eggs; served on a bed of buttered spinach and coated with cheese sauce.

folding in Enveloping one ingredient or mixture in another, using a large metal spoon or spatula

freezing Solidifying or preserving food by chilling it and storing it at 32°F (0°C)

fricassée White stew of chicken, rabbit or veal first fried in butter, then cooked in stock and finished with cream and egg yolks

fumet Concentrated broth or stock obtained from fish, meat or vegetables

G

galantine Dish of boned and stuffed poultry, game or meat glazed with aspic and served cold

garnishing Enhancing a dish with edible decorations

gelatine Transparent protein, made from animal bones and tissue, which melts in hot liquid and forms a jelly when cold

ghee Clarified butter made from the milk of the water buffalo

giblets Edible internal organs and trimmings of poultry and game, which include the liver, heart, gizzard, neck, pinions and sometimes feet and cockscomb

glaze A glossy finish given to food by brushing with beaten egg, milk, sugar syrup or jelly after cooking

goujon Gudgeons – small fish fried and served as a garnish

gratiné See au gratin

gravy 1. Juices exuded by roasted meat and poultry. 2. A sauce made from these juices by boiling with stock or wine, and sometimes thickened with flour

H

hanging Suspending meat or game in a cool, dry place until it is tender

herbs Plants without a woody stem. Culinary herbs, which are available in fresh or dried form, include basil, bay leaf, chervil, marjoram, mint, oregano, parsley, rosemary, sage, savory, tarragon and thyme. Used for their aromatic properties

hors d'oeuvre Hot or cold appetisers served at the start of a meal

J

joint 1. Prime cut of meat for roasting. 2. To divide meat, game or poultry into individual pieces

jugged Of dishes, such as jugged hare; stewed in a covered pot

K

kedgeree Breakfast or lunch dish of cooked fish or meat, rice and eggs

L

lard Natural or refined pork fat

larding Threading strips of fat through lean meat, using a special needle. This prevents the meat becoming dry during roasting

M

marinade Blend of oil, wine or vinegar, herbs and spices. Used to tenderise and flavour meat, game or fish

marinate To steep in marinade

marinière 1. Of mussels; cooked in white wine and herbs, and served in half shells. 2. Of fish; cooked in white wine and garnished with mussels

matelote In the sailor's style; e.g. fish stew made with wine or cider

meunière In the style of a miller's wife; e.g. fish cooked in butter, seasoned, and sprinkled with parsley and lemon juice

N

normande, à la In the Normandy style, e.g. cooked with cider and cream

O

offal Edible internal organs of meat, poultry and game

A to Z of Cookery Terms

P

paella Dish of saffron rice, chicken and shellfish, which is named after the large shallow pan in which it is traditionally cooked
paprika Ground, sweet red pepper
par-boiling Boiling for a short time to cook food partially
pâté 1. Savoury mixture which is baked in a casserole or terrine, and served cold. 2. Savoury mixture baked in a pastry case and served hot or cold.
pimento Green or red pepper
poaching Cooking food in simmering liquid, just below boiling point
preserving Keeping food in good condition by treating with chemicals, heat, refrigeration, pickling in salt or boiling sugar

R

reducing Concentrating a liquid by boiling and evaporation
rendering 1. Slowly cooking meat tissues and trimmings to obtain fat. 2. Clearing frying fat by heating it
roasting Cooking in the oven with radiant heat, or on a spit over or under an open flame
roe 1. Milt of the male fish, called soft roe. 2. Eggs of the female fish, called hard roe. 3. Shellfish roe, called coral because of its colour
roux Mixture of fat and flour which, when cooked, is used as a base for savoury sauces

S

salmi Stew made by first roasting game and then cooking it in wine sauce
sauté To fry food rapidly in shallow, hot fat, tossing and turning it until evenly browned
searing Browning meat rapidly with fierce heat to seal in the juices
seasoned flour Flour flavoured with salt and pepper
seasoning Salt, pepper, spices or herbs, which are added to food to improve flavour
simmering Cooking in liquid which is heated to just below boiling point
skimming Removing cream from the surface of milk, or fat or scum from broth or jam
smoking Curing food, such as bacon or fish, by exposing it to wood smoke for a considerable period of time
soufflé Baked dish consisting of a sauce or purée, which is thickened with egg yolks into which stiffly beaten egg whites are folded
sousing Pickled food in brine or vinegar, e.g. soused herrings
spit Revolving skewer or metal rod on which meat, poultry or game is roasted over a fire or under a grill
starch Carbohydrate obtained from cereal and potatoes
steaming Cooking food in the steam rising from boiling water
stewing To simmer food slowly in a covered pan or casserole
stuffing Savoury mixture of bread or rice, herbs, fruit or minced meat, used to fill poultry, fish, meat and vegetables

T

terrine 1. Earthenware pot used for cooking and serving pâté. 2. Food cooked in a terrine
timbale 1. Cup-shaped earthenware or metal mould. 2. Dish prepared in such a mould
trussing Tying a bird or joint of meat in a neat shape with skewers and/or string before cooking

V

velouté 1. Basic white sauce made with chicken, veal or fish stock 2. Soup of creamy consistency
vinaigrette Mixture of oil, vinegar, salt and pepper, which is sometimes flavoured with herbs

W

whisk Looped wire utensil used to beat air into eggs, cream or batters

Y

yogurt Curdled milk which has been treated with harmless bacteria

Index

The Good Health Cookbooks

The Publishers wish to express their gratitude for major contributions by the following people:

Editor: URSULA WHYTE — Art Director: MICHAEL McGUINNESS — Designer: SANDRA DEON-CARDYN

Diet Consultant: MIRIAM POLUNIN — Home Economist: VALERIE BARRETT — Additional Photography: PHILIP DOWELL

The Publishers also wish to acknowledge the help of the following:

Gilly Abrahams for editorial help; Fred and Kathie Gill for proof reading; Mary-Anne Joy for help with calorie counting; Terri Lamb and Carole Perks for design assistance; Vicki Robinson for indexing; and Michelle Thompson for food preparation. Additional photographic props were supplied by Graham and Green.

The Good Health Cookbooks are based on THE COOKERY YEAR, **to which the following made major contributions:**

Editorial Adviser: ELIZABETH POMEROY
Photographer: PHILIP DOWELL
Home Economist: JOY MACHELL

Writers:

Ena Bruinsma
Margaret Coombes
Derek Cooper
Margaret Costa
Denis Curtis
Theodora FitzGibbon
Nina Froud
Jane Grigson
Nesta Hollis
Kenneth H. C. Lo

Elizabeth Pomeroy
Zena Skinner
Katie Stewart
Marika Hanbury Tenison
Silvino S. Trompetto, MBE, Maître Chef des Cuisines, Savoy Hotel
Suzanne Wakelin
Kathie Webber
Harold Wilshaw

Artists:

Colour:
Roy Coombs
Pauline Ellison
Hargrave Hands
Denys Ovenden
Charles Pickard
Josephine Ranken
Charles Raymond
Rodney Shackell
Faith Shannon, MBE
John Wilson

Black and white:
David Baird
Brian Delf
Gary Hincks
Richard Jacobs
Rodney Shackell
Michael Woods
Sidney Woods

Black and white photography:
Michael Newton

Typesetting: Tradespools Ltd, Frome **Printing:** W. S. Cowell Ltd, Ipswich **Binding:** Dorstel Press Ltd, Harlow

RGHCF–16-001